The Melodramatic Thread

Interdisciplinary Studies in History

EDITOR
Harvey J. Graff

James R. Lehning

The Melodramatic Thread

Spectacle and
Political Culture
in Modern France

Indiana University Press

BLOOMINGTON & INDIANAPOLIS

This book is a publication of

Indiana University Press
601 North Morton Street
Bloomington, IN 47404-3797 USA

http://iupress.indiana.edu

Telephone orders	800-842-6796
Fax orders	812-855-7931
Orders by e-mail	iuporder@indiana.edu

The paper used in this publication meets the minimum
requirements of American National Standard for
Information Sciences—Permanence of Paper for Printed
Library Materials, ANSI Z39.48-1984.

Manufactured in the United States of America

Library of Congress Cataloging-in-Publication Data

Lehning, James R., date.
    The melodramatic thread : spectacle and political culture in modern France / James R.
Lehning.
        p.   cm. — (Interdisciplinary studies in history)
    Includes bibliographical references and index.
    ISBN 978-0-253-34900-2 (cl : alk. paper) — ISBN 978-0-253-21910-7 (pbk : alk. paper)
1. Theater—France—History—19th century. 2. Theater—France—History—20th century.
3. France—Politics and government—19th century. 4. France—Politics and government—
20th century. 5. France—History—Revolution, 1789–1799—Theater and the revolution.
I. Title.
    PN2634.L44 2007
    792.0944—dc22

2006100897

1 2 3 4 5 12 11 10 09 08 07

For Amanda and Charles

Contents

Acknowledgments

The completion of this book owes much to people who have helped me along the way. Harvey Graff first suggested to me that I write a book that became this one, and offered a place for it in his series with Indiana University Press. Harvey and Bob Sloan of IUP have both been supportive as I have written the book, and I will always be grateful for their patience. The referees for the press, especially Venita Datta, made comments that greatly improved the book. I have also learned much from friends and colleagues with whom I have talked. As always, Joan Scott's support has been crucial. At the University of Utah, Bob Goldberg, Ray Gunn, Ron Smelser, Esther Rashkin, and Bruce Dain helped with suggestions, references, and loans of books. Parts of chapter 3 were presented as a paper at the Society for French Historical Studies meeting in March 2005, and I am grateful to the commentator, Ray Jonas, and to the audience and other participants for their comments.

The Interlibrary Loan office of the Marriott Library at the University of Utah helped, as usual, to overcome the limitations of the library collection. I also thank the libraries of the University of California, Berkeley, the University of Washington, and Brigham Young University for allowing me to use their collections.

Financial support for this project came from the University of Utah Research Committee, which gave me a Faculty Research Grant for research in Paris and then extended it when my original plans did not work out. Robert Newman, Dean of Humanities at the University of Utah, has supported my work since his arrival in Salt Lake City, and I am particularly grateful for his permission to leave behind my administrative duties and head for Paris in February 2004. Liz Leckie, Assistant Dean of Humanities, also deserves thanks for taking over those duties during my absence from campus. Ray Gunn and Eric Hinderaker, chairs of the History Department during the life of this project, have also been supportive in every way possible. To all these people, and to those I may have neglected to mention, my deepest thanks.

Salt Lake City
October 19, 2006

The Melodramatic Thread

1. Introduction

On June 8, 1794, at the height of the Terror, the leaders of France and the people of Paris celebrated a Festival of the Supreme Being in central Paris. With Jacques-Louis David as impresario, the houses of Paris were decorated with tree branches, flowers, and tricolored flags to demonstrate the productivity of the soil of France and the glory of the Republic. The Tuileries Gardens, which would be the site of the first part of the festival, featured a statue representing atheism, with the inscription "only hope of the foreigner" on it. Across the Seine, the Champs de Mars, the site of previous revolutionary festivals, had been renamed the Champs de la Réunion. In the immense field rose a high mountain that would be the focal point for the second half of the celebration.

The Festival of the Supreme Being began with a cannon salvo summoning men and women from each section of the city to the Tuileries. Mothers carrying roses symbolizing mercy, young girls with baskets filled with flowers to symbolize youth, and men and boys with tree branches to represent the masculine virtues of strength and liberty all converged on the Tuileries Gardens. They were met by members of the Convention, with Maximilien Robespierre, in his role as president of the Convention, at their head. The Conventionnels also participated in the symbolism of the festival, holding shocks of wheat, flowers, and fruits.[1]

Robespierre welcomed the processions from around the city with a speech celebrating France's devotion to the Supreme Being, the source of all that was good, including the Republic and the liberty written in men's hearts. In spite of the ongoing war, the Terror, and the need for revolutionary vigilance, he urged his fellow citizens to give themselves over to joy on this day of festivities. This speech was followed by a performance by the Opera of Theodore Désorgues's song "Father of the Universe, Supreme Intelligence," set to music by François-Joseph Gossec. Robespierre then set fire to the statue of Atheism, which disappeared in flames to be replaced by a statue of Wisdom. Interpreting the pageant in a second speech, Robespierre described the disappearance of atheism and with it "all the crimes and unhappiness of the world." Only wisdom, he told his audience, could lead to the prosperity of empires.

After the ceremony at the Tuileries the members of the Convention marched in procession across the river to the Champs, surrounded by tricolored banners and children with flowers. A coach in the middle of this procession carried tools and goods made around the country, a plow covered with wheat and oak branches, and a printing press. These were placed next to a statue of Liberty, to indicate that liberty was necessary for the arts to flourish. Robespierre was at the head of this procession, exposing him not only to the cheers of the crowd but also to hecklers who accused him of wanting to be a god.[2]

At the Champs de la Réunion the Conventionnels assembled at the highest point of the mountain constructed in the middle of the field, while a hymn to the Supreme Being and a symphony were performed. The groups of men and women sang while children threw their flowers into the air. Young men drew their sabers and swore to be victorious, while elderly men gave them a paternal blessing. The festival ended with another artillery salvo, representing the national vengeance, and a fraternal embrace by all of the participants and the cry of "Vive la République!" Impressed by its perception of the festival—the beauty of the weather, the decorations, the joy of the people, the unanimity of the sentiments expressed, the speeches, and "the cordiality and order" that reigned during the ceremony—*Le Moniteur* summarized the events as "the most beautiful festival whose memory could be perpetuated in the pomp of the Revolution."[3]

Mona Ozouf has shown how the Festival of the Supreme Being marked clear divisions in the politics of the Republic. While endorsing equality of origins and celebrating agriculture, a "festival of dairy products, fruit and bread," it articulated support for the Republic against radicals on the left who supported the radical dechristianization that had been portrayed in the Cult and Festival of Reason the previous winter.[4] But it was also about reconciliation and national unity. The symbolically destroyed Atheism was replaced by Wisdom. The national representatives in the Convention were prominently featured. The ceremonies were open to, and incorporated, the entire population of revolutionary Paris.[5] The festival was therefore not only a description of the virtue of the Republic and the evil of its enemies, but also an attempt to consolidate the Revolution as part of the patrimony of France in a unified Republic of all the French. Yet, while Robespierre might urge his listeners to set aside their political concerns for a day of festival, reminders of the internal and external enemies of the Republic remained present, not only in the heckling he received but also in the need to mark the day as a hiatus in the domestic and foreign conflicts of the Republic.

At the same time as Robespierre and his allies were performing the Festival of the Supreme Being on the Champs de la Réunion, Parisian actors were performing plays for audiences in theaters in central Paris and on the Boulevard du Temple. Some of these performances were closely bound up with the events of the Revolution. Marie-Joseph Chénier's *Charles IX, ou l'Ecole des rois,* first performed on November 4, 1789, seemed to express the goals of the first year of the Revolution for reform of the monarchical state.[6] Jean-Louis Laya's *L'Ami des lois* appeared in January 1793 during the trial of Louis XVI and portrayed on stage the difficult task of reconciling Old Regime noble status with the new society created by the Revolution.[7] In October 1793, Sylvain Maréchal's *Le Jugement dernier des rois* reinforced the emphasis on popular democracy and republicanism that the Terror brought to the fore.[8] In the words of theater historian Michèle Root-Berstein, "Liberty walked among the actors on stage and exhorted the French to brave deeds and republican ideals."[9]

But while Chénier, Laya, Maréchal, and others dramatized revolutionary conflicts, most plays performed in revolutionary Paris appeared at first sight—and to later historians—to have little to do with the Revolution. Three years before the Festival of the Supreme Being, in March 1791, one of the successors to the Comédie-Française of the Old Regime, the Théâtre de la Nation, performed a new drama by one of the most popular playwrights of the period, Monvel, entitled *Les Victimes cloîtrées*. The play was popular, but it made only a few overt political references. The cast of characters in the play included a heroine, Eugènie, whose virtue was threatened; an evil abbot, Père Laurent, and his henchmen; a noblewoman in the clutches of the Catholic Church, Mme de St-Alban; a distraught (and not particularly helpful) bourgeois, Dorval, who was in love with the heroine; and a collection of representatives of the forces of progress and Enlightenment, notably Mme de St-Alban's brother, M. de Francheville. In the end, Eugènie is rescued from apparent death by the not particularly honorable device of a rebellious monk reading the private correspondence of the abbot.[10]

Monvel's play was more interesting as a diversion from the events of the Revolution than anything else, and its plot places it in a long line of French plays of the eighteenth and nineteenth centuries that feature imprisoned characters. But like the Festival of the Supreme Being, it described a world divided between virtue and threatening evil, a rescue not in heroic fashion, as in classical tragedy, but through questionable means, and an attempt to reconstruct a unified world that the events of the play had disrupted. And while civic ceremonies such as the Festival of the Supreme Being and stage plays such as *Les Victimes cloîtrées* depended to some extent on verbal articulation of their meaning through the speeches of political leaders such as Robespierre and characters such as Eugènie and Dorval, they were also representations that used different kinds of stagecraft—sets, costumes, effects such as the burning statue of Atheism—to get across their message.

There are few questions of greater importance in the early twenty-first century than those related to the development of democratic political systems, in which the exercise of power is broadly shared and limited. Political scientists recently gained interest in the process of democratization in the aftermath of dramatic changes around the world between the mid-1970s and the 1990s, a period

Samuel Huntington described as the "third wave" of democratization. Following a first wave that occurred over the century between 1828 and 1926, and a second in the aftermath of World War II, the third wave began in 1974 with the Portuguese Revolution. It continued to the fall of the Eastern European Peoples' Democracies and the breakup of the Soviet Union in 1989–91, and into the 1990s.[11] Subsequent research has speculated about the end of the third wave, about a reverse wave in which some of the new democracies would revert to authoritarian government, and about the possibility of a fourth wave.[12]

This growing concern with democratization processes reflects on the past experiences of European countries such as France as they moved from absolute monarchies to more democratic political systems. The history of this process in modern France revolves around a handful of significant themes: the impact of the disruptions of the revolutionary upheaval of 1789 and the 1790s; the establishment after 1789 of a political regime based on popular support; the creation of links between the French nation and that regime; and the struggles that resulted from divisions about the nature of the regime, especially the direct heir of the Revolution, the Republic. The conjunction of the Festival of the Supreme Being and a popular Parisian play suggests the way in which this book seeks to contribute to our understanding of that history. Examining public ceremonies and theatrical performances in tandem leads to an explicitly interdisciplinary approach, drawing on insights from the study of political culture and the methods of cultural and literary studies to understand the meaning and power of public performance. In particular, I will suggest that both political culture and theatrical performances drew heavily on a particular form of performance, melodrama, and that this "melodramatic thread" in French political culture provided a significant model for the ways in which French men and women constructed the political life of their country.

Political scientists who have studied the process of democratization in a variety of chronological and national contexts have pointed to a number of different factors that seem to have an impact on the process either of establishment of democratic institutions or on their persistence.[13] Often these emphasize elite behavior.[14] Larry Diamond and Juan Linz more broadly list eleven different categories of "sources of democratic progress and failure" in their 1989 survey of democracy in Latin America. These included leadership, institutions, the strength of the state, civil society and associational life, socioeconomic development, cleavages of class and inequality, historical factors, economic policies, international factors, and political culture.[15] Other studies have cited structural factors such as economic development, dependency and world-system role, class structure, democratic diffusion, resource distribution, and actors as the most important factors.[16] Almost all of these explanatory or functionalist models of democratization give some place to the role of political culture. As one of the most important political scientists to focus on democratization in recent years, Larry Diamond, remarked, "few problems are riper for illumination from the political culture perspective than the sources of democratic emergence, consolidation, and persistence," and "democratic consolidation can ... only be fully understood as encompassing a shift in *political culture*."[17]

It is striking, however, the extent to which different disciplines have examined political culture in different ways. Social scientists have tended to view it in terms similar to the way it was originally defined in the 1960s, as an "overarching set of social values" or "the system of empirical beliefs, expressive symbols, and values which defines the situation in which political action takes place."[18] Many social science approaches to political culture assume it to be static, giving it an inherently conservative tone. For example, many studies of democratization in Latin America have assumed that an authoritarian political culture in the region made the development of democracies there virtually impossible. Giuseppe Di Palma's emphasis on the role of elites in presenting democracy as a viable alternative in a crisis of an authoritarian regime is one response to this.[19] Another has been Larry Diamond's insistence that political culture could change in response to social and economic change, social and civic mobilization, institutional practice, historical experience, and international diffusion.[20]

But scholars in other disciplines have viewed the concept of political culture differently. In a formulation that is typical of the approaches of historians and other students of cultural studies influenced by the "linguistic turn" of the 1980s, Keith Baker defined political culture as the "discourses and practices" through which individuals and groups articulate, implement, and enforce the claims they make on each other.[21] This study seeks to bring to social scientists' concern with democratization an understanding of political culture, and ways of examining it in the past, that reflect the latter approach. In particular, I will emphasize the discursive aspects of political culture, a view that allows us to see how ceremonies and theatrical performances could contribute to the French experience with the process of democratization and create a particularly French way in which this process occurred.

To make the link between political culture and performance, we may start with one of the most influential arguments about these processes in European history, and one that has already had a significant impact on our view of the French version of this process. This came from Jürgen Habermas in a work that, while first published in German in 1962, gained influence in France and the United States only in the 1980s. In *The Structural Transformation of the Public Sphere*, Habermas argued that a rational bourgeois public sphere, articulated in settings such as coffee shops and newspapers, laid the foundation for the development of nineteenth-century liberal democracies.[22] While very limited in Habermas's original formulation, this view has been extended to take into account the obvious ceremonial aspects of those political systems.[23] We might go further and note that if, as Gary Thurston suggests, the public sphere elaborated by Habermas describes the "thinking, discussing part of society that took literature, theater, music, and museums seriously," then the representations of the public sphere, and the theatrical performances that in France had sought since before the Revolution to "arm the people with reason" and break down cultural barriers between the elite and the people, are an important aspect of the development of a democratic civil society.[24] Public ceremonies, in this view, have an educational effect similar to that of the coffee houses and press that Habermas emphasized, increasing the rationality of public discourse.

But if we follow this argument through several disciplinary perspectives, it becomes immediately apparent that it raises as many questions as it resolves. Including performance as a part of a democratic polity seems to assume that performance has a transparent ability to communicate understanding without distortion. In the eighteenth century, this question was at the heart of a dispute between Denis Diderot and Jean-Jacques Rousseau on the nature of representation, a dispute framed in both aesthetic and moral terms. Diderot thought that there was a clear distinction between the representation and the represented. But for Rousseau, representation needed to be as close as possible to what was being represented. This was a dispute with more far-reaching implications than the realms of painting or acting. The connection Rousseau posited between representation and reality—the "navel or spindle which connects the represented to its representation," in Frank Ankersmit's words—opened the possibility of the represented being corrupted by its representation, a possibility that Diderot's formulation did not allow.[25] In this view, the performance or representation of public reason might be not a source of "reasoned, progressive consensus formation," as Habermas hoped, but "an occasion for the manipulation of popular opinion," the means by which individual interests, far from being banished from the public sphere, become the coin of politics, a perversion of the rational, critical operation of the public sphere.[26]

The potential for deception and perversion of political democracy through theatrical methods has hung over the efforts to create such political systems, ironically reversing the optimism of Diderot and the pessimism of Rousseau. In recent years complete separation of representations from any underlying reality, such as Diderot optimistically posited, has been suggested as the most important danger to democracy. This was the argument Guy Debord made about the postwar society of France, a society that he called in 1967 *La Société du Spectacle*. Debord emphasized the way in which spectacles of all kinds worked to justify the existing system of economic, social, and political relations and the alienation that they generated for the individual. They turned all life into appearance rather than reality, a "material reconstruction of religious illusion."[27] With the spectacular reconstructing reality as it speaks of it, reality is completely foreign to the integrated spectacular.[28]

The broad brush strokes of Habermas and Debord inevitably leave scholars in disciplines with more empirical methodologies somewhat unconvinced. The art historians Michael Fried and Thomas Crow have explored aspects of visual culture in eighteenth-century France and related these aesthetic developments to the limited public culture of the late Old Regime and the Revolution.[29] Other art historians have claimed that the nineteenth century increased the significance of these visual aspects of French culture. In his study of the relationship between Impressionism and modernism, T. J. Clark closely connects visuality and modernism, arguing that "the circumstances of modernism were not modern, and only became so by being given the forms called 'spectacle.'" Late-nineteenth-century Paris was distinguished for Clark by the "sheer density of signals conveyed and understood, and the highly coded nature of the conveyance." In this formulation, it is not just that Paris was the location for public ceremonies and theatrical performances. It is also the ways in which these ceremonies and performances involved "contact and transaction, contests of nuance and misreading."[30] There is a history interwoven with this view, in which the narrative describes the intensification of the symbolic aspect of Parisian culture. This history was punctuated by a nineteenth-century form of viewing, the *flâneur*. This (male) strolling bourgeois figure who used the modern city as the object of his explorations was complemented by a feminine form of viewing in the increasingly commodified world of department stores.[31]

Paralleling the concerns of historians of art and capitalist consumption are descriptions of the many public ceremonies, mass public meetings, parades, and party rallies of popular nineteenth-century politics as a part of the public sphere and as a way of creating support for the state that organized the events. Mona Ozouf's study of Revolutionary festivals was a landmark work not only for inventorying the important ceremonies of the Revolution but also for suggesting their contribution to the creation of an inclusive Revolutionary movement and their expression of the ideals of the Revolution. Avner Ben-Amos has written a history of republican funerals in the nineteenth and twentieth centuries, carrying Ozouf's thesis about the consolidating effects of such public ceremonies forward in time. Matthew Truesdell has described the public ceremonies of the Second Empire, and Olivier Ihl the festivals of the Third Republic.[32] Other historians have examined events such as the *fête nationale* and the centennial and bicentennial celebrations of the Revolution.[33] In a related vein, the works of Maurice Agulhon on the symbolism of Marianne have emphasized the importance of visual representations as companions to verbal descriptions of republicanism.[34]

Historians of other countries have also examined public ceremonies as a way of understanding political culture. A series of studies of English ceremonies suggested the importance of events such as royal coronations in creating English national identity in the nineteenth and twentieth centuries.[35] American historians have shown how festivals, especially those celebrating the events and ideals of the Revolution in France, were used in the American debate over the nature of the American republic and the legacy of the American Revolution. These celebrations also provided opportunities for groups such as women, the poor, and African Americans to find a public place denied them in celebrations such as the 4th of July or Washington's Birthday.[36] Celebrations in the early Republic were also, as one Jeffersonian orator said in 1806, "so many engines, made subservient to electioneering purposes."[37] In the nineteenth and twentieth centuries parades and other public performances were an integral part of an increasingly democratic American politics.[38]

Russian historians have also described the use of a number of cultural forms, including poster art, spectacles, and theater, to rally support to the New Regime in the aftermath of the Bolshevik Revolution in 1917.[39] Spectacular public festivals in the Bolshevik regime offered an "aesthetic equivalent to the revolution in politics," a parallel that Lenin himself noted. Influenced by popular carnival theater, the organizers of public festivals in Russia broke down the separation between theatrical performances intended for elite groups and those with a more popular audience.[40] These performances also marked the moment of Revolutionary origin. A dramatization of *The Storming of the Winter Palace* presented on its third anniversary on November 7, 1920, on the site of the original event, Palace Square in Petrograd, utilized festival and theatrics to perform a foundational myth for the Soviet regime. Reflecting Rousseau's fears of distortion and Debord's insistence that performances turned appearance into reality, the performance suspended historical recollections of the event, and instead created a new version, "history the way it should have been." In a staging similar to avant-garde theater, the spectators in Petrograd in 1920 were placed in the middle of the action. The actor playing Alexander Kerensky contributed to this effect by stepping across the proscenium to ride in a car across the square to the entrance of the palace. The play could be performed only on the site of Palace Square and the Winter Palace, which reprised their roles as sets for the revolutionary drama. As James von Geldern notes, this is not theater as ritual, but a theatricalization of life itself,[41] similar to what Debord called "the society of spectacle."

Other scholars have more directly linked public ceremonies to concerns about the effects of modern consumer culture. Maurice Samuels's analysis of early-nineteenth-century French novels and theater, for example, emphasizes the commodification of spectacle and the "obsession" with the recent past that marked early-nineteenth-century French culture. For Samuels, this is a way in which French culture dealt with the aftermath of the French Revolution of 1789 and its subsequent events.[42] The cultural historian Vanessa Schwartz argues "that a culture that became 'more literate' also became more visual as word and image generated the spectacular realities" of the late nineteenth century.[43] Schwartz links this to Charles Baudelaire's *flâneur*, in which "the spectator assumes the position of being able to be part of the spectacle and yet command it at the same time." The effect of this, she says, was "the collective participation in a culture in which representations proliferated to such an extent that they became interchangeable with reality."[44]

While Schwartz describes a position of power for the *flâneur*, the strongest theme in these varied approaches has been an emphasis on ceremonies and spectacles as instruments of social control, a way in which a dominant state, or consumer capitalism, consolidates support. In the end, then, this emphasizes the mystification of an externalized "reality" about the exercise of power through the use of symbols. But this (Durkheimian or Marxian) approach too narrowly construes the relationship between symbol and politics by creating an artificial distinction between the domains of symbol and politics. The anthropologist Victor Turner argued a generation ago that "every type of cultural performance, including ritual, ceremony, carnival, theater, and poetry, is explanation and explication of life itself."[45] For Turner these performances are metacommentaries, stories a group tells about itself, "an interpretive reenactment of its experience,"[46] a means by which both actors and spectators reevaluate the social order, and are transformed in the process.[47] At about the same time, Clifford Geertz wrote about the "theater state" of nineteenth-century Bali, emphasizing the "expressive nature of the Balinese state," and its use of spectacle and ceremony in the dramatization of public issues. The state, in Geertz's reading of Bali, "was a device for the enactment of mass ritual." And while he contrasted the "theater state" in Bali, in which ceremonies were the central function of the state, with Western states, in which, he claimed, such ceremonies are peripheral to the exercise of power, he in the end suggested that an emphasis on politics as a "domain of social action" misunderstands the role of ideas. These last are not, he argues, "unobservable mental stuff. They are envehicled meanings" that must be interpreted. "The real," he concludes, "is as imagined as the imaginary," and the performances of the state were "neither illusions nor lies, neither sleight of hand nor make-believe. They were what there was."[48] More recently, and more relevant to our concern with democratization, Laurence Whitehead has suggested the use of a dramatic metaphor as a heuristic device for the study of democratic transitions, even while suggesting the importance of theatrical techniques for the success of leaders in the process. Theater thus was no longer a metaphor for Whitehead, but rather a fundamental part of the process of democratic transition as it was led by men such as Nelson Mandela, Václav Havel, and Boris Yeltsin.[49]

While the concerns of Rousseau and Diderot continue to pervade discussions about theatricality and performance in political culture, the insights of Turner, Geertz, and Whitehead suggest that representations of power actively participate in the creation of meanings about the state, the nation, and the use of power. A modern French political culture influenced by forms of public performance must have had strong implications for the creation of French political institutions and practices and for the twists and turns of that creative process, the narrative of French history that we know. But few sources speak to audience reactions to performances: Victor Hugo's description of the return of Napoleon's body in 1840, or Maurice Barrès's description of the funeral of Hugo in 1885, are famous not only because of the literary renown of their authors, but because they are almost unique as first-person accounts of these huge public events.[50]

The methods of literary analysis and cultural studies provide an alternative to relying on such anecdotal accounts. Historians, especially French historians, have long recognized the important role that literary figures played in political life, and there have been several recent efforts at increasing the links between historical and literary studies. These have most often emphasized the political roles of literary figures, intellectuals, and performers, as well as the impact of literary forms such as drama or the novel on public opinion.[51] Lynn Hunt moved away from this approach in her reading of the "family romance" of the French Revolution, emphasizing the way in which the French "collective political unconscious ... was structured by narratives of family relations," and Judith Walkowitz similarly linked narratives of sexual danger to popular culture in late Victorian England.[52] The methodological assumption of this book extends this approach chronologically to emphasize the importance not just of the role of literary figures and institutions acting in their sphere, but also of the circulation of forms of performance and spectacle in the political culture of modern France. By paying attention to the form of public ceremonies and consciously viewing them as theatrical, I suggest, we can understand better their place in French culture and their ability to resonate with the people of France. Literary critics may focus on texts such as poems or novels. But their methods lead us to think more carefully about the ways in which particular texts—not just written texts, but any collections of symbols that create meaning—accomplish their cultural tasks, and lead us to see how performances such as plays and public ceremonies create meaning.

Historians often read dramatic works and novels for their content. But I wish to focus on the form of public performances in the same way that a literary critic would analyze a literary text in terms of its structure and genre. Genre can be seen as a set of rules about how a literary text should be structured in order to create meaning. As such, it has often been prescriptive, providing the basis for literary criticism that measures the extent to which a poem, or novel, or play conforms to the rules that supposedly define Aristotle's genres of lyric, epic, and drama, or other subgenres discerned by later critics. Because of this prescriptive character, it has fallen into disfavor in recent decades. But the important point here is not the prescriptive ways in which genre has been used in literary criticism, but rather the insight that, by acting as a set of expectations, genre helps the reader to understand the work, "relating it to the world as this is defined and ordered by the prevailing culture."[53] Discerning the form of a public performance allows us to understand how a particular discourse—in this case, the French discourse about politics and especially democracy—operates to create, for French men and women over the last two centuries, an understanding of the uses of power in their political, social, and cultural institutions.

The form of performance, then, will help us to understand French political culture by giving us insight into the discourses that make up that culture. But in contrast to Habermas's assumption of an external "rationality" to bourgeois discourse, or Debord's positing of an equally external "reality" that spectacle distorts, I will emphasize the discursive constitution of both the objects available for study and the conditions under which statements about these objects may be considered "true" or "false." This process is intimately connected with power and the institutions that exercise power. Discursive power is "an opening up of fields in which certain kinds of action and production are brought about. As power disperses itself, it opens up specific fields of possibility; it constitutes entire domains of action, knowledge, and social being by shaping the institutions and disciplines in which, for the most part, we largely make ourselves."[54] Discourses about democratic politics, therefore, create the terrain within which political action takes place as well as the actors—the state, political elites and leaders, citizens—who perform. This means not only the institutional setting, such as parliaments, bureaucracies, civil society, and elections, but also the possibilities for different kinds of political action, such as revolution, compromise, political maneuvering, and even corruption. The emphasis on discourse also suggests the importance of similarities, "family resemblances" throughout a culture of the practices and sciences of that culture, as similar forms of knowledge appear in seemingly distinct forms of cultural activity.[55]

The following pages explore the extent to which the dramatic forms of nineteenth- and twentieth-century theater and film were present as well in the public performance of political power and constituted a particular version of politics. To see how this approach can help us understand French political culture, let us return to the French stage for a moment. Ten years after the premiere of Monvel's *Les Victimes cloîtrées,* a similar plot was used by another French playwright, Charles Guilbert de Pixerécourt, in a play entitled *Coelina,* performed for the first time on September 2, 1800, in the Théâtre de l'Ambigu-Comique on the Boulevard du Temple. The title character is an orphan who has inherited the wealth of her father, the Baron des Echelettes, and has been raised by her paternal uncle, Dufour. Coelina's virtue is demonstrated by her kindness to a mute, Francisque, whose tongue had been cut out several years earlier. But while she is in love with her cousin Stephany, Dufour's son, their happiness—and Coelina's virtue—are threatened by the designs of Coelina's maternal uncle, Truguelin, who proposes a marriage between Coelina and his own son.

Dufour, however, rejects the proposed marriage and instead announces that Coelina and Stephany will be engaged the next day. The celebration of this engagement opens the second act, but is interrupted by Truguelin's servant with a letter informing Dufour that Coelina is not his niece, but rather the illegitimate child of another man, none other than Francisque Humbert, the mute. Dufour orders Francisque and Coelina to leave his house, and when Stephany protests, he is also sent away. The mysteries of the plot begin to be cleared up when Dufour's doctor, Andrevon, informs Dufour that he recognized Truguelin as someone who, eight years earlier, had beaten and mutilated Francisque. He had alerted the authorities that Truguelin and Germain, his servant and confidant, were in the area, and he hoped that "at this moment they were taking them to Chambéry to deliver them to justice." The play ends with Francisque explaining that he had been secretly married to Coelina's mother when Dufour's brother met her. Truguelin, wishing to obtain the property of this new suitor, forced his sister to marry the baron. Hoping eventually to gain control of Coelina's fortune through her marriage to his own son, Truguelin pursued Francisque for years, literally silencing him to prevent obstruction of his plans.[56]

Pixerécourt's *Coelina* was the harbinger of a new dramatic form on the Parisian stage, melodrama, in which suffering heroes or heroines, villains, and well-meaning comics play a moral, humanitarian, and sentimental plot in a world divided into good and evil, where virtue is protected and vice punished.[57]

Pixerécourt had been writing plays since 1793, but with *Coelina* he found his true métier. For the next thirty years, he reigned supreme on Parisian stages, turning out hit after hit, milking for all it was worth the conflict between good and evil characters and plots that brought the characters to the brink of disaster. From its slow beginnings during the Revolutionary decade, melodrama blossomed in the first part of the nineteenth century. Even after other forms of drama replaced it in the elite theaters, melodrama remained the preeminent form of theatrical entertainment in boulevard and other popular theaters into the twentieth century. Adopted in the twentieth century by the new media of film and television, it became a staple form of modern mass culture.

If we seek to understand better the role of public ceremony and performance in French political culture, the rise and pervasiveness of the specific form of melodrama needs to be taken into account. This is especially true if we consider the argument by Peter Brooks that melodrama "is vital to the modern imagination" and that "the origins of melodrama can be accurately located within the context of the French Revolution and its aftermath." By destroying a series of certainties—Church and monarch, Christendom, organic and hierarchical society, as well as literary forms dependent on that society—the Revolution provided, in his view, the starting point for an unsuccessful response to those losses. Brooks directly connects a reading of the politics of the Revolution with the melodrama that marked the French stage in the aftermath of the events of the 1790s. "The Revolution attempts to sacralize law itself, the Republic as the institution of morality. Yet it necessarily produces melodrama instead, incessant struggle against enemies, without and within, branded as villains, suborners of morality, who must be confronted and expunged, over and over, to assure the triumph of virtue." And he goes further, to argue fundamental similarities between the melodramatic form and the ways in which the Revolution described itself. Saint-Just claimed that "Republican government has, as its principle, virtue; or if not, terror," similar to melodrama's strategy of division into good and evil and its intention to impose a new society. Robespierre, Saint-Just, and the Committee of Public Safety are final references for melodrama, personifying virtue in themselves and projecting evil onto the enemies of the Republic. Both the orators of the Revolution and melodrama are concerned, Brooks claims, with the "expression and imposition of basic ethical and psychic truths."[58]

Melodrama and the Revolution are both therefore about virtue, performing a Manichean conflict between good and evil and the reassertion of virtue. But the form was faced with an impossible task, describing not a final meaning or vision of life, but the search for that meaning. Melodrama is thus not life, but a "complete convention in the interpretation of life," a form that searches for ethical certainty even as it operates solely in the realm of representation.[59]

Similarly, as Paul Friedland has noted, the political actors of the postrevolutionary era "were always a moment away from implausibility—if they forgot their lines, if they were heckled by the parterre, or even if the audience lost interest."[60] The constant threat of rivals denouncing the entire basis of the new society—whether it be that of the Terror, the two empires, the restored monarchy, or the various republics of modern France—was a reminder not only of that potential implausibility but also of forces making it impossible to create the desired certainty.

Even if it was not ideologically committed to democratization, melodrama was democratic in its attempt to make clear its message to everyone. A representation of virtue with widespread popularity, melodrama allowed French culture to act as if it had a basis for a new morality even if the form underlined that, in the aftermath of the Revolution, it was impossible to find such a foundation. It distanced postrevolutionary French society from the violence and bloodshed of the revolutionary era by describing a world in which the virtue of the heroine was threatened only by the actions of an evil traitor, figuring the virtue of the French nation threatened by revolutionary or counterrevolutionary extremists. It is therefore a cultural accommodation to the disruptions of the 1790s. But while it represents the divisions in French culture, melodrama is inherently unable to resolve those disruptions. Virtue may triumph over vice by the end of the play, but melodrama does not perform this accommodation to the challenges faced by postrevolutionary France by describing a new society, as would comedy, or even through the communal sacrifice and transformation of tragedy.[61] Rather, it speaks only in terms of the religious, familial, and social hierarchies of the old society, purportedly absolute values that no longer existed in the postrevolutionary world. Amidst all of its shifting styles and popularity—a high point between 1800 and 1830, a decline through the rest of the nineteenth century (when it became less concerned about public virtue, more domestic, primarily "plot, suspense, excitement, the search for new categories of thrills"), and a drift in the twentieth century to film as popular theater declined—melodrama nonetheless has been a fundamental form with which modern culture can describe and understand change.[62]

Were melodrama limited to theater history, it would be of little interest for French political culture. But as Brooks suggests, it is a powerful insight into a fundamental problem faced by postrevolutionary culture in all of its manifestations, on stage and in the spaces in which political power was represented and exercised. Brooks's description of melodrama as a form seeking to create its own version of reality, operating solely in the realm of representation, bears striking similarities to the spectacles described by Clark, Debord, Samuels, and Schwartz. Its fundamental themes of threatened virtue, good versus evil, and an attempt to restore the assumed wholeness of a lost past reverberate through French political ceremonies as well.[63] The Festival of the Supreme Being, with its portrayal of virtue and vice, the triumph of the virtuous Republic opening the way to the happiness of the French people, and the tenuousness of that reassembly of the French nation in the dramatized unity of the festival, bears similarity to the travails of Coelina and Francisque at the hands of Truguelin, and the eventual capture of the villain and restoration of the happy household of Dufour.

These links between theater and public ceremony are underscored by the frequency with which theatrical performances were often a part of public festivals and performers were contributors to the festivals themselves. As recently as the events of May–June 1968, both politics and theater aimed at creating a transparent identity between the spectacle, whether of a public ceremony or a stage performance, and the viewer.[64] As the theater scholar Christophe Campos noted then, as in 1789 and 1871 "there was no need to go to the theater to commune with the gods of imagination, because they were everywhere. For several weeks [in 1968] Paris was a producer's dream, an enormous street happening; everything was theatrical, and there was no need for theaters."[65]

If we discard the prescriptive idea of melodrama as a set of rules to be followed by an author, and rather understand it as a form that creates a particular understanding of the world, we can see how speaking of both public ceremonies and theatrical performances in terms of melodrama allows us to see the similarities in these different practices of representation. It suggests not only that there was a significant theatrical dimension to modern French political culture, but that this theatricality took a particular form, a melodramatic sensibility, in the course of the nineteenth and twentieth centuries. We can also see how the French experience with democracy was informed by these ways of representing the transformation of the Old Regime into the New. As Brooks emphasized, the rhetoric of the Revolution and of later Republican leaders was melodramatic in its construction of a world of good and evil, of virtuous revolutionaries and evil counterrevolutionaries, and of the ultimate inability to eliminate the Old Regime and create the dreamt-for new society here on earth. The opponents of the Revolution similarly viewed the world as sharply divided. The interaction of theatrical form and political culture—the melodramatic thread this book describes—helped to shape nineteenth- and twentieth-century France, portraying and performing the relationship between the state and that civil society as it developed through the public debates and political upheavals that are such an important part of French history in those centuries.

This theatricality was intimately linked with the development of a mass political system as French political culture struggled to become more democratic in the two centuries after the Revolution. As French men and women came to participate actively in the exercise of power, the assumptions they learned about that process were presented in a particular form that drew on the rupture created by the revolutionary decade. It was not only that republicans such as Léon Gambetta, Georges Clemenceau, and Jean Jaurès saw themselves as virtuous workers for human progress and their opponents as corrupt reactionaries, or that monarchists (or Vichyites) saw themselves as the representatives of virtue, and republicans as the opposite. These divisions, arising from the Revolutionary crisis, we know provided the basis for many of the controversies of modern French political history.

But the process went even further. My contention here is not the unoriginal point that after the Revolution France was often divided into two political camps, one supporting the Revolution of 1789, the other opposed to it and wishing to restore some version of the Old Regime. My point, rather, is that these representations employed melodramatic forms when they were performed in the public spaces of Paris. The parallels we will see between the performances in French theaters and those on the Champs de Mars and Place de la Nation are important aspects of the French experience with mass democracy. The popularity of the genre of melodrama lent itself to solving one of the fundamental problems of mass democracy, that of attaching citizens to the institutions, processes, and decisions of the Republic. But in so doing, melodrama shaped the political culture by forcing the very complicated events and questions of French public life into the plots, characters, strengths, and weaknesses of the theatrical form. The construction through melodrama of events like the June Days in 1848, the Commune in 1871, the trial of Dreyfus, the defeat of 1940 and subsequent occupation and resistance, and the loss of empire made individuals such as Louis-Eugène Cavaignac, the Petroleuses, Alfred Dreyfus and the general staff, Philippe Pétain and Pierre Laval, and Charles de Gaulle specific kinds of characters, capable of some actions but incapable of others. They could be heroes or villains, but it was difficult to see them as compromisers. The plot line of melodrama, emphasizing a conflict between virtue and vice, right and wrong, weakened the attempts of figures such as Louis-Philippe, Adolphe Thiers, or Paul Reynaud to find a middle ground in the political disputes of the country. And the inability of melodrama to resolve its Manichean vision of the world damaged efforts to find reconciliation between the proponents and opponents of the Revolution. François Furet's essay arguing that "the Revolution is over" may be read as a hope that French political culture might find a different way of organizing its representations of the players, plots, and outcomes of French politics than through political divisions based on the disputes of the 1790s. As with Debord's spectacles, these representations drawn from the "revolutionary catechism" had seemingly cut loose from any connection with what they purported to represent.[66] The problem, it seemed, was to find a representation of French political life more in tune with the postcolonial, democratic France of the late twentieth century.

At the conclusion of this introduction, it is worth making clear what the following pages attempt to do, and what they do not. My primary goal is to describe the ways in which public spectacles in two different locations in French culture—public ceremonies on the one hand, theatrical and film performances on the other—contributed to the public life of France between the Revolution and the Fifth Republic. While we will not see rigid adherence to any supposed "rules" of melodrama in French theatrical or public culture, I will argue that the seepage of melodramatic conventions between stage and public ceremonies is an important aspect of that public life, creating a characteristic form that shaped modern French democracy as it became more participatory. In this respect French mass democracy is closely linked to the development of commodified spectacle in modern French culture. In order to make this argument, I will focus primarily, although not exclusively, on ceremonial and theatrical representations of the Republic and the Revolution of 1789.

It might be suggested, especially by historians familiar with the works of Agulhon, Ozouf, Ben-Amos, Ihl, and others, that this approach has already been made a part of our version of the French past. Certainly these studies have unearthed much about the ceremonial life of French politics, and a strong cultural tinge has pervaded our version of events such as the Revolution itself.[67] But these public ceremonies have not led to a rethinking of the story of modern France. Surveys of French history written in the late 1980s and early 1990s by François Furet and Maurice Agulhon make mention of well-known public ceremonies such as the Festival of Federation, the Festival of the Supreme Being, the funeral ceremonies for Victor Hugo, the *quatorze juillet*, the Centennial, the Bicentennial in 1989, and others.[68] But in both cases the narrative is constructed around the central theme of the actions of political leaders—the thumbnail sketches of Robespierre, Napoleon, Gambetta, Jules Ferry, Laval, and De Gaulle are brilliant pieces of character construction—and the ceremonial aspects of French political culture serve only to illustrate themes such as the contested nature of French politics.

If we were to take these accounts as typical of the way modern French history is narrated today—and there seems little reason not to do so[69]—we would have to say that the results of monographic research by historians such as Agulhon, Ozouf, Truesdell, Ory, Ben-Amos, and Ihl on the ceremonial aspects of French public life have not been integrated in any significant way into that narrative. The prevailing narrative of French history tells a story about rulers, elections, and social developments, and overwhelmingly about actions and what people have said in words. These actions and words are taken usually at face value, not analyzed as performance. Performance and ceremony are relegated to the margins, useful illustrations but not a part of the story.

The following chapters suggest that Clifford Geertz's insight about the importance of public ceremony in the theater state in Bali and Laurence Whitehead's perception of the dramatic aspects of democratic transitions may find applicability in one of the most important states in modern Europe. They sketch an outline of the interactions between French political culture and a melodramatic sensibility by examining key elements of these developments over the last two centuries. Chapter 2 discusses several significant events of the nineteenth century. In spite of such massive spectacles as the return of Napoleon's remains in 1840, this was a period in which civic performances were severely limited by the restrictions placed on French civil society by the governments of postrevolutionary France. Nonetheless, debates in the Restoration assembly, trials of republicans during the July Monarchy, and the public spectacles of Napoleon III's Second Empire allow us to trace the growing theatricality of French political culture and assess the significance of melodramatic conventions in those performances. Chapter 3 views the full-blown theatrical culture of the triumphant Third Republic after 1870 through the work of one of the most important playwrights of Belle Epoque culture, Victorien Sardou. In the series of plays that Sardou wrote using the Revolution as material, and in ceremonies such as the Centennial in 1889, we can see the specific ways in which melodrama served to define important aspects of the politics constituted by his work, especially the way in which Sardou utilized gender conventions to dramatize his version of the place of virtue and vice in France's culture.

Chapter 4 moves into the period between the two world wars, an era marked not only by the popularity of the new medium of film, but also by attempts to channel the crises and conflicts of republican politics into ceremonial forms. Both film representations of revolutionary events and the civic ceremonies of the early 1920s and the Popular Front of the 1930s reflected the deep melodramatic sensibility of French culture, especially the desire to create a postrevolutionary culture that would unify the nation. In the struggle to maintain a functioning democracy that marked the interwar period, we can see the ability of melodrama to link citizens and the republican state, as well as the limits such a sensibility placed on the viability of that state. The inconsistencies of the republican promise, however, became apparent not only, as at the turn of the century, in questions about gender, but also through the ways in which previously marginalized groups such as workers, women, and colonial subjects appeared in these performances. Chapter 5, finally, concludes our journey by examining a significant experimental theater company of postwar France, Ariane Mnouchkine's Théâtre du Soleil. In the various representations of French republican culture by the Théâtre du Soleil in the 1970s and 1980s, we will see the pervasiveness of melodramatic conventions as they interacted with post-1968 attempts to revitalize the radical message of French republicanism.

This brief overview should make clear that this book is neither an exhaustive catalogue of melodramatic forms in modern French culture nor a synthesis of the role of the memory of the Revolution in France over the last two centuries. The first is a task better suited to the theater and film historians on whose work I will draw in the following pages. My focus on performance also skews my sampling of the memory of the Revolution. The political volatility of the message of the Revolution over the last two centuries often forced it underground, leaving other topics more easily performed. It also leaves aside the most important location in French culture in which that memory was reproduced and represented, the school system. Beginning during the Revolution itself, and flourishing after the foundation of the Third Republic and the Ferry Laws of the late 1870s and early 1880s, this system has inculcated versions of the Constituent Assembly, the Convention, Louis XVI, Robespierre, and Danton in the minds and hearts of French students. So instead of a definitive narrative of theater history or memory, my concern in concentrating on the Republic and the Revolution and on theatrical performances is to provide a focus for my selection of materials related to the larger purpose of examining the performative aspects of French political culture.

In spite of these limitations, however, the following pages make an argument that moves toward a more cultural understanding of the political differences that have marked France in many of the years since 1789 and that have seemed so important, to both contemporaries and later historians, as explanations of the twists and turns of the country's political history. Like bits of glass in a child's kaleidoscope, the elements of French political culture reassembled in different ways and at different times over the last two centuries. The discourses of French culture that divided the world into a conflict of good and evil, that sought to rescue threatened virtue, and that continually hovered on the edge of exposure helped assemble the elements of French political culture into images of the world and, through them, create the processes of social, economic, and political life for French men and women.

2.   Varieties of Performance in Nineteenth-Century Paris

The period from the end of Napoleon's Empire to the Second Empire of the 1850s and 1860s marks a contradictory prehistory of Parisian spectacle, with limited examples of explicitly political demonstrations supplementing a flourishing Parisian theater life. While there were exceptions, such as the ceremonies associated with the restored monarchs or the return of Napoleon's remains in 1840, public ceremonial practices for the most part contrasted sharply with the festivity of the Revolution.[1] These moved only slowly from limited, closed settings in the restricted public sphere of the Restoration and early July Monarchy. Only after mid-century did they come to dominate the streets of a city that had been rebuilt by the Second Empire into a stage for modernist spectacle. At the same time, the Théâtre-Français on the Place du Palais Royal and the Théâtre de l'Odéon across the Seine performed the classical repertoire of Molière, Corneille, and Racine as well as new plays whose acceptance by these state theater companies marked their authors' entry into the highest levels of French culture. Further to the northeast, in the more popular districts of the city, the theaters of the Boulevard du Temple provided entertainment for Parisians of all classes, featuring melodramas whose appeal to popular audiences made it possible for these theaters to survive without state subsidies.

The contrast between the slowly developing ceremonial life of Paris and its flourishing theatrical culture forms the framework for a description in this chapter of the performative character of nineteenth-century French political culture. Against the background of the growth of Parisian theater, I will consider four moments in which public performances were used to constitute political positions in the era after the Restoration of the Bourbon monarchy in 1815. The first of these took place in the restricted circumstances of the representative assembly of the Restoration monarchy, when debates about the legacy of the Revolutionary decade demonstrated the possibilities of parliamentary politics as sites for a spectacular politics. The second involved more visual performances, in the artistic representations of revolutionary events sponsored in the 1830s by the government of Louis-Philippe. The third countered the government's representations of those events through performances in streets, courtrooms, and banquet halls by republican opponents of the July Monarchy. Finally, the Second Empire of Napoleon III demonstrated the acceleration of French political culture in a performative direction, with the use of a reconstructed Paris as a stage for the empire's ceremonial demonstration of its rule. We will also need to place these events alongside the history of the state and popular theaters in this period, in order to understand the ways in which forms of performance that Parisians saw on stages in the Théâtre-Français, the Odéon, and the Boulevard du Temple paralleled the forms of public ceremonies and demonstrations.

These different moments approach the development of Parisian spectacle in different cultural spaces, reflecting the complex ways in which public performance took place during the nineteenth century. In a way, this chapter is a journey through nineteenth-century Paris. We will walk from the cramped quarters of the Chamber of Deputies and the Hotel de Ville, where members of the political elite spoke to each other in words and images, out into the streets of the city, where politics was performed by men and women who saw themselves as the heirs of the Great Revolution. We will then move onto the new boulevards and squares of Baron Haussmann's Paris, a stage setting for public performance. In this journey we will see the twin forms of popular entertainment that the nineteenth-century capital offered its residents: the melodramas of the boulevard theaters and the great spectacles of French politics and culture.

The royal theaters of the Old Regime had been disrupted during the Revolution, but with the First Empire state-supported theaters in the Théâtre-Français on the Right Bank and the Théâtre de l'Odéon on the Left Bank again performed the classical repertoire along with selected new plays. But a popular theater had also existed under the Old Regime, and the first half of the nineteenth century witnessed growth in the significance of the theaters located on the Boulevard du Temple. Immortalized in Marcel Carné's 1945 film *Les Enfants du Paradis* ("paradise" was the nickname given the highest balcony), these theaters drew on an audience of urban workers who came from the growing working-class neighborhoods that bordered on the Boulevard du Temple, such as Belleville, Ménilmontant, and La Villette. For these audiences, "there was a back-and-forth familiarity between the daily life of the theaters, their personnel and their public.... The theater was a part of the mental universe as of their everyday lives." And while the theaters of the Temple were close to the working-class districts, they were distant from the center of the city, and so elite audiences had to make a longer journey from home to attend a performance. Thus, these theaters, until their demolition during the Second Empire, provided a form of popular entertainment that in many ways foreshadowed the twentieth-century development of the cinema.[2]

This popular stage was dominated by several specific forms that reflected the increasingly popular character of the audience for theater and conditioned the way in which historical events were presented. Most important of these forms was the melodrama that had begun during the Revolution and First Empire. As theater audiences became more popular, character and plot development were presented increasingly through action on the stage rather than through words. To a certain extent this reflected the vaudeville origins of boulevard theater, forbidden under the Old Regime from infringing on the privileges of the royal theaters that performed the classical dramatic repertoire. But it also was a way in which boulevard theater could attract a broader audience than those who attended the Théâtre-Français or the Odéon. The supposed "father of the melodrama," Charles Guilbert de Pixerécourt, claimed that "he was writing for those who could not read," and this gave a particular cast to the kinds of plays he wrote, and the ways in which actors performed them.[3] *Féeries,* a related form, were more fantastical than other melodramas, emphasizing magic and the supernatural, and especially utilizing the visual aspects of special stage effects. Relegated to popular theaters rather than the Comédie-Française by the 1830s, melodramas and *féeries* were considered inferior forms of drama, but nevertheless were more important forms of popular entertainment than the state theaters.[4]

A play such as Fabrice Labrousse's *La Bastille,* first performed in 1837 at the Théâtre de la Porte-Saint-Antoine, was a worthy successor to Pixerécourt. Set at the time of the Fronde in the mid-seventeenth century, it portrayed an evil governor of the famous prison, an unjustly imprisoned hero, and a happy resolution in which the hero's son frees him, and the guard who assists the rescue kills the prison governor.[5] That the play was set in the Bastille no doubt increased its resonance with audiences who knew the reputation of the prison that had stood not far from the theater. Early-nineteenth-century melodramas also drew on the events of the more recent French past. The Duc de Chartres and Lafayette appeared as characters on the stages of the boulevard, and there were a number of popular dramas in which Georges Danton, Camille Desmoulins, and even Robespierre gave long speeches that justified the Terror.[6] The 1840s also saw a revival of plays with revolutionary topics. In 1847 a play entitled *La Révolution française* was presented at the Cirque Olympique, describing a Revolution and a France that would liberate the peoples of Europe.[7] Alexandre Dumas was a master of the melodrama, and in 1847 he wrote and produced one entitled *Le Chevalier de la Maison Rouge ou Des Girondins,* based on a novel he had written in 1845–46.[8] Another play, *Charlotte Corday,* by Dumanoir and Clairville, was performed at the Gymnase-Dramatique in July 1847. It used Marat's assassin to portray, also in melodramatic terms, the threat to France posed by the Terror. Charlotte, in this version, plans to assassinate Marat to avenge the condemnation of her fiancé, a monarchist in the Vendée, and his brother, a soldier in the republican armies. While being cross-examined after the assassination, she compares herself to Joan of Arc, underscoring her role as figure for a threatened France. In this case, the resolution was not the salvation of Charlotte, but rather the reunification of her and her fiancé after death, both martyrs at the hands of the Republic.[9]

The two decades after 1848 saw a significant transformation of the Parisian theater industry. A law of January 6, 1864, ended the long-standing limitations on the number of theaters in the capital, allowing any individual to build and operate a theater. The numbers of theaters in the capital increased from twenty-one in 1852 to twenty-eight in 1870. This relatively modest increase in numbers, however, masked the destruction of many of the older theaters. Most notable was the demolition of all but one of the theaters on the old Boulevard du Temple, a result of the construction of the new Boulevard Prince-Eugène (now Boulevard Voltaire). The so-called Boulevard du Crime had been the home of popular Parisian theater since the eighteenth century, but two-thirds of the theaters in operation in 1870 were in new buildings, housing either new companies or companies that moved from older theaters that were torn down. These new theaters created a new geography of theater in the city: many of them were located closer to the center of the city on the Right Bank, and this made them more accessible to the middle-class audiences that were increasingly dominating the central arrondissements. At the same time, they became more difficult for the growing urban working class to attend. In the place of the neighborhood theaters on the Boulevard du Temple, located on the fringe of the working-class neighborhoods of the northeast, the newer theaters were now distant from popular neighborhoods, especially those in the newer industrial suburbs.[10]

The reconstruction of the city and its theater industry contributed to the creation of two different audiences. One was an elite bourgeois audience that patronized the Théâtre-Français, the Opéra-Comique, the Théâtre-Italien, and the Odéon, all located in the city center, and the Académie de Musique, awaiting completion of its new home, the Opéra Garnier. The second was a more popular audience that patronized newer theaters farther out in Bercy, Montparnasse, the Rue de Grenelle, the Boulevard de Batignolles, Montmartre, and Belleville. These popular theaters laid the groundwork for the café chantants and café concerts that, especially after the fall of the Second Empire, would create the popular theatrical entertainments of the Belle Epoque.[11]

But melodrama, even though now past its prime, remained an important part of Parisian theater. François Ponsard's Charlotte Corday was seen both in 1848 and in March 1850. This play, with a sympathetic heroine in the assassin of Marat, portrayed both the Girondins and France as threatened by Robespierre, who saw his own enemies as enemies of the state, and by the dishonorable Marat. Charlotte's assassination of Marat, however, only has the effect of turning him into a hero and elevating him to the Panthéon. In the end, as Charlotte goes to her own death, Danton returns to the struggle with Robespierre for the heart of the Revolution.[12] On the other side of opinion about Robespierre, but using the same plot structure, Henri Bonnais's *Le 9 Thermidor ou la mort de Robespierre* was rejected by the censor and then published by its author with the note that "a reading of the play will make it easy to understand the reasons that forbade its performance." Robespierre is portrayed as self-sacrificing, announcing that "I will go into the afterlife with joy, if the sacrifice of my life will be useful for the Republic." J-N Barras and J-L Tallien, in contrast, the men of the 9th of Thermidor, are in the pay of the Bourbons but not only are plotting against Robespierre but are planning to swindle the pretender to the throne. Of all the conspirators against Robespierre, only Carnot is portrayed sympathetically: he points out the hypocrisy of Barère in plotting against Robespierre after praising him as the Incorruptible. The final scenes of the play are set in the Convention and the Hotel de Ville, and are dramatizations of the historical record with a few asides added. The threatened heroes, Robespierre and Saint-Just, are willing to die for France, with Robespierre swearing that he "never wished anything except the happiness of humanity."[13]

The importance of theatrical forms in nineteenth-century Paris lies in melodrama's creation of a sensibility in French culture, a way of casting issues, whether it be in the family dramas that were the stuff of boulevard melodramas, the re-creation of the principal figures of the Revolution, or, I would argue, central issues of public policy and the organization of the use of power—political culture—in this period. The politicians of the Restoration, July Monarchy, and Second Republic could not stage a public performance in the same spectacular way as could the producers and actors of the Boulevard du Crime. The restrictions on political discussion, the police concern with maintaining public order, and even the limited followings of many of the participants in French public life between 1815 and 1850 made it difficult to mount a political demonstration, whether in support of or in opposition to the regime in power, in the same way as the Cirque Olympique portrayed Revolutionary France. But both locations in French culture, we will see, are strikingly similar in their tendencies to see the world as a place in which virtue exists, vice threatens it, and life is the story of how this conflict plays out through the intervention of heroic characters. They were also similar in their inability to find a resolution of the plot: on stage, virtue is not restored because the rescuer of virtue is himself or herself flawed in a serious way. In the Assemblies, courts, and streets of Paris the regeneration of the French nation also proved a flawed dream. Melodrama performed these conflicts and the inability of theatrical and political culture to find a resolution of them.

The political institutions of the Restoration, while bowing in the direction of the Revolution's practices of popular government, placed severe limitations on political participation. A Chamber of Deputies was elected by a property franchise, but its membership was limited to wealthy notables. A Chamber of Peers provided a further check on the chamber. The assemblies had little power over the government in any event, even had their members wished to oppose the policies of the restored Bourbon kings.[14] In spite of these restrictions, however, the experience of the Constituent Assembly and the Convention in the 1790s had shown the potential for debates in public assemblies to become popular performances of alternative views of how politics should be organized.[15] Twenty-five years later, several debates in the Chamber of Deputies demonstrated how even in the restricted circumstances of the Restoration, assemblies could became theaters for the performance of political culture.

The first came in 1818 with a debate on a law proposed by the government to reorganize the army, establishing conscription and creating a reserve made up of the veterans of the Revolutionary and Napoleonic wars. To conservatives the proposal seemed an attempt to insinuate the revolutionary principle of conscription and the personnel of the revolutionary armies into the Restoration army. These two aspects of the law threatened, conservatives thought, to revive the repression of the Revolution and the international aggression of the First Empire. But others minimized the danger. The Chevalier Allent, undersecretary of state for war, noted that the danger a conscripted army would pose to the liberties of individuals and to the peace would be opposed by not only "the moderation of our princes, the representations of the Chambers, a wise exercise of royal power and of our liberties" but also "the memory of the past," that it was a conscripted army that allowed Napoleon and the Revolution before him to disturb the peace.[16] The reporter of the law, the Comte Dambrugeac, supported the provision in the law that called for veterans to be used as a reserve. But, he noted, they could not completely meet the needs of the army in case of war. Being allowed to marry and form families meant that, while they could be used to garrison fortresses and to maintain order within France, they could not be incorporated into the troops of the line. They would have to be organized into special, separate corps, and could not then be used by the army without any limitations in time of war.[17]

The debate raised issues about how the restored monarchy would deal with the legacy of the Revolution. But as the debate proceeded, issues of public policy were increasingly presented in ways that resembled the performances in the nearby theaters of Paris. The principal defender of the proposal to use the soldiers of the Revolution and Empire as a reserve was the minister of war, General Gouvion Saint-Cyr. In a speech probably written by the liberal François Guizot, Gouvion Saint-Cyr played to an audience outside the Chamber when he first rejected, in the name of equality, the recruiting system, the *milice*, used by Louis XIV. Is it, he asked, "anything else than conscription striking a single class of citizens, conscription without equality?" His comment drew cries of approval from supporters in the Chamber. He pointed out that, since the Restoration, many former soldiers had rejoined, "with joy, and in great number, these arms that they had so long carried with glory." But he also firmly supported the use of these soldiers as a reserve. The point of a reserve, he said, was that it sleep peacefully "on the breast of the fatherland" in time of peace, and reawaken quickly in time of war. A reserve of Revolutionary soldiers would meet these requirements. "Old soldiers," he argued, "would not need to learn either military practices or military obedience; they may live a long time as citizens; they will always be soldiers."[18]

But Gouvion Saint-Cyr was doing more than arguing a point of public policy. Himself a former commander of imperial armies, he was publicly performing a role as defender of his former troops, extending to the troops of the line the adulation that had been given to fallen generals such as Lazare Hoche in memorial services during the Revolution and Empire.[19] And he played his role successfully, drawing his audience into the performance. As he turned directly to the qualities of these soldiers, the reporter noted that "the attention of the chamber increased, and the most profound silence was established." Having gained his audience, Gouvion Saint-Cyr praised revolutionary soldiers' devotion to France, asking if the country had two armies, two nations, one of which "will be struck by anathema and regarded as incapable of serving the King and France." "It is necessary to know," he said, "if we will still call to the defense of the country the soldiers who have given it glory, or if we will declare them forever dangerous to her safety." Gouvion decried this last opinion of soldiers that had been admirable in combat, motivated by a belief that they sacrificed their lives for the honor of France. "Would France not ask of these men, that Europe has always admired, the strength that they still had to offer?" With this last sentence, the silence in the Chamber was broken by loud cries of approval and applause, as would happen in Parisian theaters when the audience intervened in the performance of the play. A few moments later, he pressed further his elegy of these soldiers, emphasizing their virtuous devotion to the nation and the threat posed by the opponents of the law. "Our soldiers have atoned for much," he claimed, "for they have suffered much; who then will insist on continuing to reject them?" and, according to the record of the debate, a new shudder went through his audience. The record noted that when he finished, rounds of applause were heard, and upon his descent from the tribune he was met by "expressions of the profound impression produced by his speech." Like the actors in Pixerécourt's melodramas, Gouvion Saint-Cyr played out a scene in which he rescued the threatened virtue of the veterans and revolutionary France, and his speech resonated in the Chamber like a theatrical performance on the Boulevard du Temple.

The following year the attempt to seat the Abbé Grégoire as a member of a bureau of the Chamber of Deputies created a similar controversy. As a constitutional bishop, a republican, an advocate of Jewish emancipation, an opponent of slavery, and a member of the Convention (who equivocated but did not vote for the execution of Louis XVI), Grégoire was anathema to the Ultraroyalists in the Chamber. When his name was drawn in the random selection for membership in one of the nine bureaus of the new Chamber, there were calls for adjournment of the selection process. Members on the Right (notably the Comte de Villèle) objected on a technicality, insisting that it was necessary to await the verification of Grégoire's mandate and that he had not taken the oath to the king as had most of the deputies at the royal séance the previous session. But the Comte de Marcellus had already insisted, "No regicides in the Chamber," and, mounting the tribune, Villèle admitted that there were reasons other than Grégoire's failure to take the oath that caused opposition to his participation in the activities of the Chamber.[20]

While consideration of Grégoire for a position, even provisional, on a bureau was adjourned by the Chamber, a problem immediately arose when the president of the Chamber drew the name of a M. Beugnot, who had also not been present at the royal séance and also had not taken the oath. From the Left, this time, came calls to adjourn the appointment of Beugnot, with General Tarayre (whose own election in Charente-Inférieure would be contested and annulled on December 4) claiming that "the law ought to be equal for all: adjournment," while deputies on the Right objected.[21]

Beugnot's appointment was adjourned for the moment, as had been Grégoire's. But the issues arose again on December 6 when the question of verification of Grégoire's election from the Isère was debated in the Chamber.[22] To Jacques-Joseph Corbière, Grégoire's case was simple: it had to be decided if a regicide had the right to be a member of the Chamber, "bringing in his train the entire Revolution," a phrase that brought approval from the Right, and laughter on the Left. Grégoire's election was, in Corbière's view, an insult to the king. M. de Marcellus insisted that, as a member of the Convention, Grégoire had given his approval to the condemnation of Louis XVI, and for that reason, and that reason alone, his election should be annulled. In contrast, Devaux claimed that Grégoire had never been convicted of a crime and that the Chamber was setting itself up as a court in assuming him guilty of one.

Conservatives had begun with a technicality, the verification of Grégoire's election, but quickly moved on to associate him with the horrors of the Convention. His liberal defender, Benjamin Constant, argued on technical grounds that Article XI of the Charter banned penalties for past votes and opinions. But he also found ample, if uncomfortable, evidence for his side in the events of the Revolution, noting that Louis XVIII had used Joseph Fouché, a regicide, as a minister at the beginning of the Restoration. The king, Constant claimed, had shown in 1815 that he did not wish revenge, but rather fidelity to what he himself had promised in the Charter. To refuse Grégoire after the king had accepted Fouché into his councils would be for the Chamber to censure the king in front of Europe. In the end, Grégoire's liberal supporters became just as distanced from the original issue as his opponents. "It was impossible to punish the men of the Revolution," the liberals argued, "because the Revolution was France." The Ultras, in contrast, led by François-Régis Labordonnaye, held that it was the nation's duty to reject the authors of the crime of regicide. This time the Liberals were unable to carry the day and the abbé was denied his seat, albeit officially on a technicality.[23]

While these debates brought out disagreements on points of law and meaning of the Charter, they also involved public demonstrations that effectively turned the hall into a theater. Conservatives portrayed a wronged king, liberals saw Grégoire as offended, and for both, France itself was in danger. For both sides, the outcome of the debate would determine the success or failure of the deputies' defense of the nation's virtue. The public, open nature of the debate was also important. During the initial debate on December 2 concerning appointment of Grégoire, one deputy, M. Demarcay, was assailed by voices calling for him to speak to the Chamber when he spoke privately to the president. The long-standing tendency of the barrier between actors and audience to dissolve in French theaters was also apparent, as the debate was marked by constant interventions from both sides of the floor, as well as members speaking from the tribune in support of their position.[24] With calls from the Chamber to adjourn the appointment, while others demanded that the session continue, the assembly began to resemble a rowdy popular theater. With the ability of the president to control the session slipping away, the tribune only occasionally functioned as a focal point for the discussion, and calls came from around the room. Four days later, during the debate on seating Grégoire, the Chamber was also a scene of agitation. During the speech of M. Devaux, for example, the reporter noted that "a constant agitation reigned while the orator pronounced his discourse." The Left, in contrast, interrupted the speech by M. de Marcellus opposing Grégoire's validation. In all of this uproar, Constant's speech was apparently received in relative quiet. But when the president attempted to close off debate and vote on the seating of Grégoire, he was prevented from ending the session by the demands of members throughout the Chamber who claimed "we didn't vote, we were not heard.... Nothing has been put to vote. Stay in your seats, stay in your seats." When, a few minutes later, a vote was taken and Grégoire rejected, cries of "Vive le roi!" were heard throughout the Chamber.[25]

The speeches in these two debates were hardly great examples of brilliant oratory, and stand in poor contrast to the speeches of a Mirabeau or Danton during the Revolution, or of Gambetta at the beginning of the Third Republic.[26] They were even less competitive with the English tradition of parliamentary debate that had produced the two William Pitts and Charles James Fox in the eighteenth century, and Robert Peel, John Bright, William Gladstone, and Benjamin Disraeli in the nineteenth. Nor could Gouvion Saint-Cyr or Benjamin Constant match the oratory of Daniel Webster, Henry Clay, or Abraham Lincoln in the United States.[27] But the Gouvion Saint-Cyr and Grégoire incidents took place in the Chamber itself, one of the most public places in Restoration political culture, making it a theater for portraying the memory of the Revolution. The theatricality that had marked the assemblies of the Revolution and that was a part of other representative assemblies in the early nineteenth century had revived in the Restoration, even if in a more muted and less flamboyant way and in front of a more limited audience. Some deputies certainly tried to place limits on this, as did the Chevalier Allent when he argued in favor of conscription. "I have passed my life at the study (of military matters)," he said, "and have dreamed myself of other ideas, before having received the bases of this law. But are these bases independent of time and circumstance? Can they be posed elsewhere than in the council of his Majesty, and do we know, to establish them, all the information that it is necessary to consider?"[28] His claims of ignorance of the basis of the king's policies was, in effect, an attempt to limit public debate to the King's Council, and to conduct public debate in a less theatrical setting and form.

But these concerns were part of a larger debate about the nature of Restoration political culture, about the organization of the public sphere and the appropriate relationship between the monarch, the representative assembly, and the sovereign nation. While each began with a consideration of a procedural matter stemming from interpretation of the Charter, they soon began to draw the status of the Revolutionary era into the debate. And in these debates, theatricality intervened to structure the invocation of the Revolution, with a progression from a legalistic argument to one in which the participants were playing to their colleagues and the Chamber took on many of the characteristics of a Parisian theater. The parliamentary inquiries about the soldiers of the Revolution and the Abbé Grégoire bore all the hallmarks of the genre of courtroom melodrama.[29] And as in the melodramas playing on the boulevards, these debates framed these issues in terms of wronged virtue (the soldiers of the Revolution and Grégoire, for liberals, or the king and France itself, for conservatives). They sought to bring closure to the disputes of the Revolutionary decade, through either an acceptance of the events or their banishment from French public life. But if they underscore the continuance in French public discourse of the controversies that began in 1789, they also indicate the inability of postrevolutionary political culture to heal those divisions. The performances in the Chamber of Deputies could not reach a clear conclusion about what policies were right or wrong; they only emphasized the ambiguity of public life and the difficulty in French political culture to find agreement on the basis for that life.

By the 1830s, following the overthrow in July 1830 of the Bourbon Charles X and the assumption of the throne by Louis-Philippe of Orléans, the *Salle de Séances* of the Chamber of Deputies became even more obviously a stage setting for the performance of French political culture, not in words but in images. The decoration of the room in the Palais Bourbon clearly linked the representative assembly of the July Monarchy and the king himself to the events of the 1790s. The subjects for these paintings were suggested by François Guizot, the minister of the interior, and approved by Louis-Philippe in 1830. The centerpiece of the décor was a picture of Louis-Philippe taking the oath as king before the Chamber on August 9, 1830. The plan for the room was to flank this work on one side by a picture by Auguste Hesse of the Third Estate's refusal to disperse when ordered to do so on June 23, 1789, by the Marquis de Dreux-Brézé. On the other side would be a painting by Auguste Vinchon of an incident on May 20, 1795, in which the Parisian crowd invaded the Convention, killed a deputy, and presented his head at the end of a pike to the president, François Boissy-d'Anglas. But Boissy rescued the situation for the Assembly by saluting his fallen comrade and refusing to yield his chair to the revolt. The aftermath of this event forced the surrender of the popular movement, leaving the popular wing of the Revolution permanently crippled. The event therefore reflected the strength of the Assembly against the popular movement. The conjunction of these two paintings involved a forgetting of what had happened between 1789 and 1795, emphasizing the power of the Assembly but removing from the memory of the Revolution the popular movement that had driven events further and further to the left between the summer of 1789 and the end of the Terror in 1794.[30] They also emphasized the public nature of politics, as the deputies performed their roles in the public sphere.

Not far away from the Palais Bourbon, a short distance up the Seine and on the Right Bank, the Paris Hotel de Ville was also planned to be the location for decorations that would present in public a particular version of French politics, although one that would differ in emphasis from the public sphere constituted by the paintings in the Chamber of Deputies. This was a particularly significant site given the importance of not only the Parisian government but also the people of Paris in Revolutionary events, and the continuing perception of the city of Paris as the focal point for revolutionary movements. It therefore was to have been the site for the most popular version of the Revolution. Odilon Barrot's plan for the decoration of the Hotel de Ville included four paintings that, by pairing the fall of the Bastille with popular resistance to Charles X, and the appointment of Bailly as mayor of Paris with that of Louis-Philippe as lieutenant-general, represented the 1830 revolution as an event taking up the reforms begun in 1789.[31] In the Palais Bourbon the Revolution was located in the actions of the Third Estate and the Chamber of Deputies, the representatives of the nation, rather than the nation itself. But in the Hotel de Ville, the Revolution was to be given a popular component. In neither case was the Revolution represented as the work of the entire French nation. But the two images reflected the difference central to the political culture of the July Monarchy, between a revolution made by the sovereign nation embodied in the Parisian crowd and one made by the representatives in the Third Estate.

Louis-Philippe used the state's role as art patron to invoke his own military role in the Revolution, as a hero of 1792, to enhance the Orleanist claim to the throne. The theme was also developed in the refurbished rooms of the Chateau of Versailles, which were devoted to history paintings portraying the sweep of French history. In the Salle de 1792 at Versailles the military theme, and especially Louis-Philippe's participation in the wars of the Revolution, were dominant.[32] These invocations of the early wars of the Revolution were often personal in character and limited by the extent of Louis-Philippe's participation in the heroic past. For some, they became "little more than a repetitive jingoism fixed on Valmy and Jemmapes."[33] But they indicate the extent to which the actions and policies of the deputies and the king were supplemented in French political life during the July Monarchy by elements with a specifically visual quality: in the Chamber of Deputies and in the projected Hotel de Ville, politics was to be viewed rather than heard. This viewing was still indoors and limited to a small audience, and it was hardly a mass spectacle. But it echoed the theatrical performance of the tableaux that were a common feature of theatrical performances, and underscores further the relationship between political spectacle and theater.[34]

On December 15, 1840, a million spectators stood in the cold and watched a carriage carrying the remains of the Emperor Napoleon roll down the Champs Elysées to the Invalides. One of the most remarked-upon public events of the nineteenth century, the *retour des cendres* stood out both because it brought so many Parisians into the streets in a century when the government discouraged such public assemblies and because it represented an attempt by Louis-Philippe to combine his own service in the armies of the Revolution with the military glory represented by the emperor.[35] But the metaphorical leap between Louis-Philippe and the French nation in the Palais Bourbon, at Versailles, and at the Invalides found its antithesis in the identification of the nation and the Revolution by some radicals. Louis-Philippe sought to use Napoleon as the vehicle for his own regime's view of the past, but for radicals, the Revolution of July 1830 had rescued the Revolution from the dangers of the counterrevolution. In July 1831, for example, the Société des Amis de l'Egalité described the July Days in 1830 as the revival of the spirit of 1789, and called on Parisians to celebrate the *quatorze juillet* as the anniversary of both the taking of the Bastille and the Fête de la Fédération. "The 14th of July 1789," it said, "was the enthronement of the people as KING; the 14th of July 1790 was its coronation ceremony." In 1830, they argued, Parisians reconquered their liberty, as their parents had done before them.[36]

But there were other republicans disappointed by the results of the July Revolution and its failure to fulfill the goals of Paris radicals. These men also looked back to the first Revolution for inspiration, but not to the events and principles of 1789. In newspapers, speeches, pamphlets, and courtrooms they played out scripts that located revolutionary and national virtue in the First Republic of 1793. The republican newspaper *La Tribune*, edited by Armand Marrast, in its program printed in January 1833, demanded social reform through the establishment of the Republic, by which it meant "the equality of each to the judgment of all." It proposed the socialist idea of association as the way of organizing a just society in which those who worked would have the means to do so. The agent of this task would be the people, which Marrast linked to its revolutionary ancestor: "Our fathers, indefatigable workers for a revolution that did not find them weak; our fathers, so calumnied, so outraged by an unjust generation ...; our fathers, who accomplished such great things, have also left us great things to accomplish." The Parisian people of the 1830s were the same as in 1793: "moral as they always have been, intelligent, strong, calm, just, themselves making their destiny, making that of the world!"[37] In the same year a pamphlet entitled *Le Montagnard* lamented the attacks and insults that monarchists had heaped on the mountain of the First Republic, in spite of that regime's successes in "vanquishing all its enemies, pushing forward our frontiers, and reestablishing at home the calm troubled by so many diverse factions who opposed the democracy established in such a large and absolute manner by the montagnards." Without Robespierre, Marat, Saint-Just, Danton, and Desmoulins, "the revolution would have been lost forever, and on September 21st Paris, in place of being witness to the proclamation of the Republic, would have seen the entrance of the coalition armies and the emigrés." Robespierre in particular was "the apogee of virtue, the greatest and the most eloquent of men."[38]

These pamphlets illustrate the extent to which, for many republicans of the early 1830s, the Revolution and Robespierre were viewed as figures of public virtue. It was a particular part of Robespierre's work that inspired them, the Declaration of the Rights of Man he had proposed to the Convention in April 1793. Robespierre's proposals posed an important challenge to the liberal

Girondists who still controlled the Convention, and to the moderates of the 1830s. He supported the opposition to political oppression contained in the draft proposed by a committee, and his insistence that there was an eternal alliance of peoples against tyrants matched the draft's statement that "any individual who would usurp sovereignty" should be "put to death instantly by free men." But Robespierre on April 25, 1793, proposed amendments that contrasted sharply with the unwillingness of either the Constituent Assembly in 1789 or the Convention's committee in 1793 to turn the political revolution into a social one. "The committee has still completely forgotten," he lamented, "to state the duties of fraternity that unify all men of all nations, and their right to mutual assistance." He attempted to strike a balance, arguing that "[t]he extreme disproportion of fortunes is the source of many evils and many crimes, but we are no less convinced that the equality of goods is a chimera." But his proposals to remedy the "evils" and "crimes" caused by property holding defined property not as an absolute right, but as "the right of each citizen to enjoy and dispose of the portion of goods that is guaranteed to him by the law." This right to property carries with it "the obligation to respect the rights of others," and it cannot harm the security, the liberty, the existence, or the property of others. Defending his proposal against conservative critics, Robespierre rejected the "phantasm" of a *loi agraire,* the supposed confiscatory threat to private property that was used to tarnish socialist proposals in both the 1790s and the 1830s. But he did not support private property without limitation. Several of his proposed articles articulated a practical sense of fraternity, going beyond the draft declaration to define the aid needed by anyone who lacks necessities as a "debt" owed by those with a surplus, and requiring that those with a surplus must progressively, according to their wealth, support those whose incomes do not exceed subsistence.[39]

Robespierre's speech and amendments were greeted by "unanimous applause," according to *Le Moniteur,* but his amendments did not find their way into the finished declaration. Nevertheless, in the context of the early 1830s these ideas were politically explosive. Republicans who felt that the Revolution of 1830 had been stolen from the people of France by the bourgeoisie and by Louis-Philippe often found inspiration in Robespierre's Declaration of Rights. Using pamphlets, newspapers, and public trials, these groups publicized the views of Robespierre and tried to justify a revival of the radical movement of 1793 among French workers in 1830. A Société des Montagnards published the Declaration of Rights in 1832 with a preface that argued that "this declaration, an immortal monument raised by our fathers for public knowledge, contains the unchangeable basis for the happiness of the people, for its rights and its liberties; it rebuts the numerous calumnies spread about an epoch so universally and unjustly misunderstood."[40]

The Declaration of 1793 was the inspiration for the Société des Droits de l'Homme, one of the most important republican groups of the 1830s. Established in 1830, the Société grew quickly after an insurrection in June 1832. Paul Thureau-Dangin, a historian writing in the 1880s, estimated that it soon had 4,000 members in Paris, while Alain Faure's more recent estimate is of 765 militants by the end of 1832. By either estimate a significant force in Parisian republican circles, it was also at the head of a number of provincial associations. Strikes in 1833, in Paris, Lyon, Anzin, Caen, Le Mans, and Limoges, shifting the workers' movement from political to social goals, were attributed to it. But it suffered from internal divisions. In October 1832, as the economy slowed, a conflict emerged between the Comité Raspail, which wished to maintain the broad alliance of July 1830, and the Comité Lebon, which wanted a social republic. The radical Comité Lebon emerged victorious from the election of a new Central Committee in September 1833. This was a consequence of growing worker presence in the Société, and it began using the terminology of "association" that marked artisanal socialist movements at this time. By 1834, when it played a significant part in the "revolt of the *canuts*" in Lyon, a majority of its members were workers.[41]

The rhetoric of the Société reflected these political divisions. But it translated them into the terms of virtue and vice in which its members saw the Revolution and the Republic, echoing the contrast between the virtuous sansculotte and the grasping bourgeois that marked the Revolutionary rhetoric of 1793. A *Petit Catéchisme Républicain par un membre de la Société des Droits de l'Homme*, published in 1832, drew the contrast in straightforward terms. A Girondin, it said, was someone for whom "all morality consists in appearance ... who puts conveniences in the place of equity, justice, humanity ... who always wants to instruct, and who needs to learn ... who judges all men at the tribunal of the Girondin horde, of which he is by and by the master and the servant." A Montagnard, in contrast, is the opposite, the sworn enemy of the Girondin, "for whoever loves virtue should abhor crime. The Montagnard is the simple, natural man, who cultivates his sentiments and his reason, who concerns himself ceaselessly with the happiness of others, who makes war against oppressors of all kinds ..., who comforts the unfortunate, who sees in the love of the *patrie* only the love of humanity and who serves it with all his power; finally, it is the one who does to others all that he wishes others would do to him."[42] Public policies concerning the state of workers were therefore moral issues. The following year members of the Société continued to elaborate the complaint that the Revolutions of 1789 and 1830 had not addressed the need for social equality. A letter to the editor of the liberal newspaper *Le National* in August 1833 by J. J. Vignerte took the press to task for addressing only political questions, while "the greatest revolutions are not political revolutions; when they are not accompanied by social revolutions, they result in nothing or almost nothing. Authority changes hands, but the nation remains in the same state." But, again, this took on moral overtones: "Corrupt opinions, evil passions, ignorance, the resulting misery continues."[43]

The solution lay in the program outlined by Robespierre in April 1793. The Marseille section of the Société saw the Declaration as its point of departure: "there are engraved in sublime characters the eternal laws of justice and truth; there is the germ of all the healthy doctrines that the progress of the times should make clear; there are found the principles whose application alone can put an end to the sorrows of humanity." Further, it ordained in its regulations that a part of each session be devoted to the examination of the Rights of Man and Citizen, to aid "the moral and political perfection of all *sectionnaires*."[44] Similarly, the Grenoble section adopted the Declaration as Robespierre had proposed it, as the expression of its principles and as its guide in seeking its ultimate goal, "that the people recover the exercise of its sovereignty."[45]

Armand Carrel, in a report on the manifesto of the Société des Droits de l'Homme that he read to the Société de Défense Commune de la Liberté de la Presse in December 1833, also defended the proposals of 1793. But he spoke in terms that emphasized the threat posed to them and the radical Revolution of which they were a part, even by the moderate Revolution of 1789. "Let there be no mistake," Carrel said. The Declaration of 1793 was directed "against the society, against the civilization, against the principle of liberty conquered in 1789." In 1833, he argued, French democracy had to declare that it was no longer the democracy of 1789, that "it had increased in intelligence, in courage, in understanding of things and in aptitudes of all kinds." The outcome of the first Revolution had not favored these ideas. Not only had the Convention rejected the ideas of Robespierre, but after the 9th of Thermidor it had moved against the sections of Paris and pushed the *jeunesse dorée* "wearing the insignias of the *chouannerie*," against the worker faubourgs of Paris, the "homes of democratic passions." At the same time, however, Carrel defended the Declaration against accusations that it was too radical and would lead to a revival of the Terror. Robespierre's calls for social reform in his last speeches, Carrel argued, were not a part of the Terror, but rather an attempt to find an exit from "that unhappy regime." The Société des Droits de l'Homme no more believed in the agrarian law than did Robespierre or, for that matter, Babeuf. The Société looked to the Declaration of 1793 not because it is bloodthirsty, but rather because it is an expression of the philosophical Robespierre, a follower of Rousseau.[46] Virtue lay in 1793, not 1789, and Carrel and his friends would be its defenders.

But the Société des Droits de l'Homme did more than publish pamphlets. As in the first years of the Restoration, the conflict between the forces of order and those desiring a continuation of the Revolution was dramatized in theatrical form in public spaces. Public trials and attempted revolts against the government contrasted with the limited performances of the Restoration Chamber of Deputies and the art in the Palais Bourbon. While not yet the spectacle of the late nineteenth century, these performances show the increasingly democratic aspect of the interrelationship between public performance and French political culture. And as politics became more performative and democratic, it seems, it also became more melodramatic.

The subject of frequent prosecutions, the Société used each trial as "an open theater," in Thureau-Dangin's disapproving words fifty years later, "a tribune offered to revolutionary effrontery." The trial in April 1833 of the editors of *La Tribune*, Godefroy Cavaignac and Armand Marrast, allowed this kind of public dramatization of the goals of the republicans. The contrast between the promise to the proletariat of the Revolution of 1789 and the disappointing legacy of that Revolution was also emphasized in a trial of two journalists who were members of the Société, Vignerte and Pagnerre, in February 1834. Addressing the jury, Vignerte described his "crime" as having "deplored the misery of the people, I spoke of improving their situation." Republicans, he said, were not "drinkers of blood," but rather reformers who wished to improve men and not kill them. His codefendant, Pagnerre, claimed that the proletariat had been quickly returned to its "primitive state" after "a too short emancipation, in the middle of storms, at a time of dangers that menaced our country." When the avocat general, M. Berville, asked him, "Abuses, privileges, weren't these abolished by the Revolution of '89, and by that of 1830?" Vignerte replied, "What did proletarians gain from the Revolution of '89? Nothing, absolutely nothing!"[47]

Another trial, in 1834, included as defendants students at the Ecole Polytéchnique as well as members of the Société des Droits de l'Homme. François-Vincent Raspail, then a student at the Ecole Polytéchnique, suggested the conscious theatricality of the republicans as he used theatrical images to describe the relationship between the events of 1793 and his own generation. While lauding the men of 1793, and especially Saint-Just, Raspail insisted that he and his friends were a new generation, different from that of 1793. "We need new men," he argued, "and it is not in dressing as Robespierre, as Saint-Just, it is not in distributing among ourselves the roles of the terrible drama of their epoque, that we have the pretension of working for the regeneration of society." Nonetheless, he described his generation as a kind of audience for that drama: "Oh! messieurs, posterity is never ungrateful, and we here are posterity."[48] The drama of 1793, in his view, had been played for the audience of posterity, the generation of the 1830s.

Others soon played the drama out in the streets of Paris. The repression reflected in these trials forced the Société des Droits de l'Homme out of existence in the early 1830s, but it was replaced by a Société des Amis du Peuple, and then the Société des Familles. At the end of 1836, the Société des Saisons became the principal organization of the republicans, and on May 12, 1839, led by Louis-Auguste Blanqui, Auguste Barbès, and Martin Bernard, it launched a revolt in Paris against the government. The revolt began in the worker districts of the faubourg Saint-Martin, where the insurgents broke into an armorer's shop and stole weapons. They went on a "seditious parade" through the Saint-Denis and Saint-Martin quarters, disarming police posts and raising barricades. From there, six or seven hundred headed for the Ile de la Cité and the Prefecture of Police. They killed a police lieutenant at the Palais de Justice, then went to the Hotel de Ville, where Barbès read a proclamation calling (unsuccessfully) on workers to join in the insurrection. By late afternoon, municipal guards, national guards, and troops of the line had put down the revolt, arresting Barbès immediately, and Blanqui and Bernard later that day.[49] The insurrection had its theatrical elements: in melodramatic form, it portrayed the insurgents—and the Republic—as virtuous, threatened by the government. Barbès's speech at the Hotel de Ville, like all political speeches, drew on theatrical monologues. And the dénouement unfolded like that of a play. Louis Blanc described it in his *Histoire de Dix Ans* in terms that, were it not for the tragic results of the insurrection, could be read as either a script or the instructions for a state funeral.

> The day neared its end. Drawn towards the town hall of the 6th arrondissement by a new inspiration of their hopelessness, the insurgents began marching across the rues Simon-le-France, Beaubourg, and Transnonain, a sad itinerary that previous insurrections had traced in blood, and that seemed peopled with phantoms.... Then, from the end of the silent streets, the *Marseillaise* was heard, sung by melancholy and lugubrious voices. It was the insurgents who were stirring themselves for their last struggle. Three barricades were thrown up in the rue Grenetat, and the insurrection began digging its tomb.[50]

If the insurgents sought to portray the virtue of the republican regime of 1793, in the eyes of the government prosecutors the revolt of May 12, 1839, aimed not only at a return to 1793 but also at the overthrow of the current regime of property relations. "It is property that [they think] it is necessary to revise, modify, transfer; it is the conspiracy of Babeuf, passed from the status of a foolish project to bloody execution," said the prosecutor.[51] In his eyes, if virtue lay anywhere—although it was not the juste-milieu's way of viewing public life—it lay with the government established in 1830, as the paintings planned for the Palais Bourbon and the Hotel de Ville showed.

The failure of the uprising of 1839 did not end republican efforts to mobilize public opinion against the July Monarchy. Banquets and other public events could be used to this end, even if the audience usually consisted only of those already converted to the cause and the police spies who kept watch on the movement. A banquet in July 1840 was the occasion for a series of toasts that demonstrated how the concerns of the early 1830s, drawn from Robespierre's Declaration of 1793, had become commonplaces of the republican movement. Political reform, one participant said, was to give way to social reform, without which the first was insufficient. A journalist, M. Douville, drew on the memory of 1793 and repeated the theme of the stolen revolution of 1830: "Since the catastrophe of 9 Thermidor, the people have been exploited and compromised. Bonaparte profited from our revolutionary energy to create thrones.... But a revolution [in 1830] made for the people and by the people profited others." An artist echoed the theme: "They [our rights and our duties] command us to achieve the great moral and political regeneration that emerged in '89 from the ruins of the Bastille, and was so fatally suffocated by an obstructionist soldier." After a toast to the 14th of July, the 10th of August, and the 27th, 28th, and 29th of July by an *homme de lettres*, M. N. Gallois, the banquet closed with the *Marseillaise*.[52]

The different groups debating the form and content of French public life during the July Monarchy certainly disagreed about many aspects of politics, and their contestation formed the most important aspect of that debate. While issues such as public order and the misery of the working classes were significant aspects of the discussion, the legacy of the Revolution provided a language in which those issues could be framed. As with the Restoration debates about conscription and the Abbé Grégoire, political discussions in the July Monarchy reflected the revolutionary tendency to describe public life in terms of virtue and vice. Even if they could not agree on what was virtuous or evil—was Robespierre the figure of republican virtue, or was he the representation of evil?—they did agree that these were legitimate, and even overpowering, ways of viewing politics. The attempts by Louis-Philippe, Barrot, and others to portray the July Monarchy as the heir to the Revolution was also an attempt to cast public discussion in terms of the virtuous French nation. The grumbling by republicans about the "theft" of the Revolution of 1830 from the working classes also looked back on a virtuous Republic of 1793 that was under threat from counterrevolutionary forces.

This language marked the funeral ceremonies in 1845 for the republican leader Godefroy Cavaignac. One of the speakers, Louis Blanc, remembered his fellow republican in words that underscored the need for social reform in mid-century France. But he described this need in a specific form. "There are those," he said of Cavaignac, "for whom public calamities are individual evils; and he saw his country brought low beyond measure, democracy stopped in its development, the domain of the Revolution delivered to artisans of intrigue, war opened between interested parties, the old slavery maintained under the name of misery."[53] Blanc's language was not only about social reform. It was also about a virtuous France threatened by evil, and a republican movement that would rescue the Nation.

Blanc's version of Cavaignac and the situation of France resonated among his friends not only because it sought to improve the lives of the artisans who supported the republican movement in the 1840s. It also reflected and drew strength from the tendency to describe political conflict in melodramatic terms. Both republican and conservative politics of the early nineteenth century turned out to be stories that could be told using the plot lines playing on the Boulevard du Temple. For even as politicians argued about the veterans of the Revolutionary and imperial armies and seating Grégoire, while his regime was dramatizing Louis-Philippe's revolutionary ties, and the republicans were employing courtrooms and the streets to present their views, the theaters of Paris were providing ways to structure these stories.

The art historian T. J. Clark has emphasized the importance of the connection between the reconstruction of the city of Paris and the development of artistic movements such as Impressionism.[54] The official ceremonies of the Second Empire also increasingly made use of the city of Paris as a stage, employing sites in the capital that the reconstruction of the city by Napoleon III and his prefect of the Seine, Baron Haussmann, turned into veritable theaters for public civic performance.[55] These performances became spectacles that legitimized the regime by connecting it with the legacies of earlier regimes. The imperial marriage on January 29, 1853, was an early example of this, combining the pomp and symbolism of the Old Regime and the First Empire. As Matthew Truesdell has noted, the marriage was presented to the French people as a love match, a reflection of the nineteenth century's growing sense that the kind of dynastic calculation that had marked the marriages of earlier rulers was a vestige of the Old Regime, and that the emperor, like all French men and women, could follow his heart rather than diplomacy in choosing a partner. In his announcement to the nation of his decision to marry Eugénie, he drew a comparison between the rise of his own dynasty and that of romantic marriage, connecting the Bonapartist dynasty with the French people. The title of "parvenu," he claimed, was glorious "when it springs from the free suffrage of a Great people." It was better to remember his origins than to use marriage to add to his coat of arms.[56]

Thus there was a combination of modernity and tradition in the event, underscoring the regime's attempts to reconcile the conflicts of nineteenth-century French political culture. This continued in the ceremonies themselves, a civil ceremony conducted by minister of state Achille Fould in the Tuileries on January 29, followed the next day by a religious ceremony in the Cathedral of Notre Dame. While there were about a thousand guests, the civil ceremony was no different from that followed in marriages throughout the country: a brief ceremony, with the newlyweds providing the requisite answers, after which Fould declared them married. A link to the First Empire was made by the registration of the marriage in the imperial family register, last used for the birth of the Aiglon, Napoleon I's son, in 1811.[57]

The religious ceremony the next day was much more ornate and elaborate, and reflected the dual heritage of the Old Regime monarchy and the First Empire that the Second Empire claimed. At the entrance to the cathedral equestrian statues of Charlemagne and Napoleon I flanked a medieval-style portico erected for the occasion. The statues of the early kings of France that had been destroyed during the Revolution reappeared on the façade in painted images papered over the empty niches. The towers of the cathedral were decorated with frescoes of Charlemagne, Louis IX, Louis XIV, and Napoleon I, along with eagles and tricolors. The medieval cathedral had therefore been updated to reflect the lineage of the new regime, from the great kings of the past to the First Empire. Similarly, the carriage in which Louis-Napoleon and Eugénie rode to the cathedral was the same one used in the marriage of Napoleon I and Marie-Louise. The organizers rejected a *Te Deum* composed by Hector Berlioz in favor of one used at the earlier imperial marriage.[58]

The baptism of the prince imperial on June 14, 1856, followed the same combination of Old Regime and imperial ceremony. Notre Dame was elaborately decorated for the ceremony, with Eugène-Emmanuel Viollet-le-Duc attempting to remake it into a "church of the thirteenth century," in the words of Prosper Merimée.[59] A special stand of seats was built behind the altar for the bishops of the French Catholic Church, a reminder of the link between throne and altar. The ceremony itself closely followed those used for the king of Rome and for baptisms of the children of the kings of France. After the church ceremony, a banquet at the Hotel de Ville was hosted by the city of Paris in honor of the occasion, along with decorations and amusements in the city. These continued, both in Paris and in the provinces, through the next day. A painting memorializing the event was commissioned from Thomas Couture as a complement to David's *Coronation of Napoleon I*.[60]

These ceremonies stand in contrast to the limited audiences of debates in the Chamber of Deputies and the art in the Palais Bourbon and Hotel de Ville, or even the republican movement's performances in the 1830s and 1840s. They seem more obviously theatrical, closer to the performances in Parisian theaters. Even if not explicitly commercial, they seem to fit the spectacular public culture described by T. J. Clark and Vanessa Schwartz for the Paris of the Impressionists, and the fin-de-siècle Emile Zola's account of the baptism of the king of Rome in *Son Excellence Eugène Rougon* describes the "immense crowd" and "interminable lines of curious … the sea of human heads" in central Paris for the event. According to *Le Figaro* the ceremony drew people to the windows and roofs of the city, and also led people who lived along the Rue de Rivoli, on the Place de Grève, and on the Place du Parvis–Notre Dame to invite their friends or to sell places to enjoy the view. But the paper emphasized the many public performances the city had seen and pointed out that Parisians loved a good spectacle:

> [O]n these same boulevards, on these same quais, they watched Louis XVIII return, they watched Napoleon return, and then they again watched Louis XVIII return. They followed the funerals of the Duc de Berry, General Foy, Talma, and Manuel; they attended the revues of Louis-Philippe; they watched the wounded of February [1848] march past, along with the leaders of the Republic and the leaders of the Insurrection; in June '48 they invited their neighbors to watch the battle.

The French people, the paper thought, favored a military government, since they loved "fifes, drums, beautiful uniforms, handsome colonels, the éclat, the splendor, and the celebration" of military parades.[61]

Like stage melodramas, the Second Empire ceremonies were family events, and the weakness of Bonapartist spectacle is apparent in another family commemoration, the Saint-Napoleon. In proclaiming August 15, the anniversary of Napoleon I's birth, as the *fête nationale* in 1852, Napoleon III intended not only to recall the glory of his uncle's regime, but also to play on the revival of Marian devotions in French Catholicism (August 15 is the Feast of the Assumption) at this time. He also hoped to erase more recent memories, such as the republican celebrations of February 24 (the proclamation of the Second Republic) and May 5 (the anniversary of a very moderate revolutionary event, the opening in 1789 of the Estates General). The Emperor saw these republican memories as divisive, remembering "civil discord," and instead he claimed that only August 15 could rise above the passions of French politics and be a true national holiday.[62] The goal, then, was to unify a country torn by the Revolution.

The celebration of the Saint-Napoleon was organized by the state. Prefects in each department were ordered to have municipal councils organize celebrations, emphasizing the return of order, peace, and prosperity that the Second Empire had accomplished. The first celebration of the holiday, in 1852, indicated the intention of the nascent Second Empire to limit the memory of the Revolution by emphasizing the First Empire. Eagles and large letter Ns were placed throughout central Paris. A large figure of an eagle sat atop the Arc de Triomphe, and a statue of the first Napoleon was placed at the *rond-point* of the Champs Elysées. The imperial alliance with the Catholic Church was marked by a Mass at the Church of the Madeleine, followed by the more familiar invocation of national glory through a military review on the Champs Elysées. Later in the day popular entertainments continued the celebration, including theatrical performances in temporary theaters on the Champs Elysées as well as in the theaters of the boulevards. That night, in spite of poor weather, the festivities culminated with a fireworks display showing Napoleon I crossing the Saint-Bernard Pass.[63]

The festival was initially a success in Paris, while there was great variation in its reception in the provinces. In Lyon, the prefect and municipal administration attempted to make the celebration a popular one. Railroads brought country dwellers into the city for the day, and entertainments in the afternoon attracted large crowds. In the evening, the authorities illuminated not only public buildings in the center of the city but also public places such as the Place Bellecoeur, the Place des Terreaux, and the Place Napoléon at Perrache, as well as squares in the worker neighborhoods of La Guillotière, Vaise, and the Croix-Rousse.[64]

But in the long run the Saint-Napoleon proved no more able to unify the country than other festivals, and no better able to perform a basis for postrevolutionary society than the melodramas of the Boulevard du Temple. Through the 1850s and into the early 1860s, Napoleon III used the festival to increase his presence and popularity in provincial France, traveling to celebrate the holiday around the country. Whether the emperor was present or not, provincial celebrations brought together the civil, military, and judicial authorities in cities and towns for a religious service, which was followed by the choral singing and dancing that since 1789 had become features of civic festivals no matter what the regime. By the late 1850s the festival was widely accepted throughout the country, but in the course of the mid- and late 1860s its popularity declined. By the 1860s, as Napoleon III attempted to bolster his own military reputation in the aftermath of the Mexican expedition and the Italian War, he increasingly spent the day at the army camp in Chalons. In the last years of the Second Empire there were conflicts over the holiday, between the imperial administration and the city of Paris, and occasionally over the refusal of priests to honor the emperor adequately. The day remained one in which the watchwords of the empire—paternalism, union, order, and glory—were celebrated if not with public speeches, at least with the fireworks displays that entertained huge crowds. Even so, it remained a dynastic holiday, celebrating the emperor and the empress, but not France. In Lyon, a city with a radical republican tradition, the holiday came to reflect the increasingly unpopular aspects of the regime: ultimately it was a product of the party of order, with the army and police everywhere, and the clergy in public procession under their protection. The *fête Napoléon* was, in much of urban France, an imposed festival, unable to bind together the country's images of its national identity and its government.[65]

By the middle of the nineteenth century theatrical melodrama had become the distinctive form of popular theater. But it had also become a characteristic way in which French political culture described its significant events. The long period between the Restoration in 1815 and the advent of the Third Republic in 1870 saw significant steps that defined particular characteristics of modern French political culture and, as important, the ways in which those relationships were represented and given meaning. The Restoration was a period in which the melodramatic form was dominant on the stage, and this became a discursive form that political groups, on both the Left and the Right, found to their liking. The July Revolution of 1830, as well as the revolts of 1831, 1834, and 1839, consolidated this melodramatic representation of the conflicts over power in nineteenth-century France. Whatever hope there may have been in 1815 that a restored monarchy could find an English-style, limited parliamentary resolution to the conflicts that had their origin in the events of 1789 and their aftermath disappeared on the barricades of July 1830 and in the growing sense among republicans and the artisans of the cities of Paris and Lyon that, once again, the revolution that they made had been stolen from them by the bourgeoisie. Radicals after July found not the moderate memory of 1789 but the social message of Robespierre's 1793 Declaration of Rights the most attractive part of the legacy of the Great Revolution, and they increasingly saw the possibility of cooperation with their allies of 1830–derisively termed "Girondins" by radicals in groups such as the Société des Droits de l'Homme—as impossible. Thus, the melodramatic conflict between revolutionary virtue and reactionary evil increasingly defined political divisions for republicans.

The views of their opponents are more ambiguous. Moderate attempts to "end the revolution" worked against this Manichean view of political division. The liberals who controlled French politics after 1830–as well as Louis-Philippe himself—intended a political system that would not be built around the conflict of good and evil that had marked the First Republic, the last days of the Restoration, or the republican view in the 1830s. But they also intended to make this possible by eliminating active political participation for most French men, and for all French women. Their inability to control representations of the uses of power to impose their vision of a limited constitutional monarchy led them, in many instances, to begin defining themselves as the representation of good, and their republican opponents as evil. The social demands of the labor movement of the 1830s and 1840s contributed to this as well, for not only political power-sharing but also property arrangements—seemingly confirmed in

1789 and again in 1830–were put into question. The prosecutions of the 1830s, as well as the unwillingness of leaders such as Guizot to contemplate widening the requirements for political participation, confirmed this response of bourgeois Frenchmen to the challenges posed by the republican movement.

The Revolutions of 1848, both in February and in June, once again shifted the locale for this conflict from the press and the Chamber into the streets and clubs of Paris and other cities. The victory in June 1848 by Cavaignac's armies was seen by the members of the Constituent Assembly and their supporters as the triumph of good over evil, not a simple police action. Republicans portrayed themselves as the true heirs of the Great Revolution, and intended to prevent the fruits of revolution being stolen once again. But bourgeois liberals, even reformers such as Alexis de Tocqueville,[66] viewed the republicans not just as political opponents but as threats to any possibility of a civilized society, and so the repression of the June Days took on a ferocity that had occurred previously only in moments such as the Terror of 1793–94. The more organized repression of the Bonapartist regime was similarly based on the need to eradicate, at whatever cost, the dangerous threat to civilized society, and moderate politics, that the republican movement seemed to pose. By the Second Empire melodrama become a part of not only the performances on the Boulevard du Temple but French political culture as well.

3. Boulevard Spectacles of the Third Republic

The reconstruction of Paris during the Second Empire created a stage on which political French culture could become more performative. Certainly in retrospect we can see the theatrical aspects of public ceremonies or the actions of a political leader. But through social types such as the *flâneur,* or the development of department stores such as the Bon Marché, or spectacular forms of expression, such as the Musée Grévin or, especially after the turn of the twentieth century, film, theatricality became a more significant part of the way in which political groups, politicians, and individuals presented themselves to their society.[1] Watching and being watched seem to have become important axes around which the popular culture of fin-de-siècle France was organized.

This performative aspect of popular culture had implications for the new Third Republic established in 1870. For the republicans who controlled France in the 1880s and 1890s the Revolution and the Republic were the most important subjects for public performance. In this they sought to make a secular religion of the Revolution, intending the Republican regime that embodied that Revolution's principles to be the sole contributor to French political culture by linking together the Revolution, the Republic, and the French nation. The last decades of the nineteenth century therefore witnessed a remarkable cultural offensive by the republicans against any and all other contenders to speak for the French nation. The Republic, they believed, was the only instrument of progress, and they were determined to convince their countrymen of that belief. The Republic, Liberty, and the Nation would come together as the heroine of French history, and her story would be a triumph.

In this respect, the Third Republicans faced the same problem as did playwrights and film directors: how to make their audience watch, and understand, the performance? Just as the men and women who wrote, produced, and performed plays in the state theaters and boulevard theaters needed to draw in audiences, and keep them in their seats throughout the play, so also the republicans needed to convince French men and women that the Republic was a performance that deserved support. And just as those who put on plays utilized the resources of the stage to accomplish their task, so also the republicans adapted those techniques to accomplish theirs. In both instances, the staging created a version of the world, what Vanessa Schwartz termed a "spectacular reality." If in the boulevard theaters this staging created relatively innocuous worlds in which fictional heroines and heroes dealt with evil villains for a few hours before the audience returned to their lives in the streets, offices, factories, and shops of Paris, the performances of the Republic did the same with the more important issues of how the power of the state would be exercised. In the increasingly performative and theatrical popular culture of the late nineteenth century, these "spectacular realities" were able to create forms of viewing that constructed the world—whether the world on stage or the world of politics, society, and economics—in melodramatic terms.

But they were unable to accomplish this task completely. Just as the audience leaving a theater, or the Paris morgue, or the Musée Grévin was faced with the commonplaces of daily life that contradicted the world constructed by the performance, so also performances by feminists, socialists, and Boulangists of their versions of the legacy of the Revolution conflicted with that presented by the dominant republicans. There also continued to be opponents of the regime who called its fundamental principles into question as the basis for French politics and society. At the moment of her greatest triumph, the heroine of the Revolutionary narrative found herself embattled.

The public ceremonies of the Third Republic reflected the revival of the revolutionary tradition of public festivals as well as the pragmatic interests of the leaders of the Republic, both at the national level and in the villages, towns, and cities of the country. Historians of these ceremonies, such as Olivier Ihl, Avner Ben-Amos, and Pascal Ory, have detailed the place of these public ceremonies in the consolidation of a regime that did not enjoy universal support.[2] They have also investigated the relationship between republican ideology and public ceremonies. But it remains to place these ceremonies in the larger context of the development of spectacle as a form of public performance, as well as to examine the forms that these ceremonies took. In this chapter we will see that even at the time of greatest strength of the republican synthesis of French political culture, the spectacular representations of that culture continued to employ a melodramatic sensibility not only on stage, but also in its politics and ceremonies. But we will also see that this sensibility took a form specific to the Third Republic, in which the dramatic conflict reflected more general tensions in French culture.

The spectacular characteristics of public ceremonies of the Third Republic, as well as the melodramatic sensibility that they expressed, can be seen by briefly examining several of them. The most obvious political performance of the early Third Republic came in 1889, with the Parisian celebration of the Centennial of the Revolution of 1789. But the 1890s and the first decade of the twentieth century also saw public performances of political culture in the events surrounding the assassination of the president of the Republic, Sadi Carnot, in 1894, and in the Dreyfus Affair, which left its imprint on French politics from 1894 until after the turn of the century. Even a cursory reading of these events makes apparent the political divisions that marked French politics. But I would argue that they reflect more than just party divisions or the traditional division of France between those who supported and those who opposed the Revolution of 1789. The divisions performed in these ceremonies show a particular version of the inability of French political culture to find an acceptable basis for the construction of a version of postrevolutionary society that would appeal to all French men and women. To many leaders, opportunities appeared to arise to create such unanimity, in the Centennial, the funeral of the assassinated Carnot, and the cause of Captain Dreyfus. But in every case, French culture proved unable to heal the divisions that had emerged in 1789 and that remained tangible in the late nineteenth century. If the deep wound left in French culture by the Revolutionary events remained unhealed, melodrama remained a principal form in which that culture dealt with it in its politics and ceremonies.

During the Centennial in 1889, a series of events marked significant days of the Revolution, from the opening in May of the Estates General to commemoration in September of the founding of the Republic and the military victory at Valmy. The major event of the Centennial, the Universal Exposition, which opened May 6, 1889, was also used to recall the events of a century earlier. Alfred Picard, in his final report, argued that not only should 1789 be honored as a year memorable in the history of France and of all humanity, but since one of the most important conquests of the Revolution had been the "emancipation of work," it was appropriate to celebrate the anniversary of 1789 with a festival of commerce and industry.[3]

These events were used by the republican state to create a link between the Revolution, the Republic, and the French nation.[4] They also sought to eliminate other versions from French political culture. Many of the ceremonies that made up the Centennial enacted the principles of the Republic. But the inauguration of the New Sorbonne, on August 5, 1889, may be taken as a typical example of the performative characteristics of the Centennial. This was a part of a longer muncipal project supported by the city of Paris and its radical Municipal Council to enhance the university. The presiding figure at the inauguration of the New Sorbonne was Ernest Lavisse, the great figure of Republican professional history.[5] Attended by student delegations from all over France and Europe, the ceremony in the grand amphitheater of the new university buildings was attended by the president of the Republic, Sadi Carnot, and by professors from various faculties, members of the Senate and Chamber, and administrators from various government departments, as well as members of the Académie Française and other honorary organizations. Several previous ministers of education—Jules Simon, Victor Duruy, and Jules Ferry—joined the current minister, Armand Fallières, on the stage. The speakers drew a close link between the university, French identity, and the principles of 1789. The vice-rector of the Academy of Paris traced the history of the Sorbonne from its earliest days, listing the many figures who had studied there and had made it an expression of *l'esprit français.* This history culminated with the Enlightenment and the Revolution: "never has the soul of a people found a more generous expression of the work of intellectual and moral emancipation accomplished by itself than the principles of 1789, which have become like the song of civilized nations." Fallières, in his turn, reminded the assembly that French democracy had seen in learning "the always fertile, great ancestor" that understood the need, in a system of universal suffrage, to communicate the national ideal to everyone. "The Universities today take up the program outlined by the Revolution: that of the great encyclopedic schools where all of the sciences would be joined, mutually inspiring each other in a harmony comparable to that of the laws of nature and of the capabilities of the human spirit." To the assembled students, he confided, "as a guard of honor, the genius of France." "In the air breathed by every civilized man," he claimed, "there is something of France. It is not in vain that it gave to the world this double revelation: the *Discours sur la méthode* and the *Déclaration des Droits de l'homme....* To love France, isn't that ... to love humanity?" The ceremony ended with students and participants singing the *Marseillaise.*[6]

But if republicans and the Republic celebrated the Centennial of the Revolution, its opponents also found events to commemorate that called into question important aspects of the republican version of the Revolution and its link to the French nation. In 1889 Legitimists followed the watchword of the Comte de Chambord, "Reprenons le grand élan de 1789!" as, under the leadership of Charles d'Héricault and the *Revue de la Révolution française,* they attempted to organize a series of regional assemblies in 1888–89 that would draw up new *Cahiers de doléances,* listing the depredations of a century of revolution. Even the Universal Exposition in 1889 was the subject of antirepublican ridicule from commentators offended by the republican connection between industrial progress and the Republic. In this vein, Eugène Melchior de Vogué commented sarcastically in the *Revue des Deux Mondes* that, at least insofar as the exposition was concerned, the Gallery of Machines and the Eiffel Tower were contained in the Declaration of the Rights of Man: "only the fertile accord of liberty and democracy could give birth to these marvels, only the republican regime could give this great spectacle to the world!" In 1892, the anniversary of the September massacres was the subject of ceremonies in the Church of the Carmelites, and a decade later the attempts to beatify the victims would arouse further disputes.[7]

Five years after the Centennial, Sadi Carnot, who as president of the Republic had presided over the events of 1889, was assassinated in Lyon on June 25, 1894. Carnot had not led a particularly distinguished political career, and so his political obituaries were measured: the moderate *Le Figaro,* for example, noted, "The President has committed some political mistakes, but the private man is one who has always merited the respect of his adversaries, and we can forget easily the errors of the Head of State and remember only his dignity, his generosity, the correctness of his attitude."[8] The next day, the paper had become primarily interested in who would succeed Carnot as president. By the time Carnot was buried a week later, Jean Casimir-Périer had already been elected president.[9]

But the dead president bore one of the most famous names in the history of the French Revolution and the Republic, as the grandson of the "Organizer of Victory" of the Committee of Public Safety, Lazare Carnot, and the son of the *quarante-huitard,* Hippolyte Carnot. Even if he did not have the talent of his grandfather or the élan of his father, he nonetheless was no ordinary Third Republican. His funeral, therefore, took on aspects that evoked not only the Revolution but also contemporary debates. Carnot's heritage meant that he would be buried not in a cemetery, not even in Père-Lachaise, but in the republican shrine of the Panthéon. In spite of his own lack of brilliance and accomplishment, Carnot would become in death a symbol. But he was a conflicted one for both the Catholic Church and the republicans. With religious services at Notre Dame, and burial in the former church of Saint-Geneviève, which had been secularized by the Revolution, Carnot's funeral was made to carry a heavy representational burden. It allowed the Church to recall France to its Catholic heritage, while providing the opportunity for republicans to reaffirm their conquest of the nation. *Le Figaro* drew the appropriate conclusion, unable to resist pointing out that the most vehement and atheistic radicals had attended the service at Notre Dame. Carnot's funeral demonstrated not national unity but the inability of French political culture either to reconstruct the religious unity of the Old Regime or to create a new unity on the basis of the Republic. He stands, therefore, as a symbol of the melodramatic thread in French political culture in the fin de siècle.[10]

Michel Winock has noted that the Dreyfus Affair was "one of the great battles in the religious and ideological war that the French have constantly been fighting since the Reformation and the Revolution."[11] While this conflict was expressed in newspaper articles, speeches in the National Assembly, and the pleadings of lawyers at Dreyfus's trials, it was also apparent in the ceremonies that spoke to the legacy of the Affair. In 1908 a monument in honor of Auguste Scheurer-Kestner, the vice president of the Senate who had been one of the first political leaders to press for revision, was unveiled in the Luxembourg

Gardens.[12] The statue itself was located facing the Palais, on the principal axis of the gardens. It was a simple, severe statue of Scheurer-Kestner, with statues of Justice and Truth arranged on either side of him. The cermonies began with an unveiling of the statue attended by Armand Fallières, the president of the Republic; the president of the Senate, Antonin Dubost; Henri Brisson, the president of the Chamber of Deputies and head of the commission that had raised the funds for the statue; and the members of the government, including the president of the Council, Georges Clemenceau; as well as numerous other major Dreyfusards, including General André, Mme Zola, Mathieu Dreyfus, and Alfred Dreyfus himself.

After the brief unveiling ceremony out in the garden, the party moved into the great vestibule of the Luxembourg Palace, where there were several speeches. Henri Brisson formally turned the statue over to Dubost and the Senate, remarking that Scheurer-Kestner had marked himself as a "soldier of justice" and that his devotion to these principles would serve as "an example and a lesson for the youth of France." The next speech, by Dreyfus's defense lawyer Louis Leblois, was a recounting of Scheurer-Kestner's life, showing, as Le Figaro noted, that the politician had been "a slave to duty, confronting hatreds and reprisals to save a compatriot that he did not know." Scheurer-Kestner, he concluded, made a "cult of truth, of liberty and of justice."

The invocation by Brisson and Leblois of values such as justice, duty, truth, and liberty would have resonated with their listeners' conceptions of the values of the Revolution of 1789 and the Third Republic that was its expression in early-twentieth-century France. The final speaker, however, emphasized in particular the place of Scheurer-Kestner in the revolutionary lineage. Georges Clemenceau invoked first Scheurer-Kestner's Alsatian background, describing him as the last deputy elected from Alsace to the National Assembly, and thus making him a symbol of French patriotism and devotion to the recovery of the lost provinces. He also explained Scheurer-Kestner's leadership on the Dreyfus issue, in contrast apparently to the will of universal suffrage. This was, for Clemenceau, the way that the progress of humanity occurred: "general progress should necessarily result from the progressive accommodation of the masses to ideas submitted to the sanction of experience by the genius of the few." And while Scheurer-Kestner followed this process, Clemenceau noted that it was in the tradition of the French Revolution for France to recognize its faithful servants. "Our Republic has revived this great tradition. On the walls of the Panthéon, among the glorious names of Alsace and of Lorraine, we write, in great gratitude, the name of Scheurer-Kestner."

The dedication of the statue to Scheurer-Kestner provided the opportunity for Republican leaders to perform a version of the Republic that identified it with progress and virtue. But this was also a Republic that was in danger from the forces of ignorance, injustice, and counterrevolution. The aggressive defense of the Republic that the Dreyfusards had undertaken was placed in a larger framework of historical importance. As Brisson noted in his memoirs, the triumph of the Republic was the triumph of Truth and Justice. "The Republic conquers the world," he wrote, "because its will is to serve Truth, to realize Justice. . . . The Republic, Justice, and Beauty are sisters."[13]

These ceremonies are remarkable for their melodramatic characteristics. Dividing the world into virtuous republicans and evil opponents of the regime, dramatizing the ability of figures such as Scheurer-Kestner and Carnot to accomplish the re-creation of a harmonious, unified world in place of the one torn apart by the Revolution, these public events were attempts by the republicans to experience a transcendent connection with their republican predecessors and especially with the men of the 1790s who had, they thought, shown France—and the world—the way to progress, liberty, and happiness. These ceremonies, for some, were attempts to find the mysterious regeneration that the Revolution and the Republic should bring to France and its citizens. But they were also melodramas because, in the end, this did not happen. The Centennial aroused criticism and sarcasm from many sides, demonstrating the absence of national consensus about the Republic. The Catholic comments about Carnot's funeral show that the ceremony was unable to draw together the unified French nation postulated by the Republicans, and while Dreyfusards such as Clemenceau might admire Scheurer-Kestner, there were many Frenchmen who viewed him as a traitor to the nation.

The melodramatic thread in republican ceremonies echoed the resounding popularity of melodrama on the stages of the Parisian boulevard theater, and the remainder of this chapter will broaden the perspective on these public ceremonies by placing them in the context of developments on the Parisian stage. Vanessa Schwartz has demonstrated already the growing importance of commercialized spectacle in the Paris entertainment industry of the 1880s and 1890s, and the spectacles of the Centennial, at Carnot's funeral, and at the Luxembourg Palace can easily be seen as the full expression of the spectacular characteristics of public performance that, we have already seen in chapter 2, were emerging during the Second Empire. But it is also important to note the parallels between the melodramatic forms employed in these public ceremonies and those that continued to hold popularity on stages. This popularity was evident in the boulevard theaters of Paris. But it was also evident on stages in London and the United States at the same time, where melodramas such as the many versions of Harriet Beecher Stowe's *Uncle Tom's Cabin* were popular fare for much of the second half of the nineteenth century.[14] Just as the republicans used public spectacle to establish a link between their regime and the people of France, and found melodrama to be an effective form for this project, so also playwrights interested in attracting audiences found a popular audience through that genre.

One of the most important playwrights of the fin-de-siècle Paris theater was Victorien Sardou, and his work demonstrates the strong hold that melodrama continued to have on French theater. His plays were performed in state and boulevard theaters in France and in translation in London and the United States. He was a member of the Académie Française and wrote for the most famous actresses of the time, including Gabrielle Réjane and Sarah Bernhardt. Sardou made one attempt at a "masterpiece," *La Haine,* which came under virulent criticism when it opened in 1874. In response, Sardou declared that since the public did not care for masterpieces, he would not write them. He wrote instead for immediate success, and he achieved that. As Emile Zola wrote, after describing Sardou as a mediocrity, when criticized Sardou "smiles, he tallies up his popularity, he cites the two or three hundred performances of each of his works. Can a man for whom the theater has bought a chateau be wrong?"[15]

Sardou wrote numerous plays in the course of his career, but the discussion here will focus on his plays set in the Revolution, a subject he first used in 1860 with *Monsieur Garat.*[16] After the foundation of the Third Republic, Sardou frequently turned to the Revolution for material. By combining Robespierre, Barras, and Fouché with fictional people of Paris who undertake the important actions of the plays, he created works that both were popular and presented an interpretation of the Revolution as much as the literary and academic histories of Hippolyte Taine, Alphonse Aulard, or Albert Mathiez.[17] The first of these plays, *Les Merveilleuses* (performed at the Variétés on December 16, 1873), is set in Paris in 1797. It satirizes certain revolutionary customs, such as Theophilanthropy, as well as those profiting from the wars of the Directory and the upward social mobility that it makes possible. It also marks the rapid changes of the era, through the experiences of a former member of the *jeunesse dorée,* an émigré (Dorlis, real name Florival) who was forced into the Army of Italy and then returned to Paris, as if from another planet. He found himself at risk as an émigré, his wife first missing, and then divorced from him and in the process of remarrying. Against the background plot of royalist attempts to overthrow the Republic, conflicts between *muscadins* and *carmagnoles,* harassment of *merveilleuses,* jokes about the omnipresence of police spies working separately for each of the directors, and the language confusion caused by the Revolution and Thermidor, *Les Merveilleuses* follows a plot in which Dorlis attempts to find his wife, Illyrine.[18]

As the play unfolds, Dorlis and his friend Lagorille (the Gorilla) are arrested as royalist agents, while Illyrine marries Barras's chef de cabinet, Saint-Amour. The resolution of the plot comes in the course of a ball at the Petit-Luxembourg.

Characteristically for Sardou, this is through the intercession of the female characters. The *merveilleuses* (young women) appear, first, to have solved the plot by charming various directors—Rewbell, Carnot, Barthélemy—into agreeing to free Dorlis and Lagorille. But Illyrine's unwillingness to compromise her virtue with Barras undoes that plan. Lagorille then tells the women to spread the rumor that a plot has been discovered that will implicate everyone.[19] As the news spreads through the ball, members of the government flee while everyone except Saint-Amour burns incriminating documents and seeks a position in the expected new government from Barras.[20] Illyrine is rewarded for her virtuous refusal of Barras by being honored by him, Dorlis is struck, at Barras's order, from the list of emigrés, and Dorlis and Illyrine are able to remarry. Saint-Amour is considered mad, dismissed from his position, and replaced by Lagorille. As in all of Sardou's plays, this one resolves all of the conflicts in the end, with the rescue of the virtuous female character (Illyrine) through the manipulative intervention of less virtuous female characters (the *merveilleuses*) who themselves are directed by a secretive, clever male character, Lagorille. In spite of the happy ending, therefore, the scent of corruption hovers over the Revolutionary regime. Illyrine's virtue triumphs, but republican virtue does not.

Les Merveilleuses could have easily been set in the reign of Louis XIII or any other era in French history, since it is less about the Revolution than about the melodramatic virtue of Dorlis and Illyrine and the corruption of Saint-Amour and Barras. Sardou used the Revolutionary setting in the same way in *Paméla, marchande de frivolités,* first performed at the Vaudeville on February 11, 1898, and also set in Paris during the Directory, in 1795.[21] Barras again emerges as a major figure, and Sardou links politics and theater by having Barras lodging in a building owned by the theatrical producer Mme Montansier. The corrupt Barras finds his match in Pamela, a widow who owned a shop on the Rue de la Loi ci-devant Richelieu, where she sold "lace, scarves, decanters, fans, handbags, sachets, notebooks, garters" to a clientele of the wives of men profiting from the corruption of Directorial society.[22]

The plot revolves around a plan by Josephine Beaharnais, Pamela, and Mme Tallien to free the dauphin, whom they meet in the Temple prison. With maternal concern overcoming revolutionary devotion, Pamela swears that she will do whatever she can to save this "innocent child" even if she is only a woman.[23] The plan to rescue the dauphin involves tunneling into the prison from a neighboring house, substituting a dying boy who resembles the dauphin, and then spiriting the dauphin out of the prison. While the English agent Carford, to whom the plans are recounted, expresses concern that there are "so many women in this plot," the play demonstrates that women are willing to take action to save the dauphin, even when men will not, because of their maternal feelings for him. As Rochecôte, one of the conspirators, argues, "It is a question of an orphan to save, and in every woman, there is a mother ready to sacrifice herself for a child. What we do, you and me, because of royalism, she [Pamela] does for simple goodness of her soul. She has more merit than we do."[24] As the plot unfolds, however, Pamela is confronted by her republican friend, Bergerin, who has become aware of the royalist plot. Bergerin argues that the imprisonment of the dauphin is his destiny, but Pamela responds that whatever the political coloration, blue or white, "a child is sacred," whether the child of a king or of a *chiffonnier*. If a mother were to martyr her child, she says, she would be considered a monster. "And when it is the nation, mother of all, who causes the death of that little one, you do not flinch!"[25] If other women had seen what she had, Pamela claims, they would storm the prison, assaulting "this Bastille of Childhood, and today would be the 14th July of mothers!"[26]

In the end, Bergerin allows the escape to occur, relenting when the dauphin, half-asleep, puts his arms around him.[27] In the final scene, Pamela and the dauphin have joined a Chouan force in the countryside away from Paris. Bergerin comes to warn Pamela and her royalist allies that, following the death of the substitute dauphin, Barras and his agents are after them. The much larger royalist force makes Barras accept the escape of the dauphin, who is taken off by his supporters as one of the royalists compliments Bergerin for his help, declaring him worthy of being a royalist. Bergerin responds that the Chouans are worthy of being republicans. As the dauphin departs, Barras sums up the results of the play with "the child is saved, the Dauphin is dead, the Republic breathes, Pamela is ravishing, Josephine enchanting, I am satisfied! Everything is for the best! Let's go eat! Citizeness, my carriage is at your orders!" As Pamela heads for the carriage, she jokes to Bergerin, "tell me again that women don't understand politics!" Barras comments, "what a prejudice!" and Pamela responds, "then, let us into the Convention!" In the last line of the play, Barras responds, "God save us! We would not be strong enough!"[28]

Both *Les Merveilleuses* and *Paméla* countered the corruption of the Revolution by female qualities, the feminine wiles of the *merveilleuses* and Pamela and the virtues that Illyrine and Pamela bring from the bourgeois family into the public sphere. In contrast to the claims by republicans that the Republic was a repository of public virtue, Sardou portrays the Directory as corrupt, and Barras as unprincipled. The revolutionary promise of a regenerated society thus appears a false hope. It is not through the Republic that France will find virtue, but from women such as Illyrine and Pamela, who—because they are not public women, but virtuous women forced into the public by the threat of the Revolution—can create a virtuous public sphere. But even though he uses the same line about women in both plays—"all pretty women are equal before the law"—Sardou does not seek to overturn the restrictions on women's participation in the public sphere, and so, because they are women, they are unable to accomplish this.[29]

Sardou developed a similar theme in his most popular play, *Madame Sans-Gêne* (1893). Revived in 1900 at the time of the Universal Exposition, and performed more than two hundred times during the exposition, it had been performed six hundred times in Paris by the end of October 1900. The play is roughly based on the story of an orphan, Thérèse Figueuer, who followed Napoleon in male disguise. But Thérèse is transformed by Sardou into Catherine Hubscher, a regimental laundress who became the wife of a sergeant, Joseph Lefebvre, who became a marshal of France.[30]

A prologue to the play establishes the revolutionary setting and the characters of Catherine and Joseph. Set in Paris on the 10th of August, 1792, it takes place in Catherine's laundry near the Tuileries during the attack on the royal palace. As the attack appears to be going against the popular forces, Fouché arrives in the shop to get his laundry before fleeing to Nantes to avoid the royalist counteroffensive against the revolutionaries. Hearing the crowd outside launching another attack, Catherine suggests to Fouché that he should join them, but he declines to do so. There are, he says, those who fight in revolutions and those who organize them, and he is more of an organizer. In dialogue that finds its humor in the audience's knowledge of Fouché's future role as minister of police, Catherine jokes that Fouché might be a minister if the revolution succeeds, but not (given his cowardice) the minister of war. "Sooner," she suggests, "lieutenant of police!" examining the dirty laundry of everyone.[31]

But the prologue takes on a more serious tone after Fouché departs to join in the popular victory at the Tuileries. A wounded man, chased by the crowd, hides in Catherine's shop, and reveals himself to be the Comte de Neipperg, an Austrian member of the court who has been wounded in the attack on the palace. Demonstrating that her womanly role as caregiver is stronger than revolutionary and national sympathies, Catherine hides him, only to discover that the guards chasing him are led by her fiancé, Joseph Lefebvre. As in other Sardou plays, the power of Catherine's womanly qualities overcomes the more public concerns of the male characters, and Joseph helps Catherine hide Neipperg from the other republicans.[32]

The first act moves the scene to the imperial court in the Chateau of Compiègne in September 1811. The intervening years have seen great upward mobility. Napoleon is emperor, and Lefebvre has risen to the rank of marshal of France. This upward mobility is unsettling, but its dangerous implications are primarily associated in the play with female, not male, characters. In an early scene, two former nobles of the Old Regime complain about the imperial nobility and the lack of sophistication of the commoners Napoleon has ennobled. "One does not improvise a nobility," they complain.[33] Their complaints seem confirmed by a scene in which Lefebvre and Napoleon dine together. Napoleon dines after a fashion, Lefebvre tells Catherine later, eating "everything that he sees on the table, at random ... the confitures after the soup, the crème au chocolat on the fried mackerel and the cheese in the lentils. And all that in ten minutes."[34] But there are no dangers to France from either Lefebvre's upward mobility or Napoleon's poor table manners, and the complaints of the Old Regime nobles are marginalized. Instead, the plot revolves around Catherine's lack of breeding. She will always be the laundress of the Rue Saint-Anne, even if she is now the wife of a marshal of France. Napoleon even tells Lefebvre that he must divorce Catherine because she has created a scandal in the imperial court by refusing to accept her role as a duchess. She also becomes a source of humor for Sardou, with dialogue written in a lower-class dialect that makes her the butt of jokes not only for the Old Regime nobles but also for the audience.

Sardou does not confine his disdain for the society of the revolutionary era to his female characters. The well-known leader of the Revolution, Fouché, had already provided the opportunity for humor in the prologue. He reappears later in the play as the unscrupulous recently dismissed minister of police, wielding power among the members of the court because of his knowledge, gained as minister, of the secrets of the court.[35] But the desire of parvenus to emulate the Old Regime's manners is principally attacked through female characters, especially in a confrontation between Catherine, on the one hand, and Napoleon's sisters Caroline and Elisa on the other. Taunted by the princesses into avowing her background as a laundress, Catherine responds with a speech defending the people. "There are no stupid trades, only stupid people," she declares, and "if I speak in the jargon of the people, it is because I am one of the people, and in good company, I might say, with Masséna, who sold oil; Bessières, who was a wigmaker; Ney, a barrelmaker; Lannes, a dyer; Brune, a typesetter; and the brave Murat, presently your husband, who was valet to his father, a cafékeeper; as well as the one who today is called His Majesty, who in the past people might order, 'Hey, boy, change my plate!' " But while she takes the princesses to task for denigrating the sons of the Revolution whose efforts had given them a palace, her examples are all male, and she must find a way of placing herself in the public, largely military, sphere that legitimated male actions. She finally does so in a way that recalls her protection of Neipperg: she defends herself as someone who, far from being a camp follower, had traveled from the Rhine to the Danube, in the rain, snow, and hail, "helping the wounded, consoling the dying, closing the eyes of the dead!"[36]

Catherine therefore combines the private virtue of a woman and the public virtue of a citizen in ways that Illyrine and Pamela could not. The importance of this increases in the second act, when she meets with Napoleon, ostensibly for him to tell her his decision that Lefebvre must divorce her because of her conduct and lower-class manners. But Catherine refuses to be intimidated by the emperor, and when he accuses her of creating a scandal, she responds that the scandal is in the way his sisters insult the army through their attacks on her. She then reveals to Napoleon her own military record, recounting to his growing interest her participation in numerous campaigns as a *vivandière*, as well as that she was wounded and was commended by General Augereau in an order of the day for her service to the wounded. Impressed by this record, Napoleon decides to allow Catherine to remain married to Lefebvre. However, while her military record and virtue keep her from being completely cast aside, it is not enough to convince him to allow her to remain at court.[37] Only when Catherine steps away from her maternal role and adopts male manners, joking with Napoleon about a debt owed to her by the emperor himself from her days as a laundress, is she allowed to remain in the imperial court.[38] Napoleon's approval of Catherine is therefore the result not of her public or private virtue, but of her ability to play a man's game of court intrigue.

The final act of the play revolves around the consequences of Napoleon's discovery of a lady-in-waiting to Marie-Louise, Mme von Bulow, leading the Austrian Count de Neipperg into the empress's chambers. Napoleon seizes Neipperg, thinking he is having an affair with the empress, and sentences him to summary execution. But Catherine uses her newfound position with the emperor to defend, once again, the Austrian noble, and a series of narrow escapes made possible by the lack of scruple of men like Fouché save both Neipperg and Catherine. In the end Napoleon not only appoints Fouché minister of police and forgives him his corruption, but also joins in the general approval of Catherine's ability and orders Lefebvre to "keep her carefully! You will not find her equal!"[39]

The different characters in *Madame Sans-Gêne* provide a description of Sardou's version of the Revolution and First Empire that is similar to those in *Les Merveilleuses* and *Paméla*. Catherine and Lefebvre are the principal heroes of the play, representing the Revolution as virtuous and self-sacrificing, and are willing to risk their lives in the service of France. The radicalism of the Revolution—Lefebvre took part in the attack on the Tuileries on August 10, 1792—is submerged in the mobility that brought lower-class people such as Catherine and Lefebvre, as well as other Napoleonic marshals, to positions of power and national leadership. The nobility, however, is portrayed as useless or worse, both in the Old Regime nobles who complain about the imperial court and in parvenu nobles, especially the imperial princesses, who re-create the Old Regime court, with its hierarchies, protocol, and gossip, without service to the nation as a basis for their claim to social dominance. Napoleon himself, who in this play is a character of some complexity, rather than simply a figure in a tableau, appears to be in the sway of the lure of the Old Regime while at the same time frustrated by the complaints and plots of his sisters. But he also shows signs of a tendency to abuse his power: he interferes in the personal lives of his subordinates, a trait Fouché describes as "the hobby of a great man."[40]

Fouché is the representative for Sardou of the core of the Revolution. He is secretive, ambitious, cowardly, intriguing, and unprincipled. When Napoleon surprises Neipperg entering the empress's chambers, and plans a summary execution, Catherine attempts to enlist Fouché's help in saving her old friend, Austrian and royalist though he may be. But Fouché bluntly tells her his position, and it reflects Sardou's refusal to see the postrevolutionary regime as based on public virtue. "Neipperg," the Terrorist and minister of police says, "is not my friend; his safety makes no difference to me. The Empress detests me; her honor leaves me cold. Rovigo took my place; his disgrace fills me with joy. The Emperor punished me for predicting to him that this marriage (to Marie-Louise) will end badly; it is ending badly! I am revenged!" And just as easily he demonstrates the commercial basis of his actions: "Show me how I can profit by converting my rancor into devotion, and it is done!"[41]

There is also a gendered aspect to Sardou's version of the Revolution that places these melodramas firmly in the fin de siècle and sets them apart from earlier stage melodramas. The emperor's sisters are described in very unfavorable terms: small-minded, gossiping, malicious, grasping after precedence and honor yet contributing nothing to the public good. Catherine is generally a favorable character, someone loyal to her own roots in the people of Paris but also a representative of the virtuous citizens that helped make the Revolution. But she uses stereotypically feminine methods to manipulate men, whether through her physical beauty or through secretive scheming. In melodramatic fashion she is threatened unjustly because of her background, but the audience is constantly brought to the edge in anticipation of her being found out and paying a heavy price for her actions. There is an ambiguity about Catherine's feminine qualities that does not exist with the emperor's sisters, however. Lefebvre explains to her, for example, that as a soldier he can swear, whereas this is not appropriate for a lady of the court. But Catherine can also claim to have been a soldier, and therefore not to be held to the normal constraints of her gender. She also, in the end, displays a strong sense of virtue that her scheming serves. What redeems her is her honesty, her forgiveness of political differences in the face of private human attachments of sympathy, family, and affection, and her apparent willingness to accept the consequences of her actions. If Lefebvre is a simple, straightforward representation of public virtue in the service of the French nation, Catherine is a more complicated figure of this, personally virtuous but one who, in the end, is complimented by none other than Fouché for her ability to manage affairs.[42]

Nevertheless, her "feminine" lack of transparency contributes to the disorder in the imperial household. Fouché may be corrupt, but it is Catherine who represents the confusion and upheaval that the Revolution brought to France. The emperor declares that "I have the right to believe everything, and am sure of nothing! All the suspicions, and, thanks to you, miserable women, not a certainty!"[43] There is, therefore, for Sardou something—which he sees and portrays as feminine—about the Revolution and its legacy that creates ambiguity and prevents a clear-cut closure of the disruption created by the Revolution.

Les Merveilleuses, Paméla, and *Madame Sans-Gêne* used settings from the Revolution and First Empire to comment on aspects of postrevolutionary French society and culture. These plays combine the view of women as secretive and scheming with a model of the virtuous bourgeois woman whose public role was fulfilled not in public office but through her role in the family. At a time when the "New Woman" was demanding a role outside the strictures of the bourgeois family, the principal characters in these plays all intervened in public affairs, resolving public conflicts when the male characters nominally in charge were unable to do so.[44]

In two other plays using the Revolution as a subject, Sardou focused more directly on the morality of the Revolution itself. One of these was his most controversial play, *Thermidor,* performed on January 24, 1891, by the Comédie Française and set in the summer of 1794, at the end of the Terror.[45] The play used the story of Charles-Hippolyte Labussière, an actor who came under suspicion during the Terror and, under the name Charles Hippolyte, began working as a clerk for the Committee of Public Safety. He first destroyed his own file, then those of hundreds of others, saving them from the guillotine during the Terror. The story of Labussière had acquired some notoriety among right-wing opponents of the Republic by the end of the nineteenth century, and Sardou's play used this as the basis for his dramatization of the difficult choices posed by the Revolution.

But Sardou tells Labussière's story as a melodrama, a tale of unlikely love between an officer in the armies of the Revolution, Martial, and an ex-aristocratic woman, Fabienne, threatened by the Revolution itself. Fabienne is accused of planning to assassinate Héron, the agent of Robespierre and the Committee of Public Safety. After her arrest, Labussière and Martial search for someone else to substitute for the condemned Fabienne. While the play is melodramatic in its creation of concern for a threatened couple, Martial's and Labussière's playing God, determining who is to live and who is to die, becomes the source of dramatic tension in the play. As the two men desperately search through dossiers for one similar to Fabienne, Labussière reminds Martial that however tragic it would be for Fabienne to die, to substitute another for her is over-reaching their power: "Do we have the right to substitute for someone condemned to death someone else who is not?" "The right!" Martial exclaims. "It is a question of saving Fabienne at any price, at any price, at any price! That's everything!" "Even," Labussière asks, "at the price of a crime?"[46] While they are trying to make the substitution on the 9th of Thermidor, as the Convention was debating the fate of Robespierre and his allies on the Committee, they ultimately are unable to prevent the execution of Fabienne. Attempting to stop the cart taking Fabienne to her death, Martial is himself shot and killed by the police.

Beyond the concern the plot creates about the fate of the threatened heroine, the play also reflects on the general course of the Revolution, lamenting the movement away from the ideals of 1789 as it had destroyed its makers. Martial remarks early in the play that he had gone to the Convention and "searched in vain for the great men of the National Assembly who destroyed the Ancien Régime, the heroes of the Constituant who founded the new [regime], the Girondins who conquered liberty for us, the Dantonists who conquered the Republic for us. All disappeared, fugitives, *egorgés*!" And Labussière laments early in the play that the "harvest moon of liberty" had gone from being a "beautiful dream" to "finish in the horrific!"[47] This is not a blanket condemnation of the Revolution and all its works, but it reflects grudging admiration for the reforms of the early Revolution, and for Danton, as well as a rejection of Robespierre and the Terror.

The ability of a stage play to cross the boundary between art and politics is clearly demonstrated by the way in which Sardou's drama resonated in French politics. The premiere of the play, and its criticism of part of the Revolution, generated disorders in the theater that led the government to suspend further performances. It also led to a debate in the Chamber of Deputies as Joseph Reinach, Henri Fouquier, and Francis Charmes, moderate republicans who usually supported Freycinet's government, presented an interpellation of the decision by the minister of the interior in Freycinet's cabinet, Emile Constans.[48] This is a debate well known among French historians because it led, as we will see, to Georges Clemenceau's declaration of the unity of the Revolution. But it also bears close reading because of the perspective it provides on the dramatic forms that marked French political culture at this time.

One of the authors of the interpellation, Henri Fouquier, began by arguing that the problems with the play were "purely literary and artistic," and therefore not the concern of the Chamber. It was necessary to balance the maintenance of order with that of the freedom of the dramatic art, "a republican liberty like other liberties." He also argued that, even if the Revolution was, "en bloc," a great thing, "the men who played the drama were actors of greatly differing merit" who could not escape from the "legitimate critique of history." The Revolution, he said, "is a great act: I refuse to admit that it is a religion." Fouquier argued that Robespierre was the evil genius and the enemy of the Revolution and that France was saved in 1793 in spite of, not by, the Terror. He also declared that "The Republic is liberty; Robespierre is despotism." The play, he claimed, was directed not against the Republic, but against Robespierre. It was time, and it was necessary, to distinguish between the glorious and the abominable moments in the history of the Revolution, and any republican should approve a work that places outside history someone who had placed outside the law the greatest citizens of the country, "the true founders of the Republic."[49]

In Fouquier's interventions in the debate, there is a slippage between the events of 1794 and their representation as drama. He described the play as "the history of the struggle of the Convention and the Committee of Public Safety against Robespierre" but then immediately added "it is the tableau, it is the satire, if you wish, of the regime of the Terror." Immediately a voice from the extreme left added, "The Parody!"[50] Later in the debate Joseph Reinach also described the Revolution in theatrical terms, referring to "this Tartuffe who is called Robespierre."[51] Georges Clemenceau also used the reference to Molière's character in his intervention in the debate.[52] In each case, the Revolution itself seems best described in dramatic terms, and the debate—or the joking—revolves around what form of drama is best invoked.

For some participants in the debate, the problem was not so much—so they claimed—Sardou's play but the theater in which it was performed. As Jean-Claude Leygues, an Opportunist Republican, argued, "At the Porte Saint-Martin or elsewhere, the work would have passed without any resistance; at the Comédie-Française, *Thermidor* has the air of a challenge." A work of polemic, the play had no place, he thought, at the Comédie.[53] The minister of fine arts, Léon Bourgeois, argued on the other hand that state censure had never distinguished between the state theaters and other theaters. He defended his initial decision to grant permission for the presentation of the play by citing the examples of H. B. Blanchard's *Camille Desmoulins,* presented at the Théâtre-Français in 1831; François Ponsard's *Charlotte Corday,* presented in 1850 under the Second Republic; and *Le Lion amoureux,* also by Ponsard, presented in 1866, as proof that the subventions were given to the state theaters not for political reasons, but for artistic ones. The government should not censure a play simply because it disagreed with it. Only in an instance in which the opinions presented were appeals either to insurrection or to violation of laws should the play be censured. And while he thought Sardou's play unbalanced, in failing to portray the foreign threat to France, he nonetheless felt obliged as minister to allow it to be performed. However, when it appeared that the play would threaten public order, the minister of the interior was obliged to suspend performances of the play, a decision with which Bourgeois agreed. It was, he thought, not only the government's right, but its duty, to intervene if public order was threatened.[54] Emile Constans, the minister of the interior, defended his actions because of the need to protect public order, which he considered his first duty.[55]

Joseph Reinach, one of those who proposed the interpellation, argued on the contrary that the government was protecting not order but disorder by allowing the small minority who opposed the play to damage freedom of artistic expression. The disorders that accompanied the play at the Comédie would have occurred at a boulevard theater, and the government would have also intervened there to protect public order. The only problem with the play, Reinach argued, was that it attacked the Terror and the scaffold, and suspending the performance for that reason was damaging to the government and artistic freedom. The true insult to the Republic, he claimed, was not Sardou's play. Rather, the scandal was the claim by defenders of the Terror that the Revolution and Republic were only the scaffold and the men who executed the "most noble and pure republicans." Desmoulins and Danton, the men of August 10, were the true founders of the Republic, who had protested, at the cost of their lives, against the Terror.[56]

A moderate, Emmanuel Arène, supported the ban because Sardou himself admitted the play was politically motivated—to "settle his score with Robespierre"—and because it revived the hopes of royalists.[57] But the debate also included those who defended Robespierre and the Terror. Radicals such as Georges Clemenceau saw the play as an attack on the principles of the Revolution and the Republic. Explaining his vote in support of the government, and therefore of the ban on the play, Clemenceau argued that it was not a question of Danton or Robespierre, but of the Revolution. "For three days," he joked, "all our monarchists claim to wish to be the successors of Danton." Taunting Reinach for having picked through the Revolution, accepting this, rejecting that, he declared that the Revolution was a "bloc, a bloc from which one could not remove anything, because historical truth does not permit it." It had to be taken whole, 1793 along with 1789. Clemenceau also drew out the context of the attacks on the government's actions. He reminded Reinach that only a few years earlier they themselves had participated in a kind of revolutionary tribunal, the Haute Cour de Justice that had tried General Boulanger. For reasons far less threatening to the Republic than those faced in 1793, he and Reinach both had voted to "deliver politicians to other politicians, their enemies, and the condemnation was assured in advance." He downplayed the significance of the vote the Chamber was about to take: "Do you think that the vote of the

Chamber can accomplish something? Do you believe that the Chamber is able to diminish or augment the patrimony of the French Revolution?"[58]

He then turned on the right. "Don't you know," he asked Reinach, "who were the ancestors of these men of the right?" When the Baron Cuneo d'Ornano, a monarchist who had supported MacMahon's government of Moral Order during the 1870s, interjected that his grandfather was at the frontier, commanding a demi-brigade of the republican army, Clemenceau ignored the example and declared that the ancestors of the Third Republic's right were indeed at the frontier, but "on the wrong side of the frontier. They were with the Prussians, the Austrians and they marched against France.... They marched against the *patrie*, hand in hand with the enemy, and those who were not with Brunswick, where were they? They were in the Vendéen insurrection." He recounted episodes of republicans massacred by monarchists: the republicans of Machecoul, the death of Joubert, president of a district, whose hands were cut off. And, he claimed, the White Terror took more victims than the Red Terror.

The peroration of Clemenceau's speech indicated the ability of appeals to the Revolution to rally republicans as well as their inability to create a new France on the basis of its principles. "If you wonder," he said, "why a bad play is causing such emotion in Paris and in the Chamber, I will tell you. It is that this admirable Revolution by which we are [here] is not finished, it is that it is still going on, it is that we are still its actors, it is that it is always the same men who find themselves engaged with the same enemies. Yes, what our ancestors wished, we still desire. We meet the same resistance. We remain the same; we haven't changed. The struggle must go on until the victory is definitive." And he would not allow the Revolution to be soiled: "if the government had not done its duty, citizens would have done theirs."[59]

The antirepublican right made few contributions from the tribune to the debate, although there were frequent incidents of heckling from that side of the Chamber. At one point Cuneo d'Ornano sarcastically described Camille Desmoulins as a reactionary because "he demanded the appeal to the people; he was guillotined!"[60] But Clemenceau's speech presented them with an opportunity to appear as the voice of reason even while rejecting the Revolution. Albert de Mun asked Freycinet if the government shared Clemenceau's endorsement of the Terror. While the premier did not openly disavow Clemenceau's position, he did distance himself from the most radical parts of the Revolution. It was a ridiculous question, he said, and "We are the government, not of such and such group, not of such and such coterie; but the government of the republican party, instituted to direct in the best way possible the affairs of the Republic and the affairs of the entire country."[61] But Malartre on the right interpreted this to mean a rejection of Clemenceau's insistence that "the Revolution is not finished," and he regretted Clemenceau's evocation of "the most horrible days of our history, all of that because of a piece of theatre."[62] Finally, after the lengthy debate, the government insisted on a simple order of the day, which it won handily, 315–192.

The performances of the play were halted until a revised version appeared at the Théâtre de la Porte-Saint-Martin in 1896. The original version that had caused such controversy included a scene in which other employees of the Committee of Public Safety tell Labussière and Martial of the condemnation of Robespierre, but the end of the Terror occurs too late to prevent the tragic death of Fabienne. This was the consequence of the extremism of the Terror that offended Radical Republicans such as Clemenceau. But in the second version, the play was changed to allow a happier ending, with the two protagonists surviving. The revision also allowed Sardou to add two scenes to the play. The first portrayed the debate in the Convention on the 9th of Thermidor, showing the condemnation of Robespierre and his allies by the assembly. In Sardou's version, when Robespierre is unable to defend himself in the debate, Labussière himself shouts from the Convention floor that the leader of the Committee of Public Safety is "choking on the blood of Danton."[63] In the second new scene, "La Dernière charette," at the instigation of Labussière and Martial the Parisian populace seize and liberate the last group of prisoners, including Fabienne, condemned by the Revolutionary Tribunal. This demonstrates the people's opposition to the Terror, but it also underscores the element of chance at play in the outcome of these major events in French history. As Martial and Labussière attempt to organize the Parisian crowd to intercept the tumbril, they fear that the usual afternoon rainstorm will send the crowd home before they have their chance to play their positive role in the revolutionary drama. Happily, this is not the case, and all turns out well. But Labussière notes, as the rain begins to fall, "Ah! You can well fall now, happy rain, to wash away the blood! But five minutes sooner, you would have prevented victory! Thank you, Supreme Being!"[64]

The debate over Sardou's *Thermidor* allows us to see how the constructions of the world that the melodramatic form modeled for playwrights had seeped into other sectors of French culture and become "natural" ways of setting up debates in the French assembly. It is not only that the participants in this debate opposed their own (somewhat fictitious) versions of the Revolution to that of their opponents, a division that has long been recognized. It is that they invested their own positions with a moral virtue, an ability to create public virtue; that they saw their opponents as not just disagreeing but threatening; and that, in the end, they were unable to find the kind of compromise that reunifying French political culture demanded. Clemenceau's "The Revolution is a bloc!" stands not only as an expression of his willingness to accept the Terror along with the reforms of the Revolution. It melodramatically condemns the morality of his opponents and challenges their claim to a place in the French public sphere.

Sardou returned to the events of the Terror four years after the premiere of *Thermidor*. In 1895 he completed a play entitled *Robespierre*, which placed characters from the Revolution in a domestic melodrama.[65] Even Robespierre has an air of domesticity, with a pet dog and a scene of him in the home of the cabinetmaker Duplay, where he resided, listening to music while he awaits police reports. The play itself revolves around a case of hidden paternity. Once again the Terror threatens the protagonist of the play, Olivier, whose mother, Clarisse, has hidden from him the knowledge that his father is none other than Robespierre. In a third act that re-creates the Festival of the Supreme Being and features criticisms by Olivier, in the crowd, of Robespierre's dictatorship, Olivier is arrested and imprisoned in the Conciergerie. The outcome of the play then depends on his rescue from the guillotine.

In this as in *Thermidor*, Sardou changed endings. His first version was adamantly anti-Robespierrist and pro-Thermidorean, with Billaud-Varenne and Tallien, two of the opponents of Robespierre on the 9th of Thermidor, rescuing Olivier from prison so that he could kill Robespierre. In a version presented in London in 1899, however, Robespierre saved Clarisse, her niece Marie-Thèrese, and Olivier. But while Robespierre may be the incarnation of the Revolution, he is not forgiven his crimes: when he goes to the Conciergerie to find Olivier, he must wait in the prison for Le Bas to find Olivier. He is there visited by phantoms, reminding him of his crimes: Mme Roland, the sister of Louis XVI, Charlotte Corday, the Girondins, Desmoulins, Danton, and Marie Antoinette all appear to him.[66] His willingness to forgive the questionable opinions of his son Olivier stands in stark contrast with his incorruptibility in the face of the supposed crimes of other figures in the Revolution. The play ends with the same reproduction of the floor of the Convention on the 9th of Thermidor as Sardou added to *Thermidor* a few years earlier, although in this case the line "C'est le sang de Danton qui l'étouffe!" is not spoken by a character in the play; it is only called out from the floor of the Convention.[67]

An early-twentieth-century biographer claimed that Sardou was sympathetic toward Robespierre as a result of several childhood experiences, including having met the widow of Robespierre's ally Joseph Lebas at a party. A later one described Robespierre as his "bête noire."[68] *Robespierre* in both of its versions casts doubt on the character of the principal figure in the Terror, portraying him as vacillating and corrupt, an echo of Barras and Fouché in Sardou's other plays. But the play attacks him more directly, and completes a century of portraits that at times seem to reduce the Terror to the ambition and cruelty of a single man.[69] Not only is Robespierre willing to intervene to protect his own child, he also is a traitor to France itself. He seeks a secret deal with Vaughan, the agent of the English radical Charles James Fox, that would end the war between England and France and consolidate Robespierre's power in the new Revolutionary regime. To the Englishman, Robespierre describes his dream of becoming the French Cromwell, exercising power, but not for his own benefit. He dismisses out of hand a desire for pleasure and the "adulation of a corrupt court" and wants no other palace than the modest rooms he currently inhabits. He desires absolute power for other reasons: "the happiness of the people," which he alone is in a position to accomplish. He wants to give France a new religion, without churches or priests, of which he will be the pope, and truly republican legislation, based on virtue that he will enforce. "I wish," he says, "under a vigilant authority, to found the rule of perfect Equality. No more rich, no more poor, neither luxury nor misery.... To each, according to his age and his needs, the State will provide his portion, and by that, eliminate material cares; each citizen will owe, in exchange for this happiness, his work, his devotion, and his absolute submission to my paternal and sovereign will." Vaughan draws the conclusion: "It is the total suppression for the individual of all independence and all initiative." Robespierre agrees: "The individual is nothing. The State is everything."[70]

These plays may be seen as representative of the Parisian stage at the end of the nineteenth century, and as we have already seen they tell us a great deal about the way in which the theater created a discourse about the Revolution and the Republic. But to understand the importance of the ways in which Sardou created these performances we need to step back from these specific plays and see them both in the context of his other works and in contrast to another series of plays on the Revolution written at about the same time, Romain Rolland's *Théâtre de la Révolution,* and its most important play, *Le 14 Juillet.*

The revolutionary decade was a fertile field in which Sardou could find topics for his plays. His choice of subject, however, provided him with the opportunity to present the Revolution in a particular way. The plots of these plays are very formulaic—what Zola sarcastically described as exposition, in great detail, followed by action, ingeniously constructed, and ended by a denouement, "slapped together somehow," but in a manner to let the audience depart with a happy impression.[71] The plays are typically melodramatic: virtue is always in danger, with a threatened heroine, a conflict between the forces of good and evil, and—in the conclusion that aroused Zola's sarcasm— the happy ending as good triumphs over evil. Even in a play such as *Paméla,* with sympathetic characterizations of the dauphin, the Chouans, and Pamela herself, the republican audiences of the late nineteenth century could find a conclusion of unity in the amity of the two warring camps as Bergerin helps save the dauphin.

Sardou also uses the plays to comment on the corruption and decadence that the Revolution helped create. Barras becomes the archetype of the leader of the Revolution, a womanizer, unprincipled, and willing to do anything to maintain his power and to increase his wealth. Against Barras, Sardou places virtuous women such as Illyrine or Pamela. The most powerful of these female characters do not use the reason or the force that provides male characters with power. Nor is it unalloyed virtue that accomplishes these aims. Rather, their power comes from their ability to use their feminine attraction to manipulate men without compromising their virtue and to obtain the virtuous outcome that they desire. In the way typical of melodramas, therefore, Sardou always introduces doubt about the virtue of the result in his plays. As a consequence, he not only dismisses the public sphere created by the Revolution—it is made up of either tyrannical megalomaniacs such as Robespierre or corrupt men such as Barras—but he also subjects that public sphere to the emotions and manipulation of flirtatious women.

The use of gender conventions in these plays suggests a particular aspect of Sardou's works that is worth examining in more detail, because it brings out the particular way in which Sardou adapted the melodramatic form, with its emphasis on threatened virtue, to describe the legacy of the Revolution for French political culture. A useful comparison is with another of his plays, *Les Femmes fortes,* which was first performed in December 1860. It therefore is an early product of Sardou's craft, written at the same time as *Monsieur Garat* and preceding by a decade *Les Merveilleuses.* As the title suggests, however, it has as its subject matter the unsettled gender roles of nineteenth-century France. The plot of the play revolves around an inheritance: Quentin, the lead character, has advertised in the United States for living heirs of his deceased brother, intending to share the home and industrial wealth in France left to him in his brother's estate. While awaiting a response, he returns to France to discover that, in spite of the concern of their godmother, Claire, his daughters have adopted behavior that counters Quentin's patriarchal sense of proper female behavior. Jenny is engaged in a clandestine affair with a false Polish prince, Lazarovitch, while Gabrielle smokes and is an avid hunter who, when Quentin forbids her from hunting, taunts him by asking "And our liberties? You erase them!" and tutoyering him in the process.[72]

As the plot develops, it revolves around the arrival of the missing heir, Jonathan, who produces a deed of gift from Quentin's brother that makes Jonathan's deceased father the sole heir, disinheriting Quentin and the others. He orders them out of the house, and while Quentin unsuccessfully consults a lawyer to see if the donation can be broken, the women—Jenny, Gabrielle, Claire, and a stereotyped feminist, Mme Laborie—discuss ways of using their own feminine wiles to convince Jonathan to allow them to stay in the house. Claire reminds the others that "our strength ... is our good humor, our grace, our kindness, and all those gold threads with which we surround our hearts.... It is not in crying in a loud voice 'I wish!' but in murmuring in a low tone 'If you wish.'"[73] But while Jenny and Gabrielle throw themselves at Jonathan, they prove unsuccessful in attracting him. It is only at the end of the play, as Quentin's family is preparing to move out, that Claire manages to save the day in a lengthy scene in which she attracts Jonathan first by reminding him of his mother, and then through the artful use of "If you wish" to convince him to allow Quentin and his family to remain in the house. In the end, Jonathan tears up the donation, cheerfully complaining about Claire's ability to manipulate him.[74]

Les Femmes fortes is a comedy that takes place almost entirely—Quentin's visit to an attorney, which takes place offstage, aside—within the sphere of the bourgeois home. It parodies the unsettled gender relations of mid-nineteenth-century France, and the only woman who achieves her aims is the most conventional woman, the only one willing to adopt the subordinate female role of the bourgeois family model, Claire. Yet she also articulates the basis for power within the family that women were allowed in this model, with her emphasis on subtle charm and manipulation as the basis for the ability of a woman to convince a man to follow her lead by making him think it is his own decision: not "I want" but "If you wish." Within the bourgeois family, therefore, *Les Femmes fortes* describes a form of female power, one that Sardou found at best laughable but at worst subversive of the society he supported.

The comparison with *Les Femmes fortes* highlights the strong similarities between the female characters in that play, from 1860, and the characters in his later plays, especially *Les Merveilleuses* and *Paméla*. But it also suggests a significant change in Sardou's representation of these characteristics, for he has moved the action from the private sphere of Quentin's bourgeois home into the public sphere of the French Republic. *Les Femmes fortes* may have used the domestic sphere as a metaphor for public life, but that metaphorical connection could be easily missed given women's limited public status in nineteenth-century France.[75] But after 1870 Sardou's female characters became more explicitly public. In *Les Merveilleuses, Madame Sans-Gêne,* and *Paméla* the corruption of the Revolution is countered by female qualities; the feminine wiles of the *merveilleuses,* Pamela, and Catherine; and the virtues that Illyrine, Pamela, and Catherine bring into the public sphere. In contrast to republicans' claims that the Republic was a repository of or even created public virtue, Sardou portrays the Directory as corrupt, and Barras as unprincipled. It is not through the Republic, therefore, that France will find virtue, but from women such as Illyrine, Pamela, and Catherine, who—because they are not public women, but virtuous women forced into the public by the turmoil of the Revolution—can create a virtuous public sphere.[76]

Sardou's melodramas played, as melodrama had since the time of Pixeré-court, with threatened virtue. But his particular twist on this old theatrical genre was to use it to perform the problems of public virtue that Republican France faced at the end of the nineteenth century. It is not only that some French men and women did not agree with the republicans about the desirability of a republican form of government. Sardou—himself no ardent republican—underscored as well the public corruption of the Republic, portraying it not as a source of virtue, but the opposite. Only in the private virtue of his female characters did he find a source for the regenerated public sphere that many French sought. There is no evidence in these plays that Sardou himself saw a solution to this problem through a greater public role for women, and there is much evidence that he rejected this out of hand. But melodrama turned out to be an ideal way to perform one of the contradictions of republican political culture, the inability of the Republic to live up to its implicit promises of even political equality for all French men and women.[77]

If Sardou's own work provides an insight into the workings of his plays about the Revolution, another comes by comparing his work with that of the movement at the end of the nineteenth century for a more social drama. At the same time as Sardou was dominating boulevard theater, others in Paris and elsewhere were creating theater companies and writing plays that dealt with many of the same topics as did Sardou, but in a way that included sharp commentary on the social injustice of the Third Republic. In the place of the bourgeois citizenry assumed by most theaters and portrayed by playwrights such as Victorien Sardou, these groups envisioned peasants or workers as the archetypical citizens of the Republic.[78]

These attempts were of varying success, with most of the Parisian groups surviving only a year or two. In the course of this, however, Romain Rolland attempted to revive interest in the theater of the revolutionary period in a pamphlet published in 1903 entitled *Le Théâtre du peuple.* For our purposes, Rolland's effort is important in that, just like the public ceremonies of the Third Republic, it sought a way of relating the Revolution, and the Republic, to the people. At a time when politics was becoming increasingly popular, he argued that "[t]he eloquence of the orator is the only rival to the theater in its effect on the masses." He also saw clear parallels between theater and public celebrations, quoting favorably Diderot's hopeful question, "What if we were to assemble the whole nation on holidays!"[79] The Revolution played an important part in French dramatic history, and drama had been important to the

Revolution: he quotes the injunction of Joseph Payan during the Convention that the "rubbish" of the Old Regime must be swept aside, to "allow reason to enter and speak the language of liberty, throw flowers on the graves of martyrs, sing of heroism and virtue, and inspire love of law and the Patrie." The drama of the 1790s set the stage for a revitalization of the French dramatic tradition, cut short by the "whirlwind" of Thermidor. Further, he argued that it was not "genius" that would provide the basis for a rebirth of art, but the democratization of society promised by the Revolution and the consequent participation of "the people" in artistic activity. But there was still work to do: he bemoaned the decline of class distinctions in Paris, the result of the ability of the bourgeoisie to co-opt some workers into the bourgeoisie, while others sank into a state of increasing misery. "The first will not have a people's theater, and the second obviously cannot attend one." A people's theater, in his mind, would bring these two groups of workers together and give them "a collective sense of their party."[80]

At the same time as he was writing *Le Théâtre du peuple*, Rolland developed a "theater of the Revolution" intended to employ the example of the Revolution to stir the enthusiasms of the current generation of republicans. This *Théâtre de la Révolution* was originally inspired, he claimed, by seeing a performance of Victor Hugo's *Quatre-vingt-treize* in 1882.[81] But he was also deeply affected by the struggles of the Dreyfus Affair. He was therefore inclined to see the Revolution as a melodramatic struggle to defend virtue. As Roland sought to work out his own relationship with the French socialist movement, he found in his portrayal of revolutionary events a way to focus on the cultural aspects of the era and their implications for his own time. In so doing, he argued that the most radical phase of the Revolution, the Terror, could not be dismissed as a violent aberration, but rather had positive cultural aspects.[82]

By 1900 Rolland had conceived of a cycle of plays on the Revolution, originally to include ten, then twelve, and finally eight plays. The cycle was an attempt by Rolland to portray on stage the democracy and desire for justice that he saw at work in the Revolution. The third play in Rolland's *Théâtre de la Révolution*, *Le 14 Juillet*, was completed in 1901. It provides an important comparison for the perspectives on the Revolution portrayed by Sardou and boulevard theater. The dramatic action takes place in Paris on July 12 and 14, 1789, and revolves around the storming of the Bastille by the Parisian crowd. The play provided Rolland with the opportunity to retell the story of the great revolutionary event that had been celebrated by bourgeois republicans since 1880 as the *fête nationale*. In an author's note at the beginning of the published play, Rolland describes his reasons for using the 14th of July as the subject for a play: "I have endeavored to make live again the heroism and the faith of the nation in the throes of the Revolution during the Republican epoch, in order that we, a nation of greater maturity and more than ever conscious of the great destiny that awaits us, may continue and finish the work interrupted in 1794."[83] Rolland thus conflates the entire Revolution, from 1789 to 1794, and identifies it with the Republic. He also sees Thermidor as a truncation of the Revolution, leaving it incomplete and bequeathing to the French nation—a republican nation—the task of completing the work of the Revolution. The events of 1789 are therefore not just in the past, a glorious memory for France, but rather are an inspiration, and even a command, to further development of the Republic.

But the nation that he describes as the actor in this event is not made up of the usual leaders of the Revolution, who have very small roles in the play, but rather of the people of Paris, an incipient working class aware of its historic role in the struggle for freedom. The initial scene of the play in the Palais Royal sets up an opposition between the French elite and the crowd. The actress Mlle Contat of the Théâtre-Français defends Marie-Antoinette against the insults of the crowd. Jean-Paul Marat, the hero of the crowd, states the basis for the power of the crowd and himself as its representation: "If you don't know me, you are a scoundrel. I am known wherever there is virtue and poverty. I spend my nights taking care of the sick, and my days taking care of the people. My name is Marat."[84] He then describes the challenge an intellectual such as Rolland faced in using his particular literary skills in the service of the Revolution and the nation. He denounces actors who do not seek liberty, declaring that "they prefer plays!"

This play sets up a contrast between a threatened Revolution, whose ideals may be virtuous in the abstract, and its makers, who are less so. The action in the Palais Royal is taken over by the men who would become political leaders of the Revolution. Hoche is first denounced by Marat, who laments that it is "cold" men such as Hoche who defend liberty. Hoche in turn comments that Marat is "sick with virtue": the devotion of Marat to virtue in the name of the Revolution can turn into a disease in the body of the nation. As news of Necker's dismissal by the king spreads in the garden, Robespierre stands on a table and begins to read the Rights of Man; in a telling comment on the inability of Robespierre's Terror to carry the Revolution—defined as the Rights of Man—to fruition, Robespierre falters and Hoche must finish reading the Declaration. Camille Desmoulins then climbs on the table and exhorts the crowd to seek "Liberty, liberty! It is now flying just above our heads. . . . The day of bondage has passed." Taking a branch from a chestnut tree, he shouts, "In hoc signo vinces. Liberty! Liberty!"[85] But while this re-creation of the famous scene from July 12 may seem to imply a Revolution made by Marat, Robespierre, Hoche, and Desmoulins, the act concludes with Rolland's statement of the true actor against the king: the people threaten that "we must inspire the tyrants with the sacred terror of the nation."[86]

The last two acts of the play depict the regeneration of the people that the Revolution accomplishes. It is a regeneration that comes from the experience of the Revolution itself. In act 2 a man standing guard in a Paris street is challenged by Gonchon, the captain of the bourgeois militia: the man responds that he is "watching over the nation.... I am home. My home is in the street.... Yesterday, I didn't have any idea of all this.... But now everything's changed. I've got a part to play; I feel that everything belongs just a little to me.... Everybody is equal, equal and free.... I'm a king. I could walk over the world."[87] In the final act La Contat herself enters the Bastille and is captured by Swiss guards. Vintimille derides her for looking "like the goddess of Liberty herself," and the actress's only defense for her action—which runs counter to what she has been saying throughout the play—is that "I have a reason, but I can't explain it now. A few moments ago, it was so powerful, so clear to me. The feelings of those people thrill me, like the roll of thunder. Now that I am separated from them, I don't know." If La Contat found inspiration in the crowd, Vintimille denounces it, declaring that she is not herself, but that something new and strange—a poison from the mob—is in her. "It's like a wind of bestiality blown from the monstrous part of humanity."[88]

Rolland therefore attempts to describe a popular Revolution, acted out and sanctioned by the will of the sovereign people. The final act of the play, after the storming of the prison, depicts a unified nation celebrating their liberty, "not separated into this or that faction."[89] A pensioner in the Bastille tells the Swiss Guards not to fire on the crowd, establishing the popular unity that the bourgeois elite could not accomplish: "They are our relations, Frenchmen like the rest of us." A statue of the king is pulled down from a niche in the wall of the Bastille, and replaced by little Julie, the child of the people, who is the "good conscience" and the "little Liberty" for the others. Hoche, sabre in hand, sets the scene for a popular celebration by declaring that this daughter of the people of Paris, Liberty, will inspire "every enslaved nation" and that France "will carry across the universe the great banner of Equality."[90] In a universal and aggressive way, the play depicts, as a consequence of the Revolution, the entry of the people onto the historical and theatrical stage: "its finding its voice, its entry into historical time."[91]

Le 14 Juillet expresses Rolland's view of the Revolution as a founding moment of a popular democracy, capable of creating a unified, all-inclusive nation. The play ends after the taking of the Bastille with a popular festival in the Place de l'Hotel de Ville, as the people of Paris celebrate their freedom and the defeat of their oppressor. It is the moment of triumph when the characters cannot imagine further resistance to the inexorable spread of liberty: "The battle is finished," says the soldier Hulin, and his friend Hoche agrees: "There are no more enemies." The absence of future resistance means a benign people.

The divisions and horrors of the future—hinted at in the first scene—remain offstage. In a "Note on the Last Scene," Rolland insisted that "[t]his is, as the title indicates, a popular festival, the festival of the People of yesterday and today." To have its full meaning, the scene required that the audience itself participate in the singing and dancing at the end. The point, he said, is to bring about a union between the public and the work, "to build a bridge between the *salle* and the stage." To accomplish this, it was necessary to add to the scene music from the Revolutionary era: "Music, the tyrannical force that suppresses time, and gives to what it touches an absolute character." What he wanted was a *kermesse triomphante*, with the cheers of the actors and the audience mixing with the music of Gossec, Etienne-Nicolas Mehul, and Luigi Cherubini.[92]

The final scene of the play needed to overcome the dangers posed by a Marat "sick with virtue," a "cold" Hoche, or a bestial mob. The threat is raised and then left behind, but these dangers are a reminder of the melodramatic inability of France to create national unity after the Revolution. In a more practical sense, the response to Rolland's play further indicated the problems posed by his project of a theater aimed at his version of the people. Rolland had hoped that *Le 14 Juillet,* produced in 1902 by Firmin Gémier at his Théâtre de la Rénaissance-Gémier in Paris, would be the instrument to consolidate popular theater in France. But while it initially attracted attention, this quickly faded, and ultimately, after twenty-nine performances, Gémier closed the production, recouping only 5 percent of the investment by his backers.[93] In contrast to Sardou's popularity, Rolland's plays about the Revolution did not find much resonance at the beginning of the century among either middle- or working-class theatergoers. Even though Rolland's cycle was the most concentrated dramatic focus on the Revolution in French literature, it had few public performances.[94]

Romain Rolland and other participants in the popular theater movement saw theater as a form of cultural enrichment and moral elevation for the working classes, a way of preparing them for citizenship and the completion of the work of the Revolution of 1789. Seeing the French nation as somewhat childlike, Rolland felt that a People's Theatre had to be recreational and a "source of energy," but it also was to be didactic, guiding, in his words, the intelligence of the worker. The role of the people in these works was to be inspirational: the author's "soul collaborates with the nation, and receives nourishment from the passions common to all." Recommending melodrama and historical plays, Rolland thought in terms of popular festivals, not only as a part of plays such as in the last act of *Le 14 Juillet,* but also as a part of virtually all aspects of civic life. Theatricality suffused Rolland's notion of a truly democratic, republican culture.[95] His plays were an echo, performed in theaters rather than on the Champs de Mars, of the earlier emphasis on the use of theatrical forms to mobilize the revolutionary people during the early 1790s in revolutionary festivals such as the Festival of Federation and the Festival of the Supreme Being. His views also looked forward to the twentieth-century use of theatrical methods to mobilize mass participation in regimes not only in France but also in Germany and the Soviet Union.[96]

Both the republican public ceremonies of the first fifty years of the Third Republic and the theatrical performances of Sardou's and Rolland's plays indicate the importance of the melodramatic thread in the political and public culture of the period. While academic histories and school textbooks presented a unified "truth" about Danton, Robespierre, and their fellow revolutionaries, and the Third Republic imposed that view in the principal locus for the transmission of the Revolutionary memory, the school system, these representations were subverted when performed in public, either in the plays of Sardou and Rolland or in the public ceremonies that were a staple of French political culture at this time.

A crucial aspect of representations of French politics in the Third Republic is the frequent claim of an identity between the French Revolution and the French nation. Not only in the schools of the Republic but also in forms of entertainment and leisure a powerful discursive attempt was made to re-create a unified, unquestioned political culture that would be the basis for all French, for not only the political system but for membership in the French nation. Ultimately, however, while events such as the Centennial celebration and plays such as Rolland's *Le 14 Juillet* tried to find a basis for this, it proved impossible to accomplish or even perform convincingly. These performances included opponents of virtue as a part of their dramatic structure. The heroic Republic, or the dramatic hero, seemed always to suffer from some form of corruption, perhaps best captured by Sardou's fictional representations of figures from the Revolution such as Barras and Fouché. There were always dissenters who were able to point out the inconsistencies of the Republic's actions, and there were others who ignored the Revolution or saw it as irrelevant. In the end, both of these kinds of representations underscored the inability of French political culture to find a basis for unity acceptable to the entire nation. They therefore replicated melodrama's inability to reunify a world divided between good and evil.

They also represented that divided world in ways that increasingly brought into the foreground the shifting relationship between a representation and the represented that modern theorists of spectacle have pointed to as an important aspect of that cultural form. As in their particular locations in French culture the paintings of the Impressionists, the novels of Zola, the wax figures of the Musée Grévin, and the displays of department stores created a version of the world for their viewers, the ceremonies of the Third Republic created a version of the Republic, the revolutionary ideal finally achieved after a century of struggle. But those portrayals adopted a form that spectacularly misrepresented the world, whether private or public. The families of French men and women were more complex than they appeared on the stages of the nineteenth-century theater, and the public issues of the Third Republic were also more finely shaded than they appeared in the performances of republican ceremonies. The simplification of the issues, the reduction of the issues surrounding Thermidor into a love affair, for example, made for good theater, as Victorien Sardou understood better than any other playwright of his time. But as Sardou adopted public issues as the subjects for his dramas—as he wrote about Thermidor rather than bourgeois families—he brought into public discourse a form that resonated with the French public but that detached that public from the complexities of the world in which they lived. The "public melodramas" of Sardou made for good theater; they also made for a particular kind of democratic politics, a spectacular form in which a specific form of discourse, about private virtue and public vice, was imposed on the daily events of politics.

4. Spectacles of Light and Darkness between the World Wars

The First World War dramatically impacted the culture of all Europeans. Some scholars, such as Paul Fussell, have argued that it created a new form of understanding, a modern one, replacing the romantic forms of the nineteenth century with the irony that has marked the twentieth. Others, notably Modris Eksteins and Jay Winter, have tried to show how nineteenth-century forms of artistic expression and mourning were adapted and continued into the 1920s.[1] These cultural changes affected the ceremonial life of France, most obviously in the commemorative calendar that the Third Republicans had designed around the celebration of the Revolution and the Republic on the *quatorze juillet*. This was a process Danielle Tartakowsky has described as a passage from THE *fête* to several *fêtes nationales*, a reflection of a nation unable to find unity. There were several competing anniversaries from before the war that increased in importance with the political divisions that marked the 1920s and 1930s. The feast of Joan of Arc, rather than the *quatorze juillet*, was celebrated as a "national" holiday by the non-republican right. The first of May, celebrated since 1890 by the labor movement, became if not a national holiday certainly one for the working class. The war also produced its own anniversary, as the 11th of November became an annual ceremonial day, observed in cities and villages across France as a solemn, funeral occasion. It allowed the representation of France as Republic, Nation, and Fatherland, serving even better than the *quatorze juillet* to express the unity of the French nation. Until the crisis of the mid-1930s, the 11th of November, rather than the 14th of July, was the centerpiece of the ceremonial year.[2]

While the ceremonies that commemorated the Great War have been seen as funeral ceremonies aiming to provide closure for the living after the death of loved ones, it is also illuminating to consider them in the context of the melodramatic model that provided a significant form for public ceremony in postrevolutionary France. Viewed as social dramas, the commemoration ceremonies created the same kind of Manichean distinction between good and evil, as well as threatened virtue, that had been a part of stage melodramas. In the postwar period, however, the ceremonies especially highlighted the country's inability to re-create the prewar situation: both the confused ceremonial calendar and, more immediately, the continued presence, whether in Paris, in other cities, or in village cemeteries throughout the country, of the dead and of monuments to the dead were continual reminders that the damage to the national fabric done by the war could not be completely repaired.[3] While these ceremonies have been thoroughly studied already, we can illustrate these similarities to melodrama by briefly examining two of them, the *fête nationale* in 1919 and the burial of the *poilu inconnu* under the Arc de Triomphe on November 11, 1920.

The first *quatorze juillet* after the end of the war, in 1919, took on the aura of a celebration of the victory in Paris, portraying the French nation and the Republic as the embodiment of virtue, and the victory as the rescue of the threatened nation. It did this primarily through references to the Revolution and First Empire. Autrand, the prefect of the Seine, invoked the memory of the volunteers of the Year II and the grenadiers of Austerlitz in a ceremony at the Hotel de Ville on July 13 that honored Joffre, Foch, and Pétain. The 14th itself was what *Le Figaro* described as a "sacre de la Victoire," with "only one canopy, the sky; only one cathedral, Paris; only one religion, France." The ceremonies remained similar to traditional *fêtes nationales,* a celebration of the triumph of the Republic against its enemies and of the national unity that had gained the triumph. But this message did not receive complete adherence, and instead the ceremonies demonstrated again the inability of the Republic to provide a basis for national unity. For the veterans of the war, a traditional *quatorze juillet* seemed a nationalistic celebration by those who had not fought. They insisted that there had to be some recognition of the deaths of their comrades and the sufferings of the soldiers, and the government therefore organized, on the 13th, a commemoration that was different from any previously associated with the *fête nationale.* The Arc de Triomphe de l'Etoile was turned into a funeral chapel, and a cenotaph in honor of the war dead was erected under it. Various veterans' groups came on the afternoon of the 13th to leave wreaths at the Arc, and an honor guard remained overnight at the cenotaph. Clemenceau, the prime minister, visited the scene about 10 PM that evening.[4] On the 14th, the presence of *mutilés de guerre* in the ceremonies was a further reminder of the cost of the victory.[5] This first *quatorze juillet* after the war reflected the melodramatic conflict between a virtuous France threatened by Germany, and its rescue by the French people. A commemoration of the dead, rather than a celebration of the victorious nation, the *quatorze juillet* proved unable to re-create the prewar nation.

A ceremony directly focused on the war was better able to commemorate the recent sacrifices of French citizens for the nation, but these also demonstrate the difficulty in combining the symbolism of the Republic with commemoration of the war dead. In Paris on November 11, 1920, the Arc de Triomphe was the principal scene for an event that demonstrated as few others could the melodramatic characteristics of these ceremonies. As in other countries, the remains of an unidentified soldier were selected from the military cemeteries in eastern France and transferred to Paris. An initial proposal that would infuse the ceremony with republican sentiment, to bury the Unknown Soldier in the Panthéon—the holy ground of the Revolutionary tradition—was rejected, and the body was, in the end, buried under the Arc de Triomphe de l'Etoile. For veterans, the ceremonies marked their effort during the war. But socialists made allusions to the anniversary of the foundation of the Third Republic fifty years earlier, and the ceremonies attempted to connect the nation that the veterans of '14–18 had defended with specifically republican memories. The *Marseillaise* was solemnly played during the ceremonies. The procession moved from the Place Denfert-Rochereau, with its statue of the Lion of Belfort commemorating the national struggle in the Franco-Prussian War, to the Panthéon to deposit there the heart of Léon Gambetta, the principal republican leader of the early Third Republic and symbol of the national defense in 1870 against the German invaders. It then went on to the Place de la Concorde and the Arc de Triomphe.[6] Some commentators took up the theme of the ceremony, placing the *poilus* of the Great War in the van of Gambetta's efforts in the Franco-Prussian War and seeing them as preventing the destruction of Gambetta's threatened creation, the virtuous Republic.[7] The words on the tomb underscored this official connection: "Here lies a French soldier who died for *la patrie*. 1914–1918; 4 September 1870, proclamation of the Republic. 11 November 1918: return of Alsace-Lorraine to France."[8] The attempt at national unity was emphasized by the progress of the cortege to a selection of symbolic sites in Paris, weaving together the national effort against Prussia in 1870, the foundation of the Republic, the republican tradition of great men, and the national triumphs of the Napoleonic era.

But the ceremonies also suggest that the relatively fixed ceremonial spaces of the early Third Republic were in flux: Gambetta, the hero of the Third Republic, was left behind at the Panthéon, and France continued on to a more broadly resonant memory of military struggle and victory, the Napoleonic Arc de Triomphe. The military victory of 1918 became less a Gambettist, republican victory—after all, in spite of the struggles of Gambetta, France had lost the Franco-Prussian War and with it Alsace-Lorraine—and more a Napoleonic triumph, along with the others inscribed on the sides of the great Arc. And while that triumph might have been the best hope for national unity in the aftermath of the Great War, the tradition of extinguishing the flame on the grave of the *poilu inconnu* each evening and relighting it each morning emphasized the country's inability to reach a peaceful conclusion to the trauma of the war. The ceremony memorializing the soldiers of the Great War became the latest representation of the threatened nation, its rescue by its citizens, and the continued difficulty the nation faced in finding a set of principles that would restore its unity.

If the commemoration ceremonies drew on symbols that had marked republican rituals for generations, they took place in a rapidly changing popular culture that was marked by new media that increasingly placed in question the relationship between representations and the events they purported to represent. In particular, the period after the Armistice saw the rapid development of a new popular medium, film. It had been invented before the turn of the century, one of a number of popular "spectacles" that catered to a growing mass audience for entertainment and that took over the audience that, in the nineteenth century, had flocked to the theaters of Paris. Film inherited many of the conventions of these earlier spectacles.[9]

The early history of film in France is well known thanks to the work of film historians such as Richard Abel. Technical innovations in the 1880s and early 1890s culminated with the Lumière brothers' screenings in the Salon des Indiens on the Boulevard des Capucines in 1895 using their Cinématographe, a machine that could both record and project. In its first decade, the new industry grew rapidly, as Louis Lumière and then George Méliès developed new ways of producing films and created networks for their distribution and exhibition. After the turn of the century, Pathé-frères rose to industry leadership by selling reliable cameras and projectors and by catering to the mass audiences at fairgrounds, cafés, and nickelodeons. They consolidated their position at the end of the first decade of the twentieth century by beginning the practice of renting, rather than selling, films, and by creating a nationwide system of more than two hundred permanent theaters, a format that clearly was the wave of the future. Stage theaters were often converted to cinema, and movie theaters increasingly aimed, through low ticket prices and their location in working-class neighborhoods, at a mass audience. By 1911, as many people were viewing films in Paris as attended the two other most important popular entertainments, music halls and café concerts, combined. Competition from the American Eastman Kodak company, over film stock and film distribution, challenged the control of the French market by French companies, but on the eve of the First World War Pathé and the rest of the French film industry were still resisting being "colonized" by the American film industry.[10]

Early films drew on a number of forms of mass entertainment that had developed in the late nineteenth century, including café concerts, music halls, fairground theaters, illustrated magazines, and mass-produced photographs. Initially there was a wide variety of subject matter, including *actualités* or current events films, comic films, trick films, and *féeries,* which used the ability of film to fool the viewer to portray mysterious events. After the turn of the century, however, films became more of an art form, with comedy and crime serials, thrillers, and sentimental films focused on abandoned children and orphans. At the same time, they began to portray historical events. These short one-reel films were joined by "realizations," filmed re-creations of historical tableaus such as Pathé's *Le Sacre de Napoléon,* which, in the long-standing theatrical tradition, was billed as faithful to David's painting.[11]

By the end of the first decade of the twentieth century, historical reconstructions had become an important staple of the increasingly sophisticated productions of the major French studios. The Revolution provided subject matter for a number of these historical reproductions, such as the 1909 *La Mort du Duc d'Enghien* and Gaumont's 1910 *André Chénier.* Historical subjects continued to be important after the development of the multi-reel feature film, such as the 1911 production of *Madame Sans-Gêne,* based on Sardou's popular play.[12]

Immediately after the Great War, the French film industry fell into an economic slump brought on by lack of capital, loss of markets, and failure to update production facilities. The mood of the country after the horrific experience of the war also had an impact on the industry.[13] While increasingly challenged during the mid-1920s by modern studio spectaculars, historical reconstructions were a major subject in the 1920s, as a reimagining of the contemporary significance of figures and events from the past mediated French culture's attempts to deal with the war of 1914–18.[14] While there were few attempts to use the French Revolution itself as a subject, the one great exception to this is the 1927 silent film *Napoléon vu par Abel Gance.*

Abel Gance is remembered today as one of the most important innovators in the early history of film.[15] Born in 1889, he began making films just before the First World War, and his *J'accuse* (1919), dealing with the horrors and tragedies of the war, brought him acclaim. *La roue,* released in 1922, was both technically innovative, using montage and new kinds of camerawork, lighting, locations, and acting, and a commercial success, and made him one of the most important figures in French cinema.[16] In 1924 he began work on what would become his best-known film, *Napoléon vu par Abel Gance,* a cinematic attempt to recapture in the medium of film the sweeping spectacle of the Revolution and its most famous heir in a planned six-part series of films. Because of financial limitations, he completed only the first part. Released in 1927, the film initially had a tremendous impact when it premiered at the Théâtre National de l'Opéra in Paris: it was shown ten times, grossing a record 562,000 francs. A month later, a different version (without one of Gance's most innovative techniques, a triptych scene that technically prefigured cinemascope) was shown at the Apollo theater in Paris. But after that showing and brief premieres in the United States and other countries, the film disappeared from view. The original film was hardly seen until 1979, when a reconstructed version was shown at the Telluride Film Festival in Colorado and the next year in London. Two years later, in January 1981, a slightly shorter version, with original music by Carmine Coppola, was shown at Radio City Music Hall in New York. With these revivals, *Napoléon* became, as one obituary of Gance put it, the "Venus de Milo" of film.[17]

Gance made *Napoléon* to present his own vision of the meaning of the Revolution. This is generally favorable to the Revolution, seeing it as an event of progress for the human race, but also one that was often threatened by other countries as well as by its own internal divisions. The hero who rescues the Revolution, for Gance, is not the people, as in many republican versions of the story, but Napoleon. One theme of the film, therefore, is the importance of a strong figure such as Napoleon for the success of the Revolutionary program.[18] Since the film is concerned with the early period of the Revolution, Gance's focus on Napoleon means that the future emperor appears prominently, if anachronistically, in events of the Revolution.

It is also clear from other sources that Gance had a very complicated vision of popular participation in the Revolution and the role of Bonaparte in controlling that participation. In an "Appeal to the collaborators" given to striking workers from the Renault factory at Billancourt who were to serve as extras in Gance's re-creation of the attack on Toulon in 1793, Gance implored them to

> rediscover within yourselves the flame, the madness, the might of those soldiers of the Year II. Personal initiative is going to be of the utmost importance. I want to feel as I watch you a great surge of force capable of sweeping away with it all critical barriers, so that from a distance I can no longer distinguish between your hearts and your red bonnets. Quick, mad, tumultuous, gigantic, insolent, Homeric, with diminuendos, and grand orchestral bursts that make the moments of silence even more formidable; this is how the Revolution, that runaway horse, wills you to be.

But he also pointed out to them that "then comes a man who looks it in the face, who understands it, who wishes to make use of it for the good of France and who, suddenly, leaps on it, seizes it by the reins and little by little calms it, to transform it into the most magnificent instrument of glory."[19]

Gance's presentation of the Terror focuses on the leaders, with the crowd acting only as a cheering chorus. With the end of the Terror, Gance's account turns much more directly to Napoleon himself, portraying him on the one hand as a misunderstood and unappreciated military genius and on the other as the savior and representative of the Revolution itself. This is particularly visible in a scene in which Napoleon confronts the "ghosts of the Revolution." There are two versions of this scene, but both confirm Gance's view of the

Revolution in danger and Napoleon as its savior. In the current, Coppola, version of the film, Napoleon stops in the deserted hall of the Convention on his way to take command of the French armies in Italy in 1796. As he looks out over the empty hall from the tribune, the great men of the Revolution return before his eyes and come forward toward him. "The French Revolution is about to speak to you," Danton says. Robespierre admits that "we have realized that the Revolution cannot prosper without a strong authority. Will you be its leader?" "Yes," Napoleon responds. Danton asks him, "If the Revolution does not spread beyond our frontiers, it will die at home. Will you lead it into Europe?" Again Napoleon agrees, and they all applaud him. Saint-Just warns that if he forgets that he is the direct heir of the Revolution, "we will turn ferociously against you," and Marat asks him what his plans are. Napoleon responds that he seeks "[t]he liberation of oppressed peoples, the fusion of great European interests, the suppression of frontiers and the Universal Republic." The deputies applaud this realization of their vision, and while Napoleon admits that many wars may be necessary, he claims that "victories will one day be won without cannon and without bayonet." The leaders of the Revolution, with Danton in the forefront, urge him on, their images fading into a Marianne in front of a waving tricolor.

A second version of this confrontation between Napoleon and the leaders of the Revolution can be found in a scene based on the 10th of August, 1792, that Gance planned but that has not survived on film. The leaders of the Revolution represent the nation, articulating the demands of the Revolution to Louis XVI. Several of the demands strike at the heart of Louis's power, attacking royal arbitrariness and privilege. Others are not necessarily anti-monarchical, although clearly the scene is constructed to present them in this way: as each demand is made, Louis becomes more and more prostrate, until he collapses into a chair (under the weight of the demands?). An increasingly wild farandole around a bonfire by the leaders of the Revolution is inserted after each demand, suggesting an irrational popular complement to the intellectual emphasis of the demands. At the end of the scene, Gance's script notes indicate that "[a]ll the Revolutionary leaders are on their feet in a shared enthusiasm for the cause they are defending. A superb moment. A supernatural light increasingly transforms the atmosphere. . . . The rhythm is reaching its peak of intensity. Are all the giants of the Revolution dancing round in this red light? Is that why it has taken on such fantastic dimensions, as if millions of fireflies were dancing in hope of an eternal night?"[20]

In the way he relates Napoleon to the events of the Convention in this scene, Gance presents a vision in which the nation—the millions of fireflies in the second version of the ghosts of the Revolution—are on the margins of the victory of the leaders of the Convention over the king. But the scene is also watched by Bonaparte from outside the room. He becomes more and more luminous as the scene proceeds, until at the end he is surrounded by a halo and has an ecstatic expression on his face. In the end, therefore, the demands of the Convention, their victory over Louis, and the "enlightenment" of the nation are focused on the future emperor. Not only does Gance marginalize popular activity, he also presents Bonaparte as the ultimate protector and consolidator of the gains of the Revolution. As in stage melodrama, the story establishes the sharp division between good—the supporters of the Revolution—and evil: its opponents. Napoleon is cast as the defender of virtue, charged especially in these scenes with protecting the gains of the Revolution, its transformation of the world into a home for virtue.

Yet Napoleon himself is not a completely virtuous hero. The two versions of this scene have different emphases, and the most apparent is one that gives the existing version of the film a particularly aggressive tone, the injunction to Napoleon to lead the Revolution into Europe, and the statement that Napoleon plans to make Europeans a single people and abolish frontiers. While earlier in the film Napoleon several times emphasized the importance of defending France against invaders, and Danton's question suggests the necessity of extending the Revolution in order to protect it within France, Gance clearly moves beyond such a defensive notion of Revolutionary expansion. This becomes apparent in the last scene of the film. As Napoleon's army marches toward Italy, in a scene that makes powerful use of Gance's development of a triptych, or three-panel screen, a globe spins, showing the entire world, and a title tells the audience that "Napoleon's soul plays at building and destroying worlds." The earlier emphasis on the Declaration of the Rights of Man is submerged in Napoleon's campaigns of worldwide conquest. It is not the ideals of the Revolution that will create unity, but the force of Napoleon's armies.

The second half of the film also introduces a significant domestic aspect to this melodrama, as the story of the Revolution is interspersed with the story of Napoleon's infatuation with Josephine de Beauharnais. The principal victim of the Terror, in Gance's telling, is Josephine, who is imprisoned, although fortunately in the same prison as General Hoche. Gance suggests the gallantry of the nobility by showing Josephine's former husband, the Viscount de Beauharnais, insisting on taking her place at the guillotine, and bravely admonishing her to care for his children. After Thermidor, Gance shows the relief of those imprisoned in a scene that re-creates a Victims' Ball, in which Napoleon and Hoche watch with dismay the revelry, but in which Napoleon becomes infatuated with Josephine and wins her away from Hoche. Later, Napoleon leaves his staff waiting for two hours while he entertains Josephine in his office, and it is through her intervention with Barras that Napoleon gains the command in Italy that will lead to his eventual triumph and the climax of the film. On his way to Italy, while he plans the campaign, Napoleon writes Josephine a letter telling her how much he misses her. His domestic concerns counterpoint the roll call of the great generals of the Revolution such as Masséna and Augereau: he imposes his command on them, seemingly by the force of his personality, then gazes at a picture of Josephine and continues the letter to her. The film takes on many of the characteristics of a domestic melodrama in ways similar to those of other early silent films such as D. W. Griffith's *The Birth of a Nation*.[21]

If the subplot involving Josephine recalls the plays by Sardou that emphasized the role of feminine intrigue in the Revolution, it is also important to note the spectacular characteristics of Gance's *Napoléon,* and the differences between Sardou's stage plays and Gance's film. In the new medium of film Gance could present his version of the Revolution and its most prominent figure in a way that exponentially raised the ability of the representation to express claims to be identical with what it represented. While the boulevard plays of the nineteenth century might have captured the imaginations of theatergoers in ways that the state theaters and the Opera could not, the artifice involved in a Dumas or Pixerécourt play remained apparent to those in the seats of the Gaité or Ambigu-Comique, and Balzac and Stendhal's novelistic versions of the emperor were even more obviously fictions.[22] The silent film made by Gance, however, was able to create an entire world around the audience in the darkened theater, a world that they purchased by their willingness to pay admission but one that, for the moment at least, removed them from the 1920s and placed them in the Revolutionary decade. Broken only by the title cards, this world bore a strong resemblance to the "society of spectacle" that Guy Debord would excoriate in the 1960s.[23]

The ability of the new medium to create a complete world accelerated at the end of the 1920s as the previously visual medium turned into the combination of sight and sound that has marked it ever since. Gance attempted to adapt his work to this change by releasing a sound version of *Napoléon,* in 1935, with less success than the silent version. But another film of the period not only exploited the new capabilities of film but also captured the political conflicts of the 1930s. Marked by increased attacks on the Republic and the creation of a coalition of the principal center and leftist parties, the Popular Front, the 1930s also saw a vision of the Revolution more sympathetic to the broad current of political, social, and cultural democratization that marked the Popular Front era. Jean Renoir, working from a socialist perspective, brought together the different parts of the social spectrum against the monarchy in his film *La Marseillaise.*

While his career began before the era of sound, Renoir left an indelible stamp on French film of the 1930s and later. A contributor, along with Marcel Carné and Jean Vigo, to the movement called poetic realism, Renoir made a series of films that combined technical innovation, development of the aesthetics of film, and extraordinary sensitivity in the portrayal of individual characters. After making a farce, *On purge bébé* (1931), in a few days to prove he could make a commercially viable film, Renoir then demonstrated his ability to create individual, sympathetic characters in *La Chienne* (1931). *Boudu sauvé des eaux* (1932) was a comment on social hierarchies that were overturned in a carnivalesque way. In *Toni* (1934), Renoir chronicled the experiences of immigrant workers in southern France. *Le crime de Monsieur Lange* (1936), while bringing Renoir closer to the Communist Party, still retained in its political commentary his anarchic view of politics. *La Vie est à nous* (1936), his most political film, was made at the urging of the French Communist Party to prepare for the elections in April 1936. It echoes, in its presentation of the rural and industrial riches of France and the unity of the French nation, speeches made by party leaders in support of the Popular Front. His best-known films came at the end of the decade, *Grand Illusion* (1937) and *The Rules of the Game.* The latter was released in 1939 just as the Second World War began, and was recognized for its strengths only after the war.[24]

La Marseillaise was originally conceived during the height of the Popular Front, and, as many commentators have noted, it reflects the contradictions of the period in which it was planned and shot. The film was to be produced by the leftist collective Ciné-Liberté, which in 1936–37 mounted a discussion of film and censorship and produced documentary films on issues such as the conditions of workers. *La Marseillaise* was its most ambitious project, to be financed by a national subscription from advance ticket sales. But by the time the film was produced, in 1937–38, the Popular Front had collapsed, and the national unity of 1936 had given way to a revival of the differences among radicals, socialists, and communists that the Popular Front attempted to overcome. The film therefore presents not so much the success of the Popular Front as its failure to leave a permanent mark on French politics and culture. As Jonathan Buchsbaum notes, Ciné-Liberté and its political style of filmmaking was born with *La Vie est à nous* and died with *La Marseillaise.* This is apparent in several aspects of the film. *La Marseillaise* was a costume drama and, for some observers, uncomfortably close to the ways in which Hollywood portrayed events such as the American Civil War. The film itself does not include any of the major, and most symbolic, leaders of the Revolution, such as Robespierre, instead using common people to represent the Revolutionary nation. It ends—at the Battle of Valmy in September 1792—before the split between Girondins and Jacobins that marked the years of the Convention and that still resonated in conflicts between socialists and communists in France during the 1930s.[25]

Renoir's skill in portraying ordinary people is present in this film, making it a celebration of the contributions of all French men and women to the great events of the Revolution. It exhibits a melodramatic sensibility similar to that of Gance's film, although it constructs the split between good and evil in a different way, and finds a different hero than Napoleon. Renoir claimed that the subject—the downfall of the monarchy in 1792—had been chosen because it "offered the greatest similarity with our own."[26] In this sense, and in contrast to Gance's *Napoléon*, it made the Revolution a truly national epic, the foundational moment of an inclusive French identity. Renoir made all of the French characters, including Louis XVI, as sympathetic as the revolutionary figures. It is therefore a striking attempt at re-creating on film the unity of the French nation before the conflicts of the Revolution. While the court figures were fatally out of step with the new historical context in which they lived and acted, the Revolution becomes "a superior form of theater, a pageant acted out by a mass of players, all of whom—whatever their loyalties—have their own valid reasons."[27] The identification of the Revolution and the nation is complemented by the fact that the only villains in the film are foreigners, Marie-Antoinette and the Duke of Brunswick. The sympathetic French characters, from peasants to urban artisans to priests to kings to aristocrats in exile, emphasize the unity of all French men and women. Renoir's vision of the Revolution reflected a desire for national unity, which is apparent in the range of characters and their sympathy for the goals of the Revolution, as well as an understanding of the varying relationships of different individuals—or social types—to the Revolution. It is France, made virtuous by the Revolution, that is threatened by foreign enemies and that is the heroine of the film.

We can see Renoir's version of this conflict in several key scenes in the film. A scene in which Louis XVI, Marie-Antoinette, and the king's counselors consider the implications of the Duke of Brunswick's manifesto in 1792 is the closest to a costume-drama version of the Revolution, but nevertheless is marked by Renoir's representation of a French nation—including Louis—threatened by foreign invaders. It shows both an aggressive Marie and a pensive, cautious Louis, concerned about the possible consequences of a Prussian army invading France in his own name. "It is somewhat shocking to find our person cited in a manifesto containing such threats against our subjects," Louis says. He considers the manifesto with some irony and humor, before concluding that the authors of the manifesto "are waving torches close to a barrel of powder." This scene not only portrays Louis as a relatively pleasant and attractive individual, devoted to France, rather than as a tyrannical king, it also shows him to be politically adept, aware of the dangers Brunswick was creating for him, and willing to assert his own political skills when questioned by the queen. His counselors are less patriotic, and their advice ranges from a reactionary concerned with his own financial stake even at the price of France's honor to one who suggests the manifesto will create fury on the part of the crowd.

The foreign villain, Marie-Antoinette, advises an attack even though recognizing that it may lead to "ringing down the curtain" on the drama of a "king who cannot rule, subjects who no longer obey, and a war against her relatives in Austria" while her enemies—the Prussians—fight to save her and the king. Cynically, she calculates that a popular assault on the Tuileries will allow Louis's supporters to stamp out the revolution. Louis, on the other hand, realizes that it is his head that is on the block, not the Austrians'. But while Louis shows himself to be the most astute of those involved in the discussion, in the end the debate between him and Marie turns into one about the hunting ability of the emperor of Austria and the advisability of brushing teeth. Soon after, when rejected by his troops as he attempts to review the regiments protecting the Tuileries, Louis loses command of events.

Renoir's desire for national unity is fleshed out in two long shots, one of the *fédérés* about to leave Marseille, the other of their march through a square in Paris. The depiction of the volunteers leaving Marseille is not really a crowd scene but a series of close-ups of individuals and small groups: a woman and several soldiers offer a toast as they sing the *Marseillaise;* a soldier kisses several women goodbye; two soldiers, two women, and a man sing the anthem, with the man gazing almost directly into the camera; another soldier sings the verse as a solo; the mother of one of the principal characters, Bomier, helps him adjust his equipment before she collapses and the camera moves on to find several other soldiers and then, toward the back of the crowd, several women kneeling in sorrowful prayer. As the camera begins its return track across the crowd, it follows a single individual who joins Bomier and his mother singing before everyone hurriedly makes final farewells and the soldiers set off on their march to Paris. We see each individual depart as they march past the camera.

Renoir follows the same approach in the second crowd scene, in which the volunteers march through a public square as they arrive in Paris. The company is not a faceless crowd, but rather individuals who are featured as they move through the square; their supporters are also individuals, featured by the camera as it moves across them. As the camera pans behind the watching crowd, we do not see a single mass, but groups separated by space. A path clears for the Marseillais, and a man on horseback crosses the open space. People rush out to greet the troops, but a woman stops in front of the camera and looks around before passing on. Other individuals then emerge from the crowd.

The melodramatic structure of Renoir's version of the Revolution is apparent in its portrait of a unified French nation that is threatened by foreign invaders, and the heroism of the *fédérés* as they march to defend the nation's virtue. But it is complicated by Renoir's use of gender conventions, for these provide the basis for the nation's inability to gain complete unity in the face of the foreign invader. Martin O'Shaughnessy has argued that Renoir's films consistently expressed tensions caused by "fears of decadence and historical dislocation" through "narratives that domesticate or otherwise remove turbulent women and restore the broken link with a virile project of national history." This pattern can be seen in *La Marseillaise* in the relationships between two sets of male and female characters: the Marseillais Bomier and his mother, who initially forbids him to join the *fédérés* heading for Paris, and Louis XVI and Marie-Antoinette. While in much of the film Bomier and Louis are in opposition to each other, once each has shed the influence of the woman who restrains him, they are able to reconcile in the national endeavor of the Revolution.[28]

But the film also depicts public and private spheres that have been destabilized by the revolutionary crisis, and Renoir's use of gender plays a role here as well. On the one hand, in the opening scene and in the depiction of émigrés at Coblenz, the public space of the Old Regime is privatized. Louis XVI receives the news of the storming of the Bastille from La Rochefoucauld while reclining in bed eating, and a discussion at Coblenz about the prospects of the aristocracy returning to France occurs in a setting that mixes public policy with the concerns of the women present about the correct way to dance the gavotte in court society. On the other hand, the first scene depicting the Jacobin Club of Marseille, in which Louise Vauclair addresses the club, is very different. It is one, first, in which all present feel entitled to speak whenever the urge strikes them; secondly, the audience is made up of both men and women, shown by Renoir in a shot that moves from male to female listeners. Finally, Louise is not only the speaker, the focus of everyone's attention; she is also the most serious and politically articulate of those present. She discusses the king "Monsieur Veto," the queen, and the Assembly, while the men speak about their friendship with her dead lover and seem unable to speak seriously. This is a rare instance in which women are able to participate in public affairs and dominate male characters.

While Renoir's goal seems to be to portray a unified nation combating its enemies, therefore, the film presents an unstable national community unable to reconcile the broad statements of principle of the Revolution with the society of late-eighteenth-century (or 1930s) France. When one member of the club questions Louise's propriety in speaking—a woman's place is in the home, he says—he is shouted down by the crowd, and at the end of the scene he is attacked after he denounces Robespierre as a republican. Louise asserts her own membership in the French nation, and denounces the king, the queen, and the Assembly as traitors to that nation. She attacks Marie-Antoinette in particular for forgetting that "a nation cannot be led like a husband"—a reminder of the weakness of Louis XVI—and also indicates that Marie will have to face the strength of French women such as Louise. In one of the most crucial events in the film's narrative, Louise identifies the enemies of the nation and predicts that the volunteers will first deal with internal enemies before they go to the frontier to face the invading Prussians. In her radical version of the French nation she threatens the national unity created by Renoir's male characters.

A similar threat, from a female character, emerges in comments by Bomier's friends about his dependence on his mother. This makes it impossible for him to enlist in the regiment of volunteers: "You can't talk about the king's dependence on the Queen! You sacrifice honor and dignity for a woman too!" The debate about the proper role of women, and their relationship to public affairs, is continued in the following scene when Bomier attempts to convince his mother to abandon old customs that do not allow her to sit at the same table as him, the "head of the household." Her old customs become reactionary, antirevolutionary ideas as the scene proceeds, and she expresses her satisfaction that he will not join in the revolutionary fight against the aristocrats. In the end, however, he escapes as she bows to his will as "head of the family." His mother becomes not only a representation of proper gender roles, the sacrificing and suffering domestic figure, but also the facilitator of his revolutionary actions.

Renoir's film portrays the Revolution in the melodramatic terms that, we have seen, dominated these representations throughout the nineteenth and early twentieth centuries. France is identified with the Revolution's ideals, and is threatened by the invading forces of the Duke of Brunswick. Through the efforts of the people of the nation, from all different social groups, the threat is overcome, and the conclusion of the film, on the battlefield of Valmy, is an attempt to re-create, in the Revolutionary coalition, a basis for unity in the nation. But Renoir does not adopt the same approach to national unity as did men such as Victorien Sardou, who identified the Revolution with corruption and saw the maternal intervention of bourgeois women as the solution, or Abel Gance, who believed only a strong figure such as Napoleon could save the country. Nor was his solution that of Romain Rolland, who saw the working class as the potential savior of the country. For Renoir, rather, the safety of endangered France, and the creation of a unified nation, will come through the actions of all of the French people. Yet it is not a unity that has been achieved by the end of the film, as Bomier and his friends head toward the battle. In the words and actions of the female characters, the implications of the Revolution deny a simple achievement of national unity.

The model of national unity expressed by Renoir in *La Marseillaise* was as difficult to find in French politics in the 1930s as in his film. If one trajectory of modern French political culture has been to create a system similar to that of Great Britain, with elections and the alternation in power of clearly defined political parties, the inability to eliminate the rupture represented by the Revolution of 1789 meant that unbridgeable conflicts frequently reappeared. The parliamentary institutions of the Third Republic represented the first path, while the melodramatic politics that marked not only the 1790s, but also the 1830s, 1848, 1871, and 1890s was characterized by the revolutionary insistence on erasing the past and beginning anew to achieve the goal of the Revolution, the regeneration of the nation. During the period between the world wars, the relative stability of the political system and the ability until the mid-1930s of a popular national ceremonial culture to create unity, especially when focused on the Great War, prevented a reorganization of the place of popular ceremonies in French political culture. But the years after 1934, and especially the last few years before the outbreak of the Second World War, witnessed particularly sharp contention between two clearly drawn camps in French politics, each of whom saw and dramatized their struggle as one of defending virtue threatened by evil. As in Renoir's *La Marseillaise,* this struggle became tightly linked to the memory of the French Revolution and its role in defining who was a member of the French nation and who was not. As domestic political conflict grew more widespread so also did invocations of the Revolutionary legacy. The struggle against fascism was placed in the context of the previous generations of 1789, 1830, 1848, and 1871.[29] Condemnation of the Republic and the Revolution by those on the right similarly echoed previous disagreements about the legacy of the Revolution.[30]

A first phase after February 1934 revolved primarily around the Dreyfusard and anti-Dreyfusard camps, those who supported and those who opposed the Republic itself. As in the Affair a generation earlier, both sides portrayed their vision of France as that of "True France," and their political opponents as the villains threatening the virtuous nation. These tendencies intensified after 1936, when the Popular Front government was elected. The Popular Front not only mobilized antifascist forces in France, and in due course identified its political opponents as fascist, but it also legitimated the previously marginalized Parti Communiste Français (PCF). In so doing it spurred the mobilization of anticommunist forces, who saw the Popular Front as not the salvation of but the threat to the values of the French nation.[31] The ceremonial performances of these positions changed in the course of the period from 1936 to 1939 and helped to define particular, competing French national identities and versions of the political culture of the Republic.

The Popular Front developed gradually after February 1934 as various groups on the left came together in an alliance against the threat of fascism. Right-wing demonstrations in Paris on February 6, 1934, showed the Left the danger the right-wing leagues posed to the Republic, and the leftist counterdemonstration of February 12 showed that the Left itself could rally large numbers in support of the regime. The events of February also suggested that mass demonstrations could be powerful political instruments in the struggle for control of the country. A wave of demonstrations followed in February 1934, continuing into the next year, and fading only in October 1935. These occurred throughout the country—only five departments did not have at least one—and were remarkably frequent, averaging more than one a day. They also tended to be very violent. They thus reflected a process by which the political struggles of the country were increasingly being staged on the streets, as they had been in earlier moments of political crisis in the nineteenth and early twentieth centuries.[32]

In this context, the *fête nationale* of 1935 was only one of many demonstrations in the two years after February 1934 that dramatized the conflicts within France, and like many others it adopted a form that emphasized the danger to the country and the need to rescue it and reestablish national unity. Antifascist groups such as the Comité du rassemblement anti-fasciste du 14 juillet prepared for the *fête nationale* that year with a youth festival that featured readings of poems about the revolutionary past (such as Louis Menard's "Morts de Juin"), readings of letters from Jean Jaurès early in his career, and instruction in singing the *Ça Ira,* the *Carmagnole,* and the *Marseillaise.* There were also scattered demonstrations around Paris on the holiday. At the Place de la République in eastern Paris, the divisions in the country emerged in violent form. The right-wing group Solidarité Française placed flowers at the statue on the Place, sang the *Marseillaise,* and gave the fascist salute to the statue. In response, the members of the leftist Front Commun booed and taunted them with cries of "the Soviets everywhere" and "Red Front!" The leaguers responded with "France for the French!" and the two groups then descended into a small riot.[33]

While the Solidarité Française and the Front Commun might come to blows at the Place de la République, the major events of July 14, 1935, remained peaceful. But they also demonstrated the political divisions of the country and the ability of the ideals of the Revolution to work in support of very diverse political viewpoints. The military review presided over by the government headed by Pierre Laval drew on the commonplace notion of military glory, in which the *poilus* of 1914–18 had followed in the footsteps of their revolutionary and imperial ancestors as well as the men of 1870. While disdaining the *quatorze juillet,* not in its view a "*fête* for royalists," even the monarchist Action Française urged its supporters to honor the army. Two other ceremonies, however, were more popular and more clearly partisan. For the Left the major event was a Paris demonstration against the government in power. This took the form of a procession, led by blind veterans of the war, in which between 100,000 and 500,000 marched from Bastille to the Place de la Nation. The high point of the day was a rally, modeled on the Festival of the Federation in 1790, at the Buffalo Stadium in the Paris suburbs. In spite of the fact that Laval's government included Radicals, the demonstration drew leaders of the Socialist, Communist, and Radical Parties. The leaders of these three parties self-consciously remembered the Revolution as they swore "to defend democracy, to disarm and dissolve the Leagues, to put our liberties out of reach of the attack of fascism. We swear on this day, which relives the first victory of Republicanism, to defend the democratic liberties conquered by the people of France, to give bread to the workers, work to the young, and peace for humanity to the world." The marchers themselves chanted invocations of the Soviets, the need for bread, and the destruction of "all Bastilles," including economic ones. The events of February 1934 spurred a return to earlier uses of the 14th of July as a symbol of the combative Republic, restoring the meaning of the *fête nationale* for groups on the Left.[34]

Everyone in France, however, was not convinced. The conservative *Le Figaro* reported that "this was not a demonstration of revolutionary forces. Everything is weak and slack, in spite of the raised fists and slogans; we are watching only a parade of the multitude." In contrast, the fascist Croix de Feu impressed *Le Figaro* by its discipline, cohesion, and "dynamic energy" as it marched to the Place de l'Etoile, where Colonel de la Rocque relit the flame of the *Inconnu*. But even this right-wing group found something in the Revolution to use. In a speech at the Porte Dauphiné that ended with the singing of the *Marseillaise*, de la Rocque invoked the memory of the Revolution and the *quatorze juillet* not in the name of the universal principles that the Left found inspiring, but rather in the name of the French nation. "Your celebration of the *fête nationale*," he told his supporters, "is a justification of the 14th of July, a justification purely and unanimously French.... France should belong to the French and the French people do not wish hatred, but reconciliation."[35]

The formation of the Popular Front, its victory in the elections of May 1936, and the wave of strikes that followed the electoral victory brought the growing movement of republican defense to a peak in the summer of that year. The tragedy of the Great War continued to hover over any national celebration, and on July 12 a torch lit from the flame at the Arc de Triomphe in Paris was escorted by disabled veterans through Reims, Bar-le-Duc, and Souilly to a ceremony on the battlefield at Verdun.[36] In Paris on the 14th, an official military review took place at the Petit Palais, and a line of mourners passed the tomb of the *Inconnu* all day long. But July 14, 1936, was also marked by massive demonstrations in Paris and the provinces. Only two months after the Front's victory at the polls and a month after the socialist Léon Blum took office, all three political parties in the Front took part in the Parisian demonstration, a vivid public representation of the Republic and its situation in the face of economic and social attacks. The procession began at both the Tuileries and the Boule-vard Beaumarchais before joining together at the Place de la Bastille. An esti-mated million demonstrators marched then to the Place de la Nation and the Porte de Vincennes. The radical Edouard Daladier, the communist Jacques Duclos, and the socialist Léon Blum all spoke, with Blum urging the crowd of supporters to remain united forever. Marchers dressed in revolutionary cos-tumes, and floats portrayed events of the Revolution. At the July Column at the Place de la Bastille, there were giant portraits of revolutionary figures such as Robespierre, Marat, and Rouget de L'Isle.[37]

The Revolutionary symbolism on display defined the event as a defense of the liberties won in 1789, and the day was a revival of the tradition begun in the 1880s by the founders of the Third Republic of identifying the nation and the Republic. As in the past, the streets of Paris and other cities became popular theaters, in which the lessons of the Revolution were performed for the French nation. In the exhilarating days after the victory of the Popular Front, and especially on the *quatorze juillet* in 1936, the connection between performer and audience that marked theatrical performances occurred in the streets and at the Place de la Nation, a realization of the hopes of the Front and the Revo-lution.[38] A republican political culture that had sought to repair the rupture of 1789 on the basis of the ideals of the Revolution claimed, at long last, to have accomplished its goal in the summer of 1936.

But this national unity was a tenuous achievement. It was not just the French Revolution that marked the events of the summer of 1936. References to the Soviet Union, and radical symbols such as red flags and the *Internatio-nale,* tended to swamp those about 1789, and the PCF took the lead in invoking these references. The Front legitimated the PCF as a participant in French pol-itics, marking a significant expansion of the Republic's civil society.[39] As a part of this legitimation the party changed its approach to Revolutionary events, adopting a more "republican" relationship to the events of the 1790s. The cal-endar of holidays for the PCF changed from the one observed at the end of the twenties, when only May 1 and August 1, a day of opposition to imperialist war, were commemorated. After 1935, for the first time, the 14th of July was cel-ebrated by communists as well as those to their right. The memory of the Revo-lution also served the communists in attacks on political opponents. As the French Communist Party sought to identify itself with the French tradition, it tried to portray the fascist right as non-French, calling the members of the Fascist Leagues the "army of Coblentz," the German city to which many nobles had emigrated in 1789.[40] In a more positive vein, the communists increasingly identified with the Revolutionary tradition themselves. From 1935 on the party placed itself in a Jacobin tradition that was presented as both revolutionary and patriotic.[41] By 1939 the communist historian Jean Bruhat was planning a series of articles detailing events of the Revolution in each of the regions through which the Tour de France bicycle race passed.[42]

This then is the context in which we must see the Sesquicentennial in 1939, which generated a flood of recollections of the events of 1789. It took place in a political crisis, both domestic and diplomatic, but also expressed a political culture that tended to represent the Revolution, the French nation, and contemporary political issues in melodramatic terms. Plans for an international exposition on the Revolution collapsed due to a lack of funding from the state, replaced by an official celebration, organized by the state itself. But as the Sesquicentennial approached, the collapse of the Popular Front's second government in 1938 brought to power a more moderate government. This was headed by the radical Edouard Daladier, a politician in the process of moving away from the Popular Front and toward the political center. He was therefore less enthusiastic about identifying the nation with the Revolution. Diplomatic events also influenced his approach: as Daladier sought to stem the apparent tide of Nazi advance, he was unwilling to allow a full celebration of the heritage of the Revolution because this might offend the Right, to whom he was looking for political support. For Daladier the Revolution was only one basis for a national commemoration, along with the Armistice of 1918 and the *fête* of Jeanne d'Arc. With this hesitancy on the part of the government, and in a period of decreased popular demonstration, the army and the veterans of the Great War became the active representatives of the nation.[43]

The celebration of the Sesquicentennial therefore was muted at the national level and focused on liberty and human rights rather than social democracy. As in 1889, five dates were selected as particularly significant, to be marked by special commemorations, but several of these dates were different from the Centennial. May 5, the anniversary of the opening of the Estates General, was the first, and plans were made for ceremonies at Versailles. The second date was June 23, the anniversary of the confrontation between Dreux-Brézé and Mirabeau, on which ceremonies in Paris were to celebrate the events of the summer of 1789. The Declaration of the Rights of Man and Citizen was to be read on the radio across the country as a reminder of the principles given to France by the Revolution. July 14 was also an obvious choice, but the plans called for the *fête nationale* to be specifically focused not on the seizure of the Bastille in 1789 but on the Festival of Federation in 1790, reaffirming "the union of all the regions of France and of its Empire." Initially, two final dates, September 20 and 21, commemorated events of 1792: the victory at Valmy, to be celebrated in a military ceremony on the battlefield in eastern France; and the proclamation of the first Republic, which would be remembered in a huge public ceremony at the Place de la Nation in Paris. However, the president of the Republic, Albert Lebrun, feared leftist demonstrations on the 21st, and so it was dropped from the planning. The city of Paris, independently, planned to celebrate on July 12 the *Marseillaise* and the adoption in 1789 of the tricolor.[44]

The Communist Party at the same time instructed its parliamentary delegation to propose very specific features of the celebration. These certainly indicate the way in which the PCF constructed the memory of the Revolution, but they also suggest the inability of French political culture to reach agreement on basic questions of national unity. The celebration on July 14, 1939, was to be a *fête populaire,* drawing provincial delegations to Paris. There would be a pilgrimage in September 1939 to the battlefield at Valmy, where "the troops of the French Revolution were victorious against the enemies of liberty," and improvements were to be made at Valmy so that visitors could better appreciate the events that had occurred there in 1792. In contrast to the emphasis in the official ceremony on events during the Constituent and Legislative Assemblies, the communists planned to place a commemorative plaque on the spot in Paris on which the tribune of the Convention had stood. The PCF also thought that copies of the Declaration of the Rights of Man and Citizen should be sent to all schoolchildren at the expense of the state, and that the declaration should be posted in all public schools and public buildings. In a wary glance at the possible enemies of the legacy of the Revolution, the PCF insisted that the "Republican Army" should participate in the commemorative ceremonies, and that the chapel in Paris erected by royalists after the Restoration in expiation of the execution of Louis XVI should be demolished and replaced by a monument "to the glory of the French Revolution, as several generations of French republicans have demanded."[45] The PCF demands therefore combined different events of the Revolution, from the summer of 1789 to the war of 1792 and the National Convention, to support the political and social program of the party. As in 1936, it indicated the Left's dedication to the principles of 1789, contained in the Declaration of the Rights of Man and Citizen; its emphasis on a patriotic defense of France and the importance of the army; and its focus on the most radical part of the Revolution, the Convention and the First Republic.

The events of 1939 made the Sesquicentennial celebrations particularly relevant to a French political culture that tended to view the nation as threatened by hostile forces. The ceremony at Versailles on May 5, dominated by the personnel of the government, emphasized national unity, especially in the face of the growing German menace to French security. The Radical Edouard Herriot described the special meaning of the events of 1789 for Frenchmen in 1939. The Revolution, he argued, had created a nation out of a kingdom. The energy of the Revolution destroyed the old framework of French politics and society, sweeping out the vestiges of feudalism. The creation of the departments allowed the unification, in a new France, of the old diverse regions, a unity celebrated at the Festival of the Federation on July 14, 1790. Two reforms in particular were of overwhelming significance: the sale of *biens nationaux,* which created the "rural democracy that forms, still today, the invincible strength of France," and the attempts by the Constituent Assembly to begin the enfranchisement of all French through education.[46] In contrast then to the Jacobin history that was increasingly the dominant view of professional historians of the Revolution such as Georges Lefebvre and Albert Mathiez, Herriot's Revolution was Girondist, and in his view social conflict necessarily weakened the nation. He emphasized not the urban crowds that presaged the workers of the 1930s, but the peasants who provided support for Herriot's own Radical Party and who had been the ballast of the Third Republic since its beginnings.[47]

But the events could be read several ways. The Socialist Party newspaper, *Le Populaire,* was concerned that the official ceremonies on May 5 had a strong "academic" tone, and looked forward to other ceremonies that would allow greater popular participation. It also enjoyed the reminders to the government ministers of the unfulfilled promise of the Revolution. Its summary of an opening speech by Jean Zay described each section in terms of the reaction of one of the politicians on the platform. Zay's reference to the summoning of the Estates General to deal with fiscal problems evoked, for *Le Populaire,* a "bizarre smile" from Paul Reynaud, and the newspaper commented that "in a similar situation [now], one would send them on vacation." A reference to Mirabeau's famous statement to Dreux-Brézé, that "the assembled Nation cannot receive orders," led to a "surprised look" from Edouard Daladier. And it claimed that his visage darkened even further when a reference to the refusal of the people to pay taxes made them "the true motor of the night of August 4," the abolition of feudalism.[48] The more conservative *Le Figaro* viewed the ceremonies differently, emphasizing the words by Jean Zay that noted the universal applicability of the Rights of Man and Citizen, but also printing an opinion column that was lukewarm in its endorsement of the Revolution, approvingly quoting Benjamin Constant's disgust, even though he loved the ideals, with speeches about humanity, liberty, and the fatherland.[49]

If was therefore little unanimity in the initial stages of the celebration of the Sesquicentennial, enthusiasm faded in the course of the early summer, and the events on June 23 received little notice in the Parisian press.[50] For the communists, however, the days after June 23 demonstrated the way in which the memory of the Revolution could be constructed using melodramatic characteristics to convey the challenges of 1939. Rhetorically the Revolution served as the opposite of fascism in a number of opposed pairs. The French Revolution, the nation, reason, unity, social progress, a strong France, and the Popular Front were all identities linked together in communist rhetoric against a similar set made up of counterrevolution, racism, obscurantism, disunion, social regression, national treason, and the spirit of Munich. Maurice Thorez almost always made a reference to the Revolution in his public speeches of 1939, linking 1789 with the more radical 1792 and often invoking the name of Robespierre. The memory of the Jacobins of the Revolution, defenders of *la patrie en danger* and the foes of feudalism, provided a mantle in which the communists, the present-day Jacobins, could legitimize their own version of the struggle against the fascist threat.[51] Similarly, Jacques Duclos emphasized the necessity of remembering both the internationalism and the ardent patriotism of the communards of 1871, who in the communist view had relayed the Jacobin virtues of political and social radicalism and defense of France to the communists of the twentieth century.[52]

In contrast to the lack of enthusiasm in June, the ceremonies on July 14, 1939, were a great public celebration the government used to cement national unity. But it was the memory of the soldiers of 1792 that rallied many French men and women in a time of international crisis. *Le Figaro*'s headline read "Paris and All of France celebrate today the *Fête Nationale* with an exceptional brilliance. This 14 July will consecrate the unity of our Empire and Franco-British fraternity." One and a half million people crowded the Paris streets to watch the military parade that was the focus of the events. The soldiers who marched past the crowd led to comparisons with the volunteers of 1792 from Marseille.[53] President Albert Lebrun addressed his speech first to French men and women in the metropole, calling on them to associate their spirits with those of their ancestors. He then spoke to the inhabitants of the empire, telling them that the message of the Revolution was not just for the French, but for the entire world. "Let us unite ourselves today," he closed, "to wish a happy future for all men of good will." Premier Edouard Daladier spoke first to Frenchmen, telling them that the armies they had seen marching were the first recompense for the sacrifices they had been making to assure the security of the country. He then told the inhabitants of the empire that the French Federation had given them security, prosperity, and peace, "in the respect of their traditions and customs."[54]

But while there were official and unofficial attempts to celebrate the Sesquicentennial in a way suitable for the importance of the event, the onset of mobilization for war in the summer of 1939 dampened their impact. By late September France was in a state of war with Germany, and the commemoration of past martial glories had given way to rallying the country for the present war. The worsening political and diplomatic situation of the late 1930s made it more imperative than at any other time since the Great War for French political culture, and those who articulated it, to find a means of unifying France against the threat from Nazi Germany and domestic political and economic disruption. But even as by 1939 a more centrist version focusing on the Rights of Man and the military achievements of the Revolution had taken hold in official ceremonies, it proved impossible to overcome the tendency to cast the French nation in a melodramatic narrative in which it was the virtuous heroine threatened by an evil Germany, awaiting salvation by the leaders of the country or a group such as the working class. And, as in the film melodramas of Gance and Renoir, it also proved difficult to re-create the national unity that many saw as a lost part of French history.

Unable to find solutions to the problems of postwar France, the political parties and leaders of the Third Republic responded not only through the leagues and intellectual ferment that marked the 1930s, but also by an increasingly intense discursive conflict that, Serge Berstein has argued, acted as a "simulacre" for the differences in the country. The ideological conflicts that marked this *guerre franco-française* diverted the attention of policymakers away from the problems of the country posed by events such as the Depression, but they also, Berstein argues, channeled public discontents into the political culture, lessening in some ways the intensity of conflicts.[55] In this reading, the representations of French political culture were completely free of any connection with the issues faced by the country. If, as Berstein has suggested, the politics of the Popular Front era was a confrontation over symbols, with the Front defusing the bloody conflicts of the 1930s into a confrontation over symbols, it was the ultimate melodramatic spectacle in French culture, played out on the stage of public life.

The fall of France in 1940 revived the sentiments of national unity that marked the First World War, but also brought out the difficulties in maintaining that unity. The period between the defeat in 1940 and the liberation in 1945 presents the "Two Frances" in their starkest terms. But it is also important to note that for both sides in the conflicts of the Occupation, their different characters could be easily fitted into a melodramatic recounting of the story of France. For supporters of the Republic, its defeat presented the spectacle of republican virtue threatened by the German invader. For the regime's opponents, however, the corrupt Republic of the 1930s could be represented as the danger to the French nation. Because of these multiple representations of French virtue, the performance of Occupied France and its situation took several different forms.

The victory of France over Germany in the First World War was an obvious, and immediate, rallying point against the German occupation, and so the experience of the First World War continued to be visible, through commemorations of November 11 by the Resistance.[56] But in the middle of the national crisis brought on by the defeat of 1940, the domestic political crisis reflected by the two competing regimes of Vichy and Free France revived the use of Revolutionary symbolism, creating what Maurice Agulhon termed a "retrograde" form of competition between the two visions of France.[57] While Vichy used symbols based on the revolutionary past, its counterrevolutionary ideology was reminiscent of the conflicts of the nineteenth century. The Free France of de Gaulle in London and the Resistance in France both rediscovered the revolutionary idea of a "nation in arms" (transformed into a "nation of *résistants*").[58] As the Occupation continued, the symbols of the First Republic, the soldiers of the Year II and the men of the Committee of Public Safety, became more and more relevant and inspiring.[59] The 14th of July regained its prominence in the ceremonial calendar because it recalled an event in which the French had conquered in 1789 and then, in 1790, celebrated their liberty and unity. Its ready imagery made it the principal means both for leaders of the Resistance to rally French men and women against the occupier and for those people to demonstrate their support for de Gaulle and the Resistance.[60]

There are many aspects of the Occupation, but we may think of it as a performance of French political culture that lasted four years, from the defeat in 1940 to the Liberation in 1944 and 1945. It was a performance that adopted many features of melodrama. Both the Resistance and Vichy created the Manichean distinction between good and evil (even if they disagreed on the names of those characters) in the immediate aftermath of the defeat. For both, their public performances in these initial years were the dramatization of the conflict and the introduction of the savior of the threatened French nation. But the ability of the Occupation regime to re-create the prerevolutionary unity of France was undercut by the corruption of the Vichy regime, the cynicism of Laval and other public figures, and the dedication of fascists such as Marcel Déat to German ideals rather than the French nation. After the Normandy invasion, with the Liberation in progress, the *quatorze juillet* 1944 was the occasion for parades by maquis in numerous villages, a seemingly unifying conclusion to the events of the Occupation. But this drama too was marred by retributions against collaborators and the divisions of the victorious opponents of Vichy.[61] The conclusion of these dramas, played out over the course of the war, underscores the inability to achieve any final reconciliation that would restore the dreamt-for unity of the French nation.

5. Commercial Spectacles in Postwar Paris

An underlying theme of this book has been the parallels between the dramatic culture of France—the development of genres and styles that marked French theater and film—and the country's political culture. The performances I have examined thus far illustrate how, both in theaters and in more obviously political spaces, the melodramatic form, with its Manichean division of the world into good and evil, its plot centered on threats to and the rescue of virtue, and its inability to restore the unity of the world, has been a dominant mark of French culture at least since the Revolution. The era after the Liberation in 1945 in some respects seemed to move away from the simplistic vision of melodrama, however, instead addressing directly the ambiguities of a postwar France marked by increased commercialization and prosperity, but also moral complexity.

In a play presented on French radio on April 24, 1951, Bernard Zimmer illustrated these characteristics of the postwar world. Zimmer retold the story of Charlotte Corday, the assassin of Marat. His play begins not in the late eighteenth century, but in the mid-twentieth, in a meeting between the author of a play on Charlotte and a producer, a M. Grüsegott. Grüsegott suggests politely a "small change" in the play—that the man kill the woman. The author's response is one of disbelief: "What? You want Marat to kill Charlotte Corday?... Impossible!" When Grüsegott asks why, the author responds, "Because, among us, a schoolchild of seven knows that Charlotte Corday 'really' killed Marat!" Confronted not only with the reality of the past, but also that this is a commonplace in French culture, Grüsegott regretfully agrees: "What a shame! The man killing the woman is more commercial!"[1] In a few lines of dialogue, the play highlights not the clear-cut virtue and vice of melodramas but the varied pressures placed on both the author and Charlotte. These pressures included not only the long-standing ones of the meaning of the actions of Charlotte Corday and Maximilien Robespierre, and the ambiguities of those messages for France after the experience of the Second World War, Vichy, and the Occupation. Rather, the play also suggests the commercialization of representation and its distance from its referent that Guy Debord highlighted in the 1970s.

This chapter will examine the ways in which the thread of melodrama found its way into attempts to deal with the complexities of postwar French political culture. As in previous chapters, representations of the legacy of the French

Revolution play significant roles in this culture. Yet even as these dramatizations moved to escape the long-standing traditions of French theatrical and political performance, they nevertheless were influenced by the melodramatic sensibility that was such an important part of those traditions. In the experimental theater of Ariane Mnouchkine and her Théâtre du Soleil, and in the celebration of the Bicentennial of the Revolution in 1989, we will see that the spectaculars of French political culture adopted new terms for expressing the older message of the virtue of France and its Revolution, the dangerous threats that existed for that message, and the inability, even two hundred years after the Revolution, to create a new world in which the disruptions of the 1790s were resolved and French society could agree upon a single basis for its existence.

Playwrights other than Bernard Zimmer more directly portrayed a world in which not only was virtue more a private, individual quality than the public virtue characteristic of the Republic, but it seemed impossible for any character to maintain that quality. In place of the clear-cut characters of Pixerécourt and Sardou, or Gance and Renoir, the more intimate and engaged theater of Jean Anouilh, Henry de Montherlant, Jean-Paul Sartre, Eugène Ionesco, and Samuel Beckett created characters in contemporary settings who explored themes such as alienation and human struggle.[2] One of the most important influences on these playwrights was the sense of individual agency in the face of an incomprehensible world that marked postwar existentialism. But these playwrights were also part of a broader movement that revived the project of revitalizing French theater by bringing it to a popular audience. Following the Liberation, a small number of permanent theater companies were established in the provinces, breaking the Parisian monopoly on professional theater. The Ministry of Fine Arts established Centres Dramatiques Nationaux in Colmar (1946, moved to Strasbourg in 1953); Saint-Etienne (1947); Rennes (1949); Toulouse (1949); and Aix-en-Provence (1951). In combination with the existing Théâtre National Populaire (T.N.P.) in Paris, established in 1920 and located at the Palais de Chaillot, these Centres were intended not only to decentralize professional theater but also to perform for a popular audience the classics of Shakespeare and Molière as well as innovative new plays. But especially after the events of 1968, when their directors often cooperated with the opponents of de Gaulle's government, these theater companies found themselves in financial difficulties. Only in the 1980s, with the election of the socialist François Mitterrand as president of the Republic and the appointment of Jack Lang as minister of fine arts, did they enjoy increased funding. In spite of these fluctuations in support, however, they have been a site for the performance of the innovative theater of the postwar era and a means by which a regional and popular audience could be exposed to drama.[3]

In 1953 a journal, *Théâtre Populaire,* was founded by Roland Barthes, Guy Dumur, and Morvan Lebesque to further these aims. Drawing on models from Elizabethan England and ancient Athens, this journal sought a theater that would be relevant to mid-twentieth-century urban dwellers and therefore, they hoped, be revitalized. While the Centres Nationaux and the T.N.P. provided performance venues for this movement, it was given a boost by the performance in Paris in 1954 of Bertholt Brecht's *Mother Courage* by the visiting Berliner Ensemble. Favorably reviewed by Barthes in the pages of *Théâtre Populaire,* the performance sparked a wave of interest in Brecht that continued to dominate French theater well into the 1960s.[4] By that decade the Théâtre Populaire de Lorraine was discarding the classical repertoire, and instead developed plays focusing on contemporary issues, such as the steel industry in Lorraine, based on interviews with members of the worker community. At the same time a number of theaters in the Parisian suburbs of Aubervilliers, Nanterre, Villejuif, Saint Denis, and Sartrouville provided locations where younger performers and directors could develop a theater more directly relevant to the concerns of the workers who lived in these districts.[5] These plays emphasized reason and causality rather than passion, and aimed not at creating a spectacle that would enthrall the viewer, but rather at establishing a relationship between actor and audience that would show the origins of a particular action. They therefore ran against the tendency in French popular culture toward melodramas in which the performance's relationship with the world outside the theater was weakened or broken by its simplification of character and plot.

In Jean Anouilh's *Pauvre Bitos,* first performed in 1956, the Revolution was a means by which Anouilh could explore the much more contemporary topic of the Resistance during World War II and the treatment of collaborators after the war.[6] But it is a Revolution, and a Resistance, that are remarkable for their complexity, in the place of the simple identification of these elements with virtue in French political culture. The play recounts a *dîner aux têtes,* in which each guest is made up as a figure from the Revolution, and must speak and act as that character during the dinner. The evening has been planned by its host, Maxime, a bourgeois, as a way of humiliating an old schoolmate, André Bitos, an upwardly mobile student who, after serving in the maquis, has become *substitut* for the *procureur* of the Republic. In an action that many members of the Resistance would see as virtuous, Bitos has recently—and long after the Liberation—insisted on the execution of a collaborator who betrayed the maquis. He is assigned the role of Robespierre, implicitly identifying the post-Liberation settling of scores by the Resistance with the Terror.[7] While for the twentieth-century republican tradition an identification with Robespierre is a positive one, in Anouilh's play the comparison is damning, for Anouilh intends to call into question the simplistic association of Robespierre with virtue. His identification during the period between the Terror of 1793 and the postwar Tribunal marked a rejection of this most radical phase of the Revolution as an idealized model for the French Republic. It therefore called into question the Jacobin Revolution, the favorite of the French Left from Mathiez and the Radical Republicans of the turn of the century to the Resistance and the French Communist Party, as a basis for French political life in the mid-twentieth century.[8]

Yet this is not simply a counterrevolutionary condemnation of the Terror. Anouilh also drew attention to the pettiness of the bourgeois characters who use the dinner party—and their pose as figures from the Revolution—to continue to mock and harass André Bitos. While he may be guilty of blindly enforcing laws—especially those regarding collaboration—Bitos has also sinned in the eyes of Maxime and others for his single-minded pursuit of mobility into the class they have belonged to by birth. As Maxime explains, "I did not like you . . . you lacked grace."[9] The bourgeois alternative to Bitos/Robespierre does not therefore appear to be very attractive itself, in Anouilh's description. As France began the *Trente Glorieuses,* the economic growth of the postwar era, and the social distractions that came with it, Anouilh's concerns can be read not so much as a rejection of the Revolution as a description of its complex legacy, through creating the society in which Maxime and his friends were the elite as well as providing the opportunity for men like Bitos/Robespierre to rise to positions of power. What is remarkable about the play is both the ability of the Revolution to function effectively as a metaphor for Anouilh's postwar concerns, not only in the obvious if imperfect identification of Bitos with the leader of the Terror, but also in the complex portrait of a society in turmoil, and Anouilh's rejection of the melodramatic conventions that had marked many performances of the legacy of the Revolution in modern France.

Anouilh's play operated within the normal constraints of stage production, separating the audience from the stage. But in the late 1960s such practices came under criticism by avant-garde theater companies, who sought to move outside of the standard form of the theater and away from the strictures within which playwrights such as Anouilh operated. The events of 1968 gave further impetus to this, disrupting not only the industrial and educational sectors of French society, but also artistic work.[10] In the aftermath of the Events of May, forty-two directors of provincial Maisons de la Culture issued a declaration denouncing the limited financial support given to the Ministry of Arts, the official emphasis on Parisian theater, and the paternalism of the system of Maisons de la Culture. Instead, they called for a theater that would be more in tune with the concept of a *théâtre populaire,* in which theater would be in touch with the social classes for whom it could provide a useful way of representing their own social situation.[11]

Such criticism of contemporary theater led to several innovative theater companies. One of these was Ariane Mnouchkine's Théâtre du Soleil. Mnouchkine and many members of the company first joined together in 1960, when she founded a university theater group, the Association Théâtrale des Etudiants de Paris. This lasted only a few years, breaking up in 1962 as some members of the group performed their military service. Mnouchkine herself left France to travel in Japan and Cambodia, learning about the theater traditions of those countries. In 1964 the Compagnie du Théâtre du Soleil was established as a workers' cooperative. The group achieved its first success in 1966 with a production of Arnold Wesker's *La Cuisine*. This was performed in the Cirque de Montmartre, a small theater that became the group's home. In early 1968 another production, Philippe Léotard's adaptation of *A Midsummer Night's Dream*, established the Théâtre du Soleil as a rising, innovative theater company.[12]

The events of May 1968, however, created a crisis for the young company and its members. During the strikes of May–June, it performed *La Cuisine* for striking workers occupying the Renault, Citroën, and SNECMA factories around Paris, and this experience began to bring political concerns to the fore in the group's work. In the aftermath of the events, which disappointingly ended with a Gaullist election victory and the defeat of the May movement, Mnouchkine arranged for the company to use a theater near the Jura Mountains from July 15 to September 15, 1968. In retrospect, this summer appears central to the development of the company: it became more of a community, the result of living and working together, and this created the basis for its future style of production, *la création collective*. The outcome of this came in 1969, when *Les Clowns* was presented at the Théâtre de la Commune in Aubervilliers, and then again at a summer festival in Avignon.[13] After *Les Clowns*, the Théâtre du Soleil considered several possibilities for its next project. One was a production of Brecht's *Baal*, but this play was rejected because of its cost and subject matter. Another possibility indicated the increasingly obvious leftist politics of the company, a work on the Paris Commune of 1871 to be based in part on Jules Vallès's *L'Insurgé*.[14] Ultimately, however, they turned to the French Revolution and began what would become two plays: *1789*, first produced in 1970; and *1793*, which followed in 1972.

In contrast to Anouilh's rejection of the Terror, these theatrical performances saw the attempts at popular democracy during that period as an uncompleted and uncomplicated legacy of the Revolution. The productions emphasized the traditional leftist view of the Revolution as an event stolen from its makers—the people—and unable to realize the utopian society it imagined.[15] The creation of these two plays was a lengthy process to which the members of the company brought their schoolbook knowledge of the Revolution, further reading and discussions with professional historians, and their improvisational skills. What is especially interesting about these productions in the context of the argument of this book is the way in which they revive the melodramatic representation of French political culture, standing in sharp contrast to less popular dramatizations such as Anouilh's *Pauvre Bitos*.

The actors of the Théâtre du Soleil selected the Revolution as the subject of the plays *1789* and *1793* because of its familiarity and resonance with the audience. This familiarity freed the company not only to emphasize the popular experience of the Revolution, but also to adopt an ironic distance from the Revolutionary events.[16] This familiarity came from the universal exposure to the history of the Revolution in the French school system; and a revised edition of the famous Malet-Isaac textbook of the Third Republic, published for primary students by André Alba, Jules Isaac, and Charles Pouthas, gives an indication of the kind of vision of the Revolution that Mnouchkine and her collaborators, as well as their audience, received in school. The initial period of the outbreak of the Revolution and the Constituent Assembly appears as the result of Louis XVI's inability to lead the Revolutionary movement, which therefore employed violence against him. The major events of the period, which together led to the destruction of the political and social Old Regime, are the transformation of the Estates General into the National Assembly (June 17); the storming of the Bastille (July 14); the "end of feudalism" on the night of August 4; and Louis's forcible removal from Versailles to Paris on October 6, 1789. In the place of the anarchy caused by the collapse of royal authority, the Fête de la Fédération (July 14, 1790) served to cement national unity, and this event appears to be the foundational moment of a French nation brought together by the "freely expressed will of its population." But Louis's flight to Varennes in June 1791 created new difficulties. In this context, the constitutional monarchy created by the Constitution of 1791 could be only a precarious compromise. The Declaration of the Rights of Man and Citizen of 1789 was praised in the text as "the program common to liberals and democrats of all nationalities," but the Le Chapelier law made the condition of workers worse, and the Assembly is described as taking the side not of the peasants, but of the seigneurs.[17]

Subsequent sections of the text attempt a relatively neutral recounting of events that had been controversial in France since the 1790s. The declaration of war by the Legislative Assembly led to the fall of the monarchy on the 10th of August 1792, and then the replacement of the Legislative Assembly by the Convention. This assembly, always a lightning rod for partisan controversy over the Revolution, was described as "tumultuous and tragic." After the fall of the Girondins on June 2, 1793, the "revolutionary crisis" occurred in a "paroxysm" with the establishment of the Terror and the "moral dictatorship" of

Robespierre. The Terror did succeed in dealing with both internal and external threats. Citing the work of Aulard and Mathiez, the text describes the Revolutionary Government as a provisional regime necessitated by the international threat to France, although it concedes that the regime did break "brutally" with the ideals expressed in the principles of 1789.[18]

The final judgment of Alba, Isaac, and Pouthas on the First Republic was generous and in the tradition of the Radical Republicans if not the socialist and communist Left. The fall of Robespierre meant the ruin of the egalitarian and democratic policy he had defended, and after the 9th of Thermidor, "the Republic, turned away from the democratic path and without further means, could only oscillate between the Jacobin peril and the royalist threat." This was the "victory of the bourgeoisie" who had been threatened by Saint-Just's laws expropriating property. "But it was also the victory of politicians and speculators without shame." After Thermidor the Republic had lost its original energy and virtue, and pursued a path of mediocrity. Bonaparte was the inevitable result of this descent, and in that sense the 9th of Thermidor prepared the 18th of Brumaire. "The Republic," it concludes, "died of the blow that struck Robespierre." In sum, whatever the failings of the Convention and the Republic, students should not fail to recognize the grandeur and patriotic inspiration of the Convention. The safety of the *patrie,* meaning national defense and protection of national territory, had always been its supreme law.[19]

While the actors of the Théâtre du Soleil claimed that the *ligne conductive* of the production came from the common knowledge of the Revolution that was "the only patrimony received by all French," they adopted a particular version of the French past. This owed much to the company's leftist politics and the then still vibrant Marxist version of the Revolution articulated in histories by Albert Mathiez, Georges Lefebvre, Patrick Kessel, Daniel Guerin, Madeleine Rebérioux, and Albert Soboul.[20]

The two plays therefore drew heavily on a particular, leftist interpretation of the Revolution. The political views of the actors and the other materials they brought to the production made 1789, and especially 1793, interpretations of the Revolution that emphasized the actions and agency of "the people" and rejected the historical role of the "great figures" of the Revolution, such as Louis XVI, Danton, and Robespierre. They also emphasized the bourgeois capture of the popular revolution. The company certainly saw the Revolution as a subject familiar to their audience. But it was also a fundamental moment in the history of capitalism and the formation of a class society for them, one in which the motive force of history came from a popular revolution such as they had witnessed in 1968.

But if the plays remained within the revolutionary catechism of the French Left, they broke through the prevailing restrictions on the physical organization of theatrical production. In ways similar to those attempted by Romain Rolland at the beginning of the century, they sought to make the the-atrical performance a participatory experience for the audience rather than a distant spectacle. In the summer of 1970, the company took over an aban-doned factory, the Cartoucherie, in Vincennes, and converted its open interior into performance space. These new facilities helped to maintain the commu-nal creative process that had become its trademark. The openness of the Car-toucherie allowed full rein to the company's imagination, and both *1789* and *1793* made innovative use of staging and audience seating to bring the actors of the plays and the audience members close together. Presented without the usual trappings of Parisian theater, such as reserved seats and ushers, the plays swept their audiences along in the enthusiasm of the first years of the Revo-lution. The audience stood, enclosed by a series of platforms and bridges on which the action took place. For a scene portraying the storming of the Bas-tille in *1789*, actors stationed themselves in the audience, explaining the tak-ing of the fortress to groups of the audience who clustered around them. The final capture of the fortress sparked a popular festival, with acrobats and other amusements. Members of the audience could move from place to place, enjoy-ing the different activities, as if they were at a fairground.[21]

The plays are therefore a combination of orthodox Jacobin history and avant-garde staging. *1789* is, from its opening moments, a play that portrays the Revolution as a revolt against feudalism and the privilege of the monar-chy, the aristocracy, and the Church. This Revolution was caused by the mis-ery of the popular classes brought on by their exploitation by these privileged groups. The *dîme*, the *champart*, and especially the *gabelle* are mentioned in the opening scene as dues that bishops and lords wanted to protect, even if, as a peasant woman exclaims, "I paid everything! I've given everything to the sei-gneur. I have nothing more to get along with!" And when the woman attempts to make a soup out of some water, a character called "le gabelou" (a tax col-lector, derived from the salt tax, *la gabelle*) tells her that everything she wishes to do is forbidden: "Touch water? Forbidden! Touch salted water? Forbidden! Touch fish? Forbidden!"[22] The narrator explains that "in that year, throughout the kingdom, the most terrible famine raged: women were too weak to nourish their infants and men spent all day looking for food, but returned with empty hands." At the end of the scene, a father kills his infant child because he cannot provide for it.[23]

The remainder of the play develops an account of the Revolution that emphasizes a bourgeois revolution instituting liberty and equality in French politics. Scenes portray the convocation of the Estates General; the drafting of the *cahiers de doléances;* the confrontation on June 23, 1789, between Mirabeau and the Marquis de Dreux-Brézé; the king's dismissal of the popular favorite

Necker and his attempt to use foreign troops to disperse the National Assembly; the storming of the Bastille; the abolition of feudalism on August 4; the passage of the Declaration of the Rights of Man and Citizen; and the women's march to Versailles and the return of the king and queen to Paris in September 1789. But these events are surrounded by increasing emphasis on popular action and the radical Jacobin emphasis on social equality and popular participation in government. At the end of the play, there is a lengthy debate about the limits of liberty and equality that refers to the Conspiracy of Equals in 1795.

While the play touches on a series of textbook events in the first year of the bourgeois Revolution, it brings to these events a strong sense of the belief in the power of spontaneous popular action that characterized the student movement of May 1968. The storming of the Bastille is portrayed not at the prison itself, but at a popular fair on the boulevards, showing the people hearing the news of their triumph elsewhere in the capital city. The crucial part of this scene begins with the telling command, by a banker, to "unloose the people!" soon amended, after a long silence, by his comment, "I said unloose the people, I didn't say arm the people."[24] To the sound of drums growing louder, the actors draw the audience into small groups and begin to recount, ever more excitedly, the storming of the Bastille. Finally, shouts come from all sides that "It's been taken, the Bastille, it's been taken!" A man brings the news that the king has withdrawn the soldiers surrounding Paris and recalled Necker to office, and will come to Paris the next day to receive the national cocarde. "Tomorrow," he tells the crowd, "the demolition of the Bastille will begin, and we will dance on its ruins. The People," he shouts, "have conquered!"[25]

This scene is reminiscent of the final scene of Rolland's *Le 14 Juillet,* a popular celebration of the victory of the people. But in *1789* the end of the scene retelling the storming of the Bastille also describes the appointment of the Marquis de Lafayette as commander of the Paris National Guard. As the music of the fair and the celebration of the triumph of the people continue around him, Lafayette declares, "I forbid any festival, any festivity, any rejoicing, all movements of happiness that may in any fashion disturb the order of proprietors, and understand one thing well: The Revolution Is Over!"[26] In the aftermath of 1968, it seemed difficult for the actors of the company to ignore the repression of the popular movement that would follow the summer of 1789. But they also insisted on the continued importance of the democratic movement. As the crowd departs following Lafayette's order, a man emerges from the crowd carrying a sick girl. He walks up to a "great doctor," Jean-Paul Marat. "The Nation is sick, doctor Jean-Paul Marat," he says, "can you heal her?" Marat's response, in words drawn from Marat's writings, is that he "swears to use his glory to instruct the people in their rights, to fill them with the courage to defend them, and harangue them every day until they have recovered them."[27]

The play also refers to the revolutionary debate over the limits of liberty and the action of the people, concerns that infuse the scene in which the king and queen are brought back to Paris in October 1789. The scene begins with a debate about the Declaration of the Rights of Man and Citizen, a milestone in the creation of a regime of liberty. But as the debate ends, a bishop removes his costume to reveal himself as a juggler representing the General Will, debating the king's veto. A second juggler, a black woman, draws attention to the failure to apply the declaration to the slaves of Saint-Domingue. Finally, a woman in the crowd denounces the actions of bakers and grain merchants, and the crowd forces the king and queen back to Paris. At this moment, three deputies step forward and declare martial law, insisting to the crowd that the deputies themselves, not the crowd, will act to protect order and legality. "The Revolution," they proclaim, "is over."[28] Again Marat, the voice of popular action, emerges, declaring that the Revolution had occurred only because of popular riots.[29] The deputies' response is to limit participation to proprietors of wealth, and again Marat denounces the replacement of an aristocracy of birth by one of wealth. Barnave responds that "if the revolution takes one more step, it cannot do so without danger; one step further along the line of liberty, and it is the abolition of the monarchy; one more step further in the line of equality, and it is the death of property! The Revolution is over!"[30]

1789 certainly rises above the usual melodramatic drama that marked much of French theatrical performance in the nineteenth and twentieth centuries. Nonetheless, it still divides the world into the virtuous proponents of the radical Revolution, personalized by Marat but broadened to include the people, and its villainous opponents, represented by Lafayette. The apparently reunifying conclusion—the successful storming of the Bastille and the popular celebration that follows, involving not only the fictitious "People" of the play but also the real "People" of the modern French Republic in the audience—proves unable in the end to resolve the conflicts of French society and politics. This inability is represented in the continuing threat to the Revolution by a counterrevolution now defined as the bourgeois opponents of popular democracy. Lafayette's ominous "The Revolution Is Over!" and the 1968 attempts at enlarging the scope of a version of popular democracy hover over the play.

The Théâtre du Soleil's production of *1789* turned out to be an immense success, both in France and in other countries. It averaged nine hundred people attending each performance, evidence not only of the attraction of the subject matter and the experimental and innovative form of the production, but also perhaps of the power of its melodramatic characteristics.[31] In 1972 it was followed by *1793*, which continued the story of the Revolution from July 1792 until September 1793, and was seen by the company as a representation of the acquisition by the people of a voice in public affairs. It became, therefore, an examination of sans-culotte attempts, unsuccessful in the long run, to create a direct democracy. The time period represented in the play was that during which, in the view of the company, "the people of Paris experienced intensely direct democracy."[32] In the view of one reviewer the subject of the play was, in fact, the delegation of popular power, and it showed how everyone to whom the people gave power moved slowly away from the Revolution. It highlighted the conflict that emerged during the Terror between those on the Left, the Enragés, who argued that democracy meant direct popular participation, and the partisans of Robespierre and the Committee of Public Safety, who claimed that democracy did not necessarily mean that a continually mobilized people regulated public affairs.[33] For another reviewer, however, the two plays had very different approaches to the Revolution: '89 represented hope, '93 disenchantment.[34]

Staged in a fashion similar to that employed for 1789, 1793 attempted to involve the audience in the experience of the democratic process. The play is set in a section—Mauconseil in Les Halles quarter—and while prominent characters of the Terror, such as Robespierre or Marat, are referred to, they do not appear on stage. Instead, the different characters represent the different occupations that were present in the section meetings of Paris during the Terror, showing this central moment in the development of French democracy not from the perspective of the elite but from that of the ordinary people of the city.

The play continued from the very beginning the leftist, *soixante-huitard* perspective that had informed 1789. The framing "Parade" that begins the performance introduces the principal characters, from Louis XVI and Marie-Antoinette to the Legislative Assembly, and, almost as an afterthought, "the people of Paris."[35] In rapid succession, the audience is informed of the events of 1791 and 1792 that preceded the Terror: the "great crime" of Louis XVI, his flight to Varennes in June 1791; the massacre of the Champs de Mars, when National Guards under Lafayette's command fired on the sans-culotte crowd; the continued treason of the king, and his appeal to foreign powers; the declaration of war in April 1792, followed by a series of defeats; and the growing demand for the end of the monarchy in the summer of 1792.[36]

The play proper carries the Revolution from late July 1792, when Mauconseil drafted a petition to the Legislative Assembly calling for the end of the monarchy, to the last popular victory of the Revolution, the institution in September 1793 of the general maximum (price controls) as a result of sans-culotte demonstrations. Four days later, on September 9, the Committee of Public Safety forbade sections to meet in permanence, an attempt to break the sans-culotte movement. Combined with the departure for the armies of many of the men who had been the spokesmen for the movement at the local level, this ended the popular revolution. Unusually, therefore, the play ends the Revolution only three months after the Mountain, the most radical faction in the Convention, gained power and a month after the beginning of the Terror. Like the events of 1968 that had been so formative for Mnouchkine and others in the Théâtre du Soleil, the first French Revolution ended in disappointment for the people of Paris. At the very end of the performance, the audience is reminded of the cost, in a roll call of men from Mauconseil and the popular movement, left for the front, arrested, executed, victims (there are no apparent victors) of the vagaries of revolution. But the play does not end there. A final text is read, from Immanuel Kant's *Jugement porté sur la Révolution française*, underscoring not only the significance in world history of the French Revolution—these "first hours of liberty"—but also the necessity for other peoples of "rebeginning the experience" of an event "too entwined with the interests of humanity and of too great an influence on all parts of the world" to be forgotten.

Telling the story of the most radical phase of the Revolution from the perspective of a sans-culotte section introduces elements into the narrative that do not affect accounts that focus on elites. Hunger and high prices, so important to the Parisian population in these years of shortage, are mentioned so frequently—and often by women—that they appear to be the principal cause of the Revolution. The insecurities created by the war are highlighted: as men from the section leave to join the armies, they leave behind wives unsure not only about the safety of their husbands but also about their own economic well-being. The radical movement, which insisted that "the first right of man is to exist"[37] and which played to these popular concerns of the people of Paris, is emphasized. Marat and Jacques Roux are therefore the heroes of these sans-culottes, and their deaths great tragedies. In contrast, Robespierre almost appears a counterrevolutionary. The activities of women are prominently portrayed, with scenes in a laundry house and a workshop illustrating the roles of women in the late-eighteenth-century domestic and manufacturing economies. But they participate in the Revolution almost entirely in their domestic roles. Through a character from Saint-Domingue, the slave rebellion there is brought into the story, and Toussaint Louverture joins Marat, Roux, and Joseph Bara as the heroes of these women.

The focus on the Revolution in the local setting of Mauconseil also places the spotlight on the question of democracy and its meaning. Early in the play a scene portrays the selection by the Mauconseil section of commissioners to meet at the Hotel de Ville and determine the course to be followed after the Assembly ignored petitions calling for a Republic in August 1792. As each candidate comes forward, they are questioned about their devotion to the Revolution, their participation in the insurrections since the 14th of July 1789, their occupation and income, and their plans for the future. A butcher who plans to "butcher the fat pig Capet" is defeated; a journalist who quotes Robespierre at length, condemning the independence of deputies from their electors and calling for sacrifices to achieve victory, is elected by acclamation; while a *fédéré* marvels at the women voting just as the men.[38] The scene therefore shows popular democracy, but also the tendency for elites to take over the Revolution. The following scene reinforces the dominant role of "intellectuals" as a *fédéré* from Marseille recounts his journey from the Midi to Paris. His earthy account of the hardships encountered is gradually overcome by the more mythical one written down by a Citizen Clerk, who thoughtfully inserts a reference to the *Chant de Guerre de l'Armée du Rhin*—the *Marseillaise*—even though the *fédéré* did not mention it.[39]

As the play proceeds, the tension over the meaning of popular sovereignty between the more radical men and women of the section, on the one hand, and the defenders of the Legislative Assembly and Convention, on the other, becomes more apparent. The laundry women quote Marat's injunction that the Convention be constantly under the surveillance of the people. The men approve a proposal that officers will be elected by their soldiers. The clause of the Declaration of the Rights of Man of 1793 making insurrection "the most sacred right and the most indispensable duty" is quoted approvingly.[40] Because the most radical version of popular sovereignty is identified with the sans-culottes, because their locale, the Mauconseil section, is the setting for the play, and because the most sympathetic characters embody this version of the Revolution, the audience is drawn onto the side of the sans-culotte movement as the play proceeds.

But the Mauconseil section is not the determinant of the policies of the Revolution, and the Convention is portrayed as lax in its willingness to implement the policies of Marat, Roux, and the sans-culotte movement. The conflict finally comes to a head in the final scene, a civic banquet on August 23, 1793, to commemorate the *levée en masse* of volunteers. A farce is played illustrating the high price of food; a grocer in the farce, who refused to adhere to the maximum, in the end is denounced and executed for his crime. While the people of the section celebrate this just end for a profiteer, a debate emerges between Baptiste Dumont, the journalist who quoted Robespierre on the 9th of August, and more radical sans-culottes. Dumont insists that such performances arouse the people against the administration; it is necessary, instead, to respect the laws and have confidence in the representatives in the Convention. Democracy, he says, is not a state "where the assembled people continually rule by themselves all public affairs." The only accounting by the revolutionary government is to its own virtue. The people should therefore "elect virtuous men" and have confidence in their representatives. The sans-culottes, in contrast, insist that their representatives should make laws that the people want, that the people alone have the right to make laws, that the deputies are not "representatives" but "mandataries" of the people, that the government and democracy are the people reunited in its assemblies, exercising all of its rights. Sovereignty, they claim, is not delegated; "a represented people is not free. The [general] will is not represented." If the sections do not have the right to criticize the Assembly, then an aristocracy of representatives will be the successor to the aristocracy of nobles of the Old Regime. With these disagreements about the very meaning of the central goal of the Revolution, there can be no happy ending: the scene ends with a baker arguing that, with the open war of the rich against the poor, it is necessary that terror be the order of the day. In the final roll call, we learn that Baptiste Dumont, good Robespierriste, was named commissioner by the Committee of Public Safety, but executed on the 12th of Thermidor, three days after the end of the Terror. His principal opponent at the banquet, Charles-Henri Le Breton, good sans-culotte, was arrested in October 1793, and executed in February 1794.[41]

The Revolution of 1793 is therefore one with many sides to it. The point, as one reviewer noted, was "to relive (and not reconstruct) an historical moment seen and lived by the people of the provinces and of Paris."[42] But while the Revolution is complicated, the play in the end constructed a series of events in which virtue always lay with the People, and that virtue was threatened by the other participants in the Revolution. Mnouchkine's "manicheism" was becoming more apparent. Bloody events like the storming of the Tuileries and the September massacres in 1792 are passed over rapidly.[43] The Vendée is mentioned only as a threat to the Republic and in the recounting of the massacre of a republican priest urging submission to the Republic by his parishioners.[44] This did not necessarily affect the theatrical experience. Gilbert Chateau, an avowed fan of Mnouchkine, claimed that "what matter Mme Mnouchkine's manicheism (no bums [salauds] among this version of the people) and her somewhat simplified version of the affair? Enthusiasm, faith, generosity. And no intellectualism. That's it, the theater."[45] Chateau's enthusiasm may have been widespread, but it was tempered by Jean Ristat's comment that one did not have to speak of the Revolution to be revolutionary, and by his complaint that the "interminable, repetitive" speeches made him feel as if he was attending a history class illustrated by a series of tableaux vivants.[46]

However successful Mnouchkine and the Théâtre du Soleil were in these plays in using dramatizations of the Revolution to raise questions about the French past and its relationship to French democracy, or even about the nature of democracy itself, the story ended pessimistically. The conclusion of 1793, with the suppression of the sections in September 1793, showed the inability of the popular movement to overcome the pressures of bourgeois and military power. Both of these plays, therefore, were representative of the postwar attempts to create a more democratic theater, as through their staging and the different effects employed they created a closer bond between actor and audience. Because of the political perspective of Mnouchkine and her company, they also were more favorable to the Revolution than Anouilh's play *Pauvre Bitos* had been.

But in the end they illustrate the presence in French culture of a melodramatic thread that was related in complex ways to the experience of the original Revolution of the 1790s and its place in French popular culture. For a variety of reasons—their schooling, the historical works that influenced them, their own experiences of revolution in 1968—Mnouchkine and her company ignored the complexities of revolution that authors such as Anouilh had found so obvious immediately after the Second World War and that the Soviet invasion of Czechoslovakia in August 1968 had underscored. As interesting and finely drawn as the characters in *1789* and *1793* are, they nonetheless remain within the boundaries fixed by the Jacobin and Marxist interpretation of twentieth-century France. And that interpretation is in form melodramatic: good versus evil, flawed heroes, and inability to resolve the contradictions created by the revolutionary moment. If the Théâtre du Soleil provided a vision of the complex world of Revolutionary France, it also performed the inability of the French nation to find an unproblematic unity in the aftermath of that event.

The work of Mnouchkine and her collaborators represents a particularly acute example of a key problem that French political culture shared with melodrama in the second half of the twentieth century, the inability to legitimize itself through reference to some absolute principle. By choosing an obviously historical subject, the French Revolution, the Théâtre du Soleil seemed at first glance to follow firmly in the footsteps of the Third Republican politicians and historians who had insisted before the Great War that there was a single, true version of the events in France in the 1790s, and that this provided a basis on which postrevolutionary France could be constructed. Yet *1789* and *1793* provided constant reminders of the artificiality of those claims, in spite of the innovative staging. In ways that recall Guy Debord's angry denunciation of twentieth-century culture as a "society of spectacle" in which representations were deceptive and detached from their referent, the plays reminded their viewers of their own textuality as well as the discursive nature of the claims of all participants in the Revolution. From the constant proclamations that "the Revolution is over," to the citizen clerk who inserted the *Marseillaise* into the *fédéré*'s account of his march to Paris, to the contentious sans-culotte play about the price of food, these two plays tell us that the world consists of representations with multiple meanings, not the one version claimed by nineteenth- and early-twentieth-century partisans of the Revolution.

The Bicentennial of the Revolution of 1789 provided the moment for the greatest celebration of late-twentieth-century French political culture. The events of that celebration have been carefully documented and analyzed, and there is no intention here to repeat those efforts.[47] But the Bicentennial is an important complement to the performances of *1789* and *1793* because of its much more overt melodramatic sensibility. Both the importance of melodrama and its characteristic inability to resolve the deep divisions in French political culture became especially apparent in the events in Paris in mid-July, the climax of the Bicentennial and its most public performance of the meaning of the Revolution for late-twentieth-century France. The celebration began on July 13, when the president of the Republic, François Mitterrand, presided over a commemoration of the Declaration of the Rights of Man. With thirty heads of state in attendance at the Palais du Trocadero, and the Eiffel Tower as a backdrop, the declaration was recited, its articles interspersed with readings from revolutionary figures such as Sieyès and Condorcet. That evening, the Opéra de la Bastille, a symbol of Mitterrand's emphasis on redeveloping the working-class eastern districts of Paris, was inaugurated by the president of the Republic and his distinguished guests, while Parisians celebrated in the neighborhoods of the city with open-air dances.

The 14th began with a military parade on the Champs Elysées in the morning. Later in the day, at the traditional free *quatorze juillet* matinée, the Comédie-Française performed Beaumarchais's *Le Mariage de Figaro*. After the performance, the actor who had played Figaro, Richard Fontana, recited the *Marseillaise* to the audience. But the main event was in the evening. With the Place de la Concorde as the official focal point, a parade designed and prepared by the theatrical producer Jean-Paul Goude unfolded over two and a half hours. The Bicentenary Commission had charged Goude with preparing a celebration that would accomplish two goals. It should evoke the *quatorze juillet* as the Fête de la Fédération of 1790 and with it the adhesion of the French people to the principles of 1789. But it should also honor the *Marseillaise,* because, as the head of the Bicentennial Commission, Jean-Noel Jeanneny, wrote in his final report, "our national hymn is able to touch the entire world."[48] Within this broad charge, Goude's intention was to focus on the idea of fraternity among all men, and the participants in the events showed this international emphasis.[49] Groups drawn from every corner of France, including Corsica and Guadeloupe, and from around the world marched past the official reviewing stand and thousands of paying spectators in the Place to the booming of drums and occasional attempts to play music. The climax came with the appearance of the African American opera singer Jessye Norman, wearing a flowing blue, white, and red gown, on a stage built around the Luxor obelisk in the center of the Place. With a huge wall of water on the Tuileries side of the square as a backdrop, Norman sang the *Marseillaise,* accompanied in French and other languages by participants in the parade. African percussionists and Maghrebin dancers underscored the emphasis on the universal appeal of the *Marseillaise* and the Revolution.

The singing of the *Marseillaise* was followed by groups representing the United Kingdom, the Soviet Union, and Guinea. A corps of drummers, the Tambours du Bronx (from the French railway town of Nevers) led a life-size float of a steam locomotive in a scene from the film *La Bête humaine,* recalling two major interpreters of the Revolution's message, the Popular Front director Jean Renoir and the novelist Emile Zola. The final group in the parade was the Florida A & M University marching band, a predominantly African American group that moonwalked through the Place. The evening ended with a fireworks display in the sky over the city.

As Steven Laurence Kaplan has noted, Goude himself cautioned against too profound a reading of the celebration he organized.[50] But a number of themes are apparent. There was the triumphalism of a celebration that was, against all odds, successful. With over a million people attending the events, many more watching on television around the world, and much of France's elite intentionally absent, it had the popular dimension that finally, on the 14th of July, made the Bicentennial an event for all French men and women. It was also an event that, to the dismay of some, and especially the extreme Right, not only reflected the Americanization of French culture but also celebrated a very diverse conception of French identity.[51] The earlier emphasis on the Declaration of Rights as the universal legacy of the Revolution not just for France, but for the world, was echoed in the inclusion in the parade of groups from former French colonies, French possessions outside of Europe, and indeed from around the world. While for some this internationalization of the message of the Revolution made it more relevant to late-twentieth-century concerns, others were appalled: *National Hebdo,* the newspaper of the Front National, denounced it as "a stupid, insulting, and grotesque presentation."[52] The Bicentennial therefore reflected the ambiguity of the Revolutionary legacy and French national identity in the late twentieth century: a foundational event of the nationalism of the nineteenth and twentieth centuries, which nonetheless could be "turned" to reflect the diversity of the contemporary French population and the increasing globalization of population movements. The event also reflected the spectacular presentation that, in the course of the twentieth century, had become increasingly a part of French political culture. Its theatricality stood in sharp contrast to the muted performance of the recitation of the Declaration of the Rights of Man the previous day, or Fontana's reading of the *Marseillaise.* The 14th of July was a massive spectacle that aroused controversy in part because it so clearly utilized the performance techniques of stage and screen, and the ultimate message about the meaning of the Declaration of the Rights of Man and Citizen was presented not so much in words as in the clash of stage effects and marching bands.

Indeed, even if considered only in the tradition of stage performances of the memory of the Revolution, the *gouderie* (the French term for the ceremonies) stands out for its blatantly commercial qualities. Very different was the event that ended the Bicentennial year, the pantheonization of the Marquis de Condorcet, Abbé Grégoire, and Gaspard Monge on December 12.[53] While the *quatorze juillet* seemed much like a Las Vegas stage show, the pantheonization clearly referred to the solemn republican ceremonial tradition. Mitterrand had revived the importance of the Panthéon in republican symbolism through his visit there on the day of his inauguration as president of the Republic in 1981. The subsequent installations of René Cassin in 1987 and Jean Monnet in 1988 continued his use of the building as a symbolic reference point.

One aspect of this ceremonial tradition was the clear statement of the meaning of the narrative, the attempt to fix the ambiguities of the performance through speeches that, like voice-overs, told the audience what they were supposed to see. In December 1989, the principal speech at the Panthéon, by Minister of Culture Jack Lang, described how the three revolutionary heroes, one from each of the three Estates, represented the commitment of the Revolution to human progress and generous concepts of equality, fraternity, and liberty. He concluded by linking the events of 1789 with the contemporary world, insisting that the French Revolution continued to inspire people around the world: "1789 is reborn in Prague in 1989, in Berlin in 1989, in Moscow in 1989, in Budapest, in Sofia, in Santiago, in Beijing in 1989." Pantheonizing three intellectuals, he argued, was particularly appropriate given the reemergence of intellectuals such as Václav Havel and Andrey Sakharov in the struggle for liberty.[54]

Lang's speech gave way to the interment of the three bodies. On each catafalque was inscribed an epitaph, a further attempt to fix the meaning of the event. For Condorcet, this was his formula "What is the first rule of politics? It is to be just. The second? To be just. The Third? To be just." For Monge, it was the motto of the Ecole Polytéchnique: "For the *patrie*, science, and glory." For Grégoire, who was denied the last sacraments by the archbishop of Paris, it was his final request, "O God, have mercy on me and pardon my enemies." Only Mitterrand entered the republican temple as, to the sounds of the *Marseillaise*, Mozart's Masonic funeral music, and Beethoven's "Ode to Joy," the Bicentennial came to an end.[55]

But as with all celebrations of the Revolution, the pantheonizations were not without controversy, and they demonstrated, as had the events of July 14th, that while public ceremonies might portray the virtue of the Revolution and the Republic, French political culture remained unable to close the revolutionary disruption and create the unified culture dreamt of since 1789. In particular, the Abbé Grégoire again was a focal point for the ambiguous relationship between the French Catholic Church and the Revolution, as he had been during the Restoration. Selected for his sponsorship of the emancipation of Jews, Grégoire became instead a symbol of the religious upheaval of the Revolutionary years. *Le Figaro* noted that Grégoire had not opposed the massacres of September 1792, nor did he raise his voice against the war in the Vendée. Perhaps most controversially, he had opposed Rome, "dreaming of breaking the tutulary link [between the papacy and the French church], and establishing a republican and gallican Church." But, the paper noted, it was ironic that the only representative of the Church at the Panthéon was the apostolic nuncio, Msgr. Lorenzo Antonetti. The French episcopate, in contrast, appeared to boycott the ceremony, in spite of numerous supporters of the pantheonization among them. One of these, the bishop of Cambrai, Msgr. Delaporte, noted that the absence of French bishops at the ceremony could "astonish" some Christians, a reaction he could understand. The vicar-general of the Mission of France, Père Jean-Marie Pioux, defended Grégoire in existential terms: "The Abbé Grégoire participated in the redefinition of French society; he was willing to dirty his hands." On the other side of the debate, however, the bishop of Rennes, Msgr. Julien, regretted that the ceremonies would leave "in the shadows" the priests massacred during the Revolution because they refused to take the constitutional oath.[56]

But the attitude of the French episcopate toward the Revolution and its Bicentennial was more complex than appeared on the surface of the controversy about the pantheonization of the Abbé Grégoire. The archbishop of Paris, Jean-Marie Cardinal Lustiger, described his hopes for the Bicentennial in an interview with the historian François Furet before the events began. Expressing his desire for reconciliation between the Church and Republican France, Lustiger nonetheless insisted on the importance of the controversial massacre of French priests in September 1792 in the Carmelite monastery in Paris. These events, he argued, were a part of the memory of French Catholics, and needed in some way to be dealt with if the reconciliation he hoped for was to take place. But this relatively conciliatory position at the end of the interview seemed to conflict with Lustiger's insistence, when pressed by Furet, that the basis of the Revolution and of modern democracy, the Rights of Man, are purely subjective. They cannot therefore be the basis for a just society. This, he argued, could come only from a conception of rights "founded by reference to the transcendence of God who is revealed and explained in history."[57] Lustiger therefore directly formulated the problem of postrevolutionary French culture that, we have seen, appeared frequently in public performances of the Revolutionary legacy: how was France to heal or replace the Old Regime's damaged foundational assumptions? His solution, however, appeared to imply a return to the prerevolutionary basis of a transcendent God as that foundation, precisely the conception that heirs of the Revolution had been struggling to replace for two hundred years.

Lustiger also voiced doubts about the nature of the Bicentennial celebration. If the French Republic was going to celebrate the success of the Revolution, he thought, it should also recognize and regret the excesses and crimes of the event. As for Grégoire, Lustiger thought that French Catholics could accept the abbé as a great figure of the Revolution only if those clergy and Catholics against whom he campaigned, as constitutional bishop, were also recognized. Grégoire therefore became for Lustiger a symbol of the forces that massacred French Catholics. Nonetheless, the cardinal expressed willingness to work to create a reconciliation. And while only his absence at the ceremony in the Panthéon on December 12 was widely reported, Lustiger had presided over a funeral mass for Grégoire at the church of Saint-Etienne-de-Mont, next to the Panthéon, the previous day.[58]

There were also disagreements outside the Church hierarchy. The former communist Annie Kriegel wrote that the pantheonization underscored the anticlerical and secular ideal of the Republic, especially in the aftermath of the Affaire du Tchador in October 1989, but that in attributing Jewish emancipation to a Catholic priest, it raised disturbing questions about Jewish agency in the aftermath of the Holocaust.[59] A Jesuit priest, Michel Riquet, responded that Grégoire was not an apostate from the Catholic faith nor from his priestly functions, but a priest profoundly influenced by the spirit of the Gospels. Emphasizing the mainstream Bicentennial theme of the Rights of Man, Riquet reminded his readers that Grégoire was being honored for his devotion to civil rights for Jews, Huguenots, and blacks, indeed for all men, an eminently Christian cause. "Honoring the Abbé Grégoire for his famous *Mémoire sur la regénération physique, morale et politique des juifs* ... does not imply that one equally agrees with his viscerally antimonarchist political views." Grégoire should be honored as a champion of the Rights of Man, as Pope John XXIII and the second Vatican Council had recognized and proclaimed them.[60] Jeanneny, in his turn, claimed in his final report to welcome the controversy, arguing that Grégoire's selection had generated healthy debate over contemporary issues. This was, he thought, precisely the mission of the Bicentennial.[61]

The *quatorze juillet* and the pantheonizations of the Bicentennial were revivals of traditional republican dramas, public performances of the meaning of the Revolution. As with earlier celebrations of the Revolution, French theater companies also presented performances intended to contribute to the celebration. In the Nord/Pas de Calais region, the Théâtre des Pays du Nord put on a cycle of plays from the Revolutionary era, reviving the works by Chénier, Laya, Maréchal, and others that had been so prominent two hundred years earlier. Eventually the company brought these plays to Paris itself. At the

Bataclan theater on the Boulevard Voltaire *Cousin Jacques, Le Jugement dernier des rois,* and *L'Interieur des comités révolutionnaires,* an ideological potpourri from the theater of the 1790s, were performed. At the Hachette on the Place Saint-Michel, a play called *Les Mystères de la Révolution* was performed, "An Evocation in images and scenes, the history as one dreams it, cruel and comic, terrible and marvelous." A "Spectacle sung and danced by masked actors" depicted *Les Héros de l'An II* at the Montorgueil, a group of "disabused and aggressive sansculottes remaking the Revolution in a little part of the provinces in 1790." Romain Rolland's *Robespierre* was performed at the Théâtre Romain Rolland in Villejuif in the Paris suburbs. At the same time a film version of the Théâtre du Soleil's *1789* was shown at the Studio des Ursulines.[62]

The melodramatic characteristics of the Bicentennial performances are readily apparent. By drawing so heavily on Third Republican traditions of civic celebration, the public celebration of July 14th and the pantheonizations of December 1989 easily constructed a virtuous Revolution and Republic, evil opponents, and a dramatic resolution that futilely sought to resolve the complexities of French political culture. From the concerns of the Catholic Church, Vendéens, and even Gaullists such as Jacques Chirac about the nature of the commemoration, the Bicentennial illustrated again the inability of public performance to resolve the conflicts created by the Revolution. Whether on stage or in public ceremonies, the divisions in France that had contributed to the development of melodrama in the time of Pixerécourt continued to mark the central public performances of Mitterrand's presidency.

One of the ironies of the Bicentennial and French theater is that the play *1789*, which had done so much in 1970 to bring the memory of the Revolution alive for theatergoers, was not performed on stage during the year. But almost two decades after the performances of *1789* and *1793* had dramatically and successfully presented a *soixante-huitard* version of the French Revolution to the French public, Ariane Mnouchkine teamed with Hélène Cixous to create a film, *La Nuit miraculeuse,* commissioned by the Bicentenary Commission of the French Revolution. Cixous had become a frequent collaborator of the Théâtre du Soleil in the course of the 1980s, writing plays on Cambodia (*L'Histoire terrible mais inachevée de Norodom Sihanouk, roi du Cambodge,* 1985) and India (*L'Indiade, ou l'Inde de leurs rêves,* 1987) that were produced by the company. The increasing practice of working from scripts produced by writers such as Cixous marked one of the shifts that had occurred in the company since the days of the collectively authored *1789* and *1793*. Another was the apparent move away from the approach sympathetic to Marxism that those plays took. This did not necessarily mean that the politics of the company or Mnouchkine had moved to the right. Indeed, Mnouchkine had frequently acted in public as a strong advocate of human rights, campaigning for workers, immigrants, and HIV/AIDS communities, and she would conduct a hunger strike in 1995 to protest the inaction of Europe and the United States in Bosnia.[63]

La Nuit miraculeuse (filmed in September 1989 and broadcast on French television on December 20, 1989) may be taken as emblematic of the waning, which the Bicentennial seemed to confirm, of the radical memory of the Revolution and the growing strength of the melodramatic thread in French spectacles that were more and more disconnected from the events of 1789. It depicted the passage of the Declaration of the Rights of Man and Citizen in August 1789 by the National Assembly, and in that sense adopted the Bicentennial's version of the meaning of the Revolution. But it turned away from the leftist orthodoxy that marked *1789* and *1793*. Instead it dealt with the Declaration of Rights in a way that turns one of the most radical statements of the Revolution, the call for radical change that had made the Revolution such an inspirational event for two hundred years, into a relatively safe, sentimental comment on the past. By focusing on the Declaration of Rights, it reflects the continuing search for a basis on which to reunify French political culture in the aftermath of the Revolution, as well as the inability to accomplish that task. But by presenting the Declaration in the context of a magical story, it separated the document and its principles from the context within which it was created.

La Nuit miraculeuse tells the story of the debate and passage of the Declaration from several perspectives represented by characters in the film. One is that of a pessimistic young man who has organized an exhibit of mannequins of figures of the Constituent Assembly for a Bicentennial display in the Palais Bourbon. His sadness is caused by the realization that, with the end of the Bicentennial, the display is to be sold to a M. Batala, the villain of the film, who will use the figures in the *grands magasins* of Paris, commercializing and thus tainting the ideals of the Revolution. The movement of the leaders of the Revolution from the political space of the Palais Bourbon into the commercial spaces of the *grands magasins* emphasizes the "spectacular" disjuncture between the reality of the Revolution and its representation in the mannequins. Throughout the film, he attempts—in a melodramatic and eventually slapstick portrayal of the class struggle—to save "his" revolution from being sold out to M. Batala and his evil henchmen. A second perspective is that of a small boy, who is introduced at the beginning of the film selling small puppets of members of the Constituent Assembly on the street. In his innocence he represents the utopian promises of the Revolution. The third perspective is that of a woman, an attendant in the *toilette des élus* in the Palais Bourbon, who comes to reflect the ability of the ideals of the Revolution to inspire people in the twentieth century.

Most of the film takes place in the Palais Bourbon, in the chamber of the National Assembly, as the deputies—the mannequins come to life, identified by the awestruck citizens of 1989–debate and attempt to pass the Declaration of the Rights of Man and Citizen. But its passage is cast into doubt—in the film at least—by the fractiousness of the deputies, notably the Marquis de Mirabeau, older brother of the more famous *comte* and a defender of the Old Regime's privileges. It is also threatened by a bomb placed in the Palais by Batala's men, which leads to a long sequence as the heroes of the film follow a wire around the Palais to the bomb. They act with increasing desperation, fearing that they will not find it in time and the Assembly will be destroyed before it passes the Declaration of Rights. Eventually the various hurdles are overcome, and the declaration passes, to the relief of the onlookers.

The film is therefore another melodrama in a long line of performances that portray the legacy of the Revolution as threatened virtue and that seek to restore unity to French political culture through the dramatic rescue of the principles of the Revolution, the Rights of Man. In this instance it is the commercialism satirized by Bernard Zimmer in 1951 and attacked in the 1970s by Guy Debord, rather than counterrevolutionaries, that threatens republican virtue. The tone of the film may have been necessary to hold a popular television audience. But while that tone detracts from the seriousness of its message, the film does raise at least three significant issues concerning the relevance of the Declaration of the Rights of Man and Citizen to the France, and the world, of the late twentieth century.

One of these issues is immigration and membership in the French national community. As the deputies debate the declaration inside the Palais Bourbon, the camera shifts to the exterior and then looks through the iron fence that surrounds the Palais across the high brow of the Pont de la Concorde. In the night, marching through a snowfall, appears a stream of people, representatives of every possible immigrant group. This stream of immigrants evokes consternation on the part of the parents of the boy, who watch from the steps of the Palais. But the boy himself is filled with joy, and he rushes to the fence to open the gate and welcome the immigrants. As the debate continues inside, Arabs, Vietnamese, Muslims, Africans, and Hassidic Jews fill the gallery of the chamber to watch the debate on the declaration that will provide the basis for their membership in the French nation.

The importance of the declaration to France and to the world is underscored by the other participants in this march across the Pont and into the chamber, a collection of historical figures from France and other countries, men and women who have helped advance the cause of human rights. Victor Hugo, Alfred Dreyfus, Emile Zola, Jean Jaurès, Emily Pankhurst, Desmond Tutu, Martin Luther King Jr., and Mahatma Gandhi all enter the Palais, an international Panthéon that suggests that the Enlightenment religion of humanity is still alive, and that its home is in France. After the passage of the declaration, these distinguished figures stand together and introduce themselves to each other, in what might be taken as a reminder to viewers of the film that the struggle to fulfill the promise of the Revolution has been, and continues to be, the defining theme of world history. Gandhi tells the Constituents, "we are grateful to you and all your friends" for the Revolution as the source of human progress.

The third theme, revolutionary violence, is only hinted at obliquely, through the character of Robespierre. In *La Nuit miraculeuse,* as in so many other dramatic presentations of the Revolution, the leader of the Terror assumes his habitual role as representative of the violence that seems to undercut the revolutionary message. Early in the debate Robespierre accuses the Constituents of wanting a revolution without revolution. And after the passage of the declaration, as everyone else celebrates, Robespierre ominously foreshadows the future: "Nothing is done," he says, "everything begins."

The promise of the declaration, and its identification with the Revolution, clearly dominated the film, as it dominated the entire Bicentennial. At a time when the anti-immigration Front National was gaining political strength in France, and other anti-immigration groups were becoming significant political players in Germany, Austria, and elsewhere, the Declaration of the Rights of Man seems, in the film, to absolve France of problems in absorbing the immigrants who marched across the Pont de la Concorde. At a time when the ability of the Revolution's message to inspire the rest of the world, not to mention French men and women, seemed to be in question, the characters in the film all seemed to find it awe-inspiring and central to their lives. And after two centuries of French history, with additional evidence from many other countries, that seemed to suggest the difficulty of implementing the declaration without violence, Robespierre was marginalized. In his place Gandhi and Martin Luther King Jr., the apostles of nonviolence, stood in the center of the chamber. The film took seriously the revolutionary promise of human happiness, even if this tended to sentimentalize the radicalism of the Revolution in ways that Mnouchkine's earlier plays did not.[64] This sentimentality is, perhaps, Mnouchkine's response to the roll call of those who paid heavily for the gains of the Revolution that ends 1793.

The sentimentality of the film, however, creates some of its most powerful moments. As the British suffragette Emily Pankhurst watches the debate— notable for its lack of concern with women's rights—the attendant of the *toilette des élus* stands next to her and tells her, "You were my first hero.... I know your life by heart." She shows Pankhurst a snapshot of a 1932 demonstration in Paris for women's votes, and points to herself in the photo, standing next to a person she thinks is Emily Pankhurst. The moment is weakened, however, by the fact that in 1932 French women were still seeking the vote, when in most other European countries women had obtained it in the aftermath of the First World War. A second, even more striking moment comes soon after a handful of *déportés*, with shaved heads and concentration camp garb, file in and sit in the gallery. A few moments later, a Hassidic Jew across the gallery stands up and begins shouting to his brother Jacob, whom he has recognized among the *déportés*. The tearful reunion depicts France as the home of human rights, obscuring how Jacob might have found his way to the camps, and what the role of French citizens, French police, and a French government might have been in his journey.

La Nuit miraculeuse and its adoption of the Bicentennial's mainstream version of the Revolution is remarkably different from the attempts in *1789* and *1793*, Mnouchkine's works of the early 1970s, to portray the Revolution as a popular, and empowering, event. Whereas the canonical figures of the Revolution are almost totally absent from the two plays, in the film they are central in what becomes almost a trivia contest on Revolutionary history: can you recognize that figure from the schoolbooks? Whereas in the plays, the French people make their Revolution, at the Bastille and in the Mauconseil section, in the film they watch passively from the gallery while the members of the assembly—speaking mannequins—discuss their future rights. The conjunction of the plays and the film raises important questions about the Revolution and its contemporary relevance. Do men and women have rights because the major figures of the Revolution managed to pass the declaration, or because they are human beings? And were those rights acknowledged—France's claim to a central place in world history—because of the men of the Constituent Assembly or because of the sans-culottes of Mauconseil?

The bitterness and ambiguity that marked the plays of Bernard Zimmer, Jean Anouilh, Eugène Ionesco, and Samuel Beckett, and the films of Jean-Luc Godard and François Truffaut, held a tenuous place in French culture by the last decades of the twentieth century. These works may have burnished France's cultural reputation in the postwar era, but they struggled against the certitudes of a popular culture that constructed plots around good and evil and threatened virtue. The melodramatic thread that had been such an important part of the initial French response to the events of the 1790s remained significant, and even seeped back into attempts such as *1789* and *1793* to perform political issues. By the time of the Bicentennial in 1989, the characteristics of the melodrama were the comfortable way of commemorating the virtues of the Republic—the Rights of Man—and the dangers those virtues faced in the modern world.

It would be too mechanical to connect directly the increasingly commercial aspects of the representations of the Revolution in Fifth Republican France with the economic growth and commercialization that the *Trente Glorieuses* brought to the country in the aftermath of the Second World War. But the theatrical and ceremonial aspects we have seen in this chapter suggest the importance of the distance between the message of the Revolution and its representation in the last third of the twentieth century. Even as the principles of the Declaration of the Rights of Man became the central part of the Revolutionary message, the performative aspects of French political culture seemed to submerge that message in the form of the representation. The representations we have examined in this chapter—the plays of the Théâtre du Soleil, the *gouderie* and pantheonizations of the Bicentennial, and the film dramatization in *La Nuit miraculeuse*—all point to the characteristic way in which French culture has framed the Revolution. The events of 1789 were not simply political conflict. Rather, they were the expression of the dream of a virtuous world, but one threatened by evil represented by the opponents of the Revolution. Those virtues survived—France, after all, was still around, still the incarnation of virtue—but they did not triumph. History, by the end of the twentieth century, had proved that the world torn apart by the storming of the Bastille could not be reunified through the theatrics of a Festival of Federation.

6. Conclusion

This book has been explicitly interdisciplinary, drawing its emphasis on political culture and spectacle not only from historians but also from political theorists, art historians, and literary critics, and its interpretive methods from historical, cultural, and literary studies. Disciplines, we know, are not natural, preordained forms of inquiry that excavate preexisting truths about the past, or about literature, or about social behavior. Rather, they are structures of knowledge that create their own subjects for inquiry and rules for determining the validity or falseness of an assertion about those subjects. Interdisciplinary projects such as this one, therefore, may clash with the expectations of practitioners of different disciplines. But the end result of the methodological perspective of this book is greater understanding of the French past than would be possible by remaining within the bounds of mainstream historical approaches or by adhering more rigidly to the limits of the disciplines from which I have borrowed.

The previous chapters have sketched out an interpretation of French political culture that focuses on the form adopted both in French theater and film on the one hand, and in public ceremonies on the other. I have argued that this was often melodramatic, a theatrical form that builds dramatic tension around a Manichean conflict between good and evil, and in which the plot traces a threat to a virtuous character from an evil one, the rescue of virtue through means that are themselves corrupt, and as a consequence a conclusion that does not re-create the stable, unified situation at the beginning of the plot but rather seeks, without achieving, a new basis for stability and unity. While the revolutionary era certainly had an impact outside France, and indeed outside Europe, it particularly affected French political culture. It is especially important, therefore, that, following Peter Brooks's view of French melodrama as a form that grew out of the disruptions of the French Revolution in French society, politics, religion, and culture, we understand melodrama as a form in which French culture performed its conflicts, its desire for unity, and its inability to find a satisfactory basis for a stable postrevolutionary society.

The popularity of melodrama in French theaters and films over the last two centuries has made it a commonplace in French entertainment, a dominant form in which French culture tells stories. That it was also common in public ceremonies suggests both that it had utility as a way of establishing communication between the organizers of the ceremonies and the viewing audience of citizens and that it played an important role in creating the connection between the increasingly participatory French state of the nineteenth and twentieth centuries and many, even if not all, of the citizens that it attempted to rule.

If the melodramatic form helped political regimes communicate with their citizens, and established legitimacy for them, it did this by limiting the ways in which French political culture could tell stories about the uses of power. This does not mean that the form could not be stretched as these stories were told, just as playwrights and screenwriters found ways to extend the melodramatic form even as it limited the ways in which they could tell stories on stage and film. But even avant-garde authors and directors such as Romain Rolland and Ariane Mnouchkine found themselves pulled back into the form. It was still more difficult for the pageant-masters of the Republic to escape a plot in which the Republic, identified with France, was endangered by internal or external enemies, to be rescued by the heroism of the republicans, the citizens of the Republic, or the people of the French nation. That the conclusion of the plot, or of the pageant, always seemed to be an incomplete resolution seemed to resonate with both theater audiences and citizens. But while the characters in melodramas do not have to deal with the consequences of how they have saved virtue from vice after the curtain falls, it was not so with the performances of French political culture. The Republic and its citizens must face the implications of its political tactics, whether those be the violence of the Terror, the corruption of the Third Republic's parliamentary politics, the Fifth Republic's immigration policies, or the ultimate inability to create the utopia on earth that lies at the heart of the radical version of French republicanism.

But if melodrama has been a part of French culture since the Revolution, it has not always been the same, either in theaters or in public ceremonies. Drawing the parallel between theatrical melodrama and public ceremonies serves to highlight the ways in which the melodramatic form shifted to reflect pressures in French culture coming from broader changes in French society and the increased visibility of groups such as workers, women, and immigrants. Old characters took on new meanings, new characters were introduced, and plots became more complicated as the issues that dominated French society and politics in the early nineteenth century gave way to those of the late nineteenth and twentieth centuries. Also, as many commentators have noticed, public performances became more commercial, more spectacular in Debord's sense. This was the case even if it was not universally so: the contrast between the *gouderie* of July 14, 1989, and the pantheonizations five months later demonstrates the continuation to the late twentieth century of the solemn forms of Revolutionary and nineteenth-century spectacle even as the commercialized events of the late nineteenth and twentieth centuries became more important. The stage for public melodrama therefore changed over time, as French popular culture itself became dominated by the emphasis on performance that the spectacles on the Champs de Mars and the boulevard stages reflect.

We may gain some understanding of the importance of the melodramatic thread in French political culture by placing the preceding analysis in the context of discussions about democratization and, especially, about the role of political culture in that process. As an example of the process of democratization, France holds a particular empirical position for the "frequency with which both democratic and undemocratic regimes have collapsed," an interpretation of French political history that reproduces the narrative of French history as one divided between supporters and opponents of the Revolution.[1] The alternation of two empires, two monarchies, and five republics in the years between 1789 and the late twentieth century has been variously attributed to French difficulty in agreeing on an acceptable institutional basis for political activity, the persistence of competing political ideologies and the failure to develop broad-based support for democratic (or "republican") political institutions, and the absence in France of civil society organizations supportive of democratic institutions.[2]

The latter explanation in particular has spurred recent historical investigation, as historians have developed a history of the public sphere and civil society in France. This account begins with the coffeehouses, clubs, salons, and newspapers in which Jürgen Habermas thought European bourgeois rationally and critically discussed the policies of the expanding nation-state, beginning in the eighteenth century.[3] At the same time, audiences in theaters and viewers of art contested the royal administration's attempts to control these cultural activities.[4] David Bell has argued that this civil society was of "fundamental importance" in the growing sense of French national identity that he sees in the 1750s and 1760s.[5] The idea of civil society has been the conceptual underpinning for a cultural history of the French Revolution and subsequent attempts in France to establish a democratic government. But the Revolutionary era shows the ambiguity of the concept when applied to the French experience. The First Republic of 1792 was a period of remarkable popular mobilization, in the numerous organizations—*armées révolutionnaires* that sought grain in the countryside during the Terror, clubs, informal networks in neighborhoods—that served to organize and mobilize the crowd. But it was also a period in which the boundary between the state and a protected sphere of individual activity became most permeable, even nonexistent in the law on suspects of the Terror.[6]

After the Terror, different regimes attempted to establish limits on the democratic impulses that were a legacy of the Revolution. Ironically, this often meant increased state intervention into the workings of civil society. The

Directory (1795–99) formalized the moderate gains of the early Revolution. But this project was aborted by the more authoritarian Bonapartist Consulate and Empire.[7] During the nineteenth century, while the police were carefully monitoring the more democratic factions in French politics, a number of different kinds of associations developed in spite of legal restrictions. Political clubs appeared in 1848. Electoral committees also began in the early days of the Second Republic, and while the Second Empire attempted to limit the existence of these groups, the electoral politics of the Empire led both Bonapartists and republicans to continue to develop this form of association. *Sociétés d'action,* which had dominated radical politics under the July Monarchy, also continued but tended to decline in importance after the failure of the resistance to the coup d'état in 1851. Groups such as the voluntary Sociétés d'Emulation in Alsace that helped to organize bourgeois civil society also continued and became more overtly political especially after the fall of the empire in 1870. Increasingly in the late 1860s the state became a prominent player in the organization of civil society, an important feature of the French experience in the process of democratization, by instituting a growing number of quasi-state organizations that allowed electoral practice. Republicans also significantly reconstituted civil society in the years just before 1870.[8] There was a widespread discussion of decentralization in the late Second Empire and the growth of "a sizeable literate political community …, constituting a body of 'informed opinion' within the wider political community," that developed by the end of the 1860s. There were also groups such as the Comités des Travaux Historiques, both encouraged and limited by the state in their attempts to preserve the local monuments of the French provinces.[9] These developments articulated an elite version of civil society, but nonetheless point to attempts to reformulate the relationship between the French state and its society, and set the stage for post-1870 French history as a process of democratization of this civil society. Yet as recently as 1968, French political life was disrupted by violent disagreements, in the Events of May, over the relationship of civil society to a French state reinvigorated by the increase in presidential power granted by the constitution of the Fifth Republic. Even more recently, violence has erupted over the presence of immigrant groups in metropolitan France.[10]

The recent emphasis on the public sphere and civil society is the result of the influence of approaches to democratization and political culture in the contemporary world that have employed this concept. Yet the social science literature on democratization is almost always ambiguous about the aspects of political culture that support democratic transitions and consolidation. In some respects this is a continuation of the civic culture literature that began in the 1960s with the work of Gabriel Almond and Sidney Verba. For example, Larry Diamond has noted that "we observe during democratic consolidation the emergence of an elite political culture featuring moderation, accommodation, restrained partisanship, system loyalty, and trust. These norms enhance the predictability and mitigate the intensity of political conflict."[11] More recently, he has spoken about "beliefs about democratic legitimacy" as central in democratic consolidation, and about an acceptance of democracy as "the only game in town," but without being more precise.[12] Robert Putnam attributed the same virtues of honesty, trust, and law-abidingness to a civic community supportive of democracy in Italy.[13] Ronald Inglehart has argued that "with rising levels of economic development, cultural patterns emerge that are increasingly supportive of democracy, making mass publics more likely to want democracy and more skillful at getting it." He has also defined those cultural patterns as emphasizing "self-expression values" as opposed to "survival values" that are less supportive of democracy. He concludes that not only is development linked to changes toward rational, tolerant, trusting, and postmodern (self-expression) values, but also that the historical culture of the society (Protestant, Orthodox, Islamic, Confucian) creates culture zones that also affect democratic prospects.[14]

Civil society has also been posited as the source of cultural or attitudinal consequences supportive of democracy. While one version emphasizes the ability of civil society organizations to attack authoritarian governments (as Solidarity and other such organizations seemed to have done in Eastern Europe in the 1980s), neo-Tocquevilleans such as Robert Putnam view them as settings in which citizens create social capital and learn the processes of negotiation, accommodation, and compromise that have long been cited as the cultural underpinnings of democracy. This occurs especially through participation in associations with strong horizontal links that encourage equality, in contrast to vertically linked associations dominated by a single patron or a small elite.[15] Others working in this vein have emphasized the importance that these organizations be structured around ties that are "mutual, cooperative, symmetrical, and trusting." Civil society organizations based on "political equality, reciprocal communication, mutual respect, and the rule of law" help socialize citizens into "democratic norms" and contribute to the deepening of democracy by inculcating the "deeper values of democratic citizenship," such as "tolerance, moderation, a willingness to compromise."[16]

However, the concept of social capital used by Putnam and others remains ambiguous, especially in its dependence on or independence from social structures.[17] Empirical studies also do not seem to provide unqualified support for the proposition that strong civil society institutions necessarily lead to democratic outcomes. Civil society organizations may create civic virtues that are not uniquely democratic: in different political and constitutional contexts the social capital created in civil society can support undemocratic regimes such as nazism in Germany, fascism in Italy, or apartheid in South Africa. While civil society associations may contribute to the creation of democracy, they seem to be a necessary but not sufficient condition for democratic development. As Philip Nord concluded after a review of essays on a number of European countries in the nineteenth century, "civil societies come in many shapes and ... not all configurations, vibrant in constitution as they might be, are conducive to democratic government."[18]

We need, therefore, to understand political culture better in this process. Seeing how French political culture framed questions about the changing relationship between state and society can help overcome the inability in the civil society literature to distinguish between specific aspects of political culture or get beyond its vague concepts of trust and accommodation. In this inquiry the interpretive method of analysis I have adopted provides important insights. For the most part dependent on polling data as the basis for statements about values and beliefs, social scientists have not pursued the kind of analysis of discourses that has marked the work not only of poststructuralist literary critics, but also of scholars in cultural studies and cultural history. This kind of analysis—the second interdisciplinary influence on this book—leads not so much to a political culture "generated and flowing within societal institutions," but rather toward the "symbolic, linguistic, and interpretive elements through which people make sense of politics."[19] It also allows a version of political culture that is not simply supportive of institutional and other structural aspects of democracy, but plays an active role in determining the possible outcomes of democratization by its ability to structure the ways in which actors understand the process and its possible outcomes.[20]

This book, then, suggests a more precise description of French political culture. It describes not only the ways in which that political culture—viewed as discourses about the use of power—constructs broad issues such as trust and the acceptance of democratic regimes, but also how political issues are framed. It would be foolish to reject the insights about economic development, institutional factors, and leadership that have marked the vast social science and historical literature on democratization. But we must also recognize that their statements about political culture can be improved upon through analysis of the way these interpretive elements make sense of politics.

The preceding chapters have focused on the ways in which French political culture has construed public debates. I have spoken less about specifically "civic" virtues in modern France than of the ways in which French men and women have structured their discussions about political institutions and the narratives they have told about political conflict. Whereas in the civic culture literature political conflict is dealt with through the habits of compromise and negotiation that support democracy, the French experience seems to suggest that a pervasive aspect of French political culture since the Revolution has been the framing of political conflict in terms of threatened virtue, evil opponents, and brave heroes who rescue the threatened heroine yet are unable to re-create a posited unity that existed before the threat. If in French republican thought civil society was more a "civic" society made up of "a community of citizens who ideally practiced 'civic virtue' by participating in public life and devoting themselves to the common good," then the melodramatic thread I have traced here suggests a further complexity to that "civic virtue."[21]

One consequence of this approach is to emphasize the importance of discursive practices as a central component of modern French history, rather than the individual actors—Robespierre, Napoleon, Thiers, Gambetta, Pétain, de Gaulle—who have formed the central thread of many accounts of French history. This is not to deny the roles of these actors in the course of French history. But in the same way that recent versions of literary history make it less dependent on the genius of individual authors, and make it more about discursive practices of writing and representation, modern French history becomes separated from the talents and heroic—or villainous—actions of the leading men of the nation's past, and becomes more the product of the ways in which the history of France has been constructed by the structures within which it has been understood.

We might then make two final points about French history in this context. First, France provides an example of a country in which the process of democratization was affected in a very specific way by the political culture within which that process took place. The melodramatic thread in French political culture narrated political conflict in terms that ran counter to the emphasis on negotiation and accommodation that political scientists have consistently seen as important cultural supports to democracy. Second, this insight into France's political development suggests the importance of recognizing that "the fate of democracy is open-ended," that it may weaken or effectively disappear through either collapse of formal institutions or "insidious processes of decay." This suggests the importance of activities after the establishment of electoral democracy to "deepen" the hold of democratic institutions, practices, and values.[22] In this respect the reading of public performances in modern France that I have offered in the preceding chapters argues that the pervasiveness of melodramatic forms not only on the French stage but also in its civic ceremonies has created a particular way of framing public issues that has at times contributed to the hollowing out of French democratic institutions. The division of the world into threatened virtue and threatening evil, the tendency to see the development of political issues as heroic rescue of the virtuous heroine (who often turns out to be the Republic, or France), and the inability to create a unified resolution to the tensions contained in the plot have made

French political history a narrative that is primarily not about compromise and national unity, but about conflict, defense of fundamental values, and a willingness to accept an incomplete final resolution.

The use of the form of melodrama in our analysis of these performances is therefore not simply an unnecessary borrowing of the language of one discipline by another. Rather, stage and film melodramas show us the ways in which these versions of the world are structured, the ways characters develop, and the difficulties they have in achieving complete resolution. These were enhanced by the spectacular performance style of modern French theater and ceremony, and persisted over the course of the changes in social and economic organization of the country. They suggest the interconnectedness of different representations of the uses of power in modern France and the independent role of political culture as a part of the process of democratization. They suggest not only how these melodramatic public performances linked to their audiences—if melodrama played well on the boulevards, why not on the Champs de Mars and the Place de la Nation?—but also what discourses guided the perception of public issues by the citizens that the French Republic claimed to empower.

But the concept of melodrama, both in Peter Brooks's formulation and as it has often been played out on French stages, in French films, and in French public ceremonies nonetheless contains the desire for a unified resolution. We must remind ourselves that in melodramas the villains are vanquished, the heroine is rescued, and the characters who remain on stage at the final curtain believe themselves to have achieved a happy ending. It is only we as spectators who can see the underhanded methods that have saved the situation, and who appreciate the incompleteness of the plot resolution. In the end, then, let us recall the optimism of Robespierre's injunction at the Festival of the Supreme Being that his fellow citizens give themselves over to joy for that day, and Le Moniteur's conclusion that it was "the most beautiful festival whose memory could be perpetuated in the pomp of the Revolution." The Revolution may have disrupted the fabric of French culture and ended the possibility of creating a new society and polity based on a different universally accepted principle. But the Revolution was also about hope for a better world, and melodrama has continued that desire.

Notes

1. Introduction

1. The festival is described in Alphonse Aulard, *Le Culte de la raison et le culte de l'Etre Suprême* (Paris: F. Alcan, 1892), 52–59. See also, for background developments, Michel Vovelle, *The Revolution against the Church: From Reason to the Supreme Being*, trans. Alan José (Columbus: Ohio State University Press, 1991), 98–122.

2. Aulard, 318, attributed the heckling to François Bourdin de l'Oise and Antoine Merlin de Thionville, in a rehearsal for the 9th of Thermidor.

3. *Le Moniteur Universel* 265 (25 Prairial An II): 86.

4. Mona Ozouf, *Festivals and the French Revolution*, trans. Alan Sheridan (Cambridge, Mass.: Harvard University Press, 1988), 115.

5. Ibid., 111.

6. Marie-Joseph Chénier, *Charles IX ou L'Ecole des rois*, in *Théâtre de la Révolution*, ed. Louis Moland (Paris: Garnier Frères, 1877), 29–88, esp. 53, 84, 27; on the controversy surrounding the play, see Paul Friedland, *Political Actors: Representative Bodies and Theatricality in the Age of the French Revolution* (Ithaca: Cornell University Press, 2002), 260–67, and Susan Maslan, *Revolutionary Acts: Theater, Democracy, and the French Revolution* (Baltimore: Johns Hopkins University Press, 2005), 30–57.

7. Jean-Louis Laya, *L'Ami des lois*, in Moland, 227–98.

8. P. Sylvain Maréchal, *Le Jugement dernier des rois*, in Moland, 305–26.

9. Michèle Root-Bernstein, *Boulevard Theater and Revolution in Eighteenth-Century Paris* (Ann Arbor, Mich.: UMI Research Press, 1984), 223–224, 227.

10. Monvel (Jacques-Marie Boutet), *Les Victimes cloîtrées*, in *Monvel: Théâtre, discours politiques et réflexions diverses*, ed. Roselyne LaPlace, 295–370 (Paris: Honoré Champion, 2001).

11. Samuel P. Huntington, *The Third Wave: Democratization in the Late Twentieth Century* (Norman: University of Oklahoma Press, 1991), 13–26.

12. Larry Diamond, *Developing Democracy: Toward Consolidation* (Baltimore: Johns Hopkins University Press, 1999), 24–63, 261–78.

13. The distinction between creation of a democracy and its subsequent consolidation and persistence was first posed by Dankwart A. Rustow, "Transitions to Democracy: Towards a Dynamic Model," *Comparative Politics* 2 (1970): 337–63. For more recent research utilizing Rustow's argument, see Lisa Anderson, ed., *Transitions to Democracy* (New York: Columbia University Press, 1999).

14. Robert Dahl, *Polyarchy: Participation and Opposition* (New Haven: Yale University Press, 1971); Rustow; Juan J. Linz, *The Breakdown of Democratic Regimes* (Baltimore: Johns Hopkins University Press, 1978); Giuseppe Di Palma, *To Craft Democracies: An Essay on Democratic Transitions* (Berkeley and Los Angeles: University of California Press, 1990). But see the critiques by Diamond in Larry Diamond and Juan J. Linz, "Introduction: Politics, Society and Democracy in Latin America," in *Democracy in Developing Countries,* Vol. 4: *Latin America,* ed. Larry Diamond, Juan J. Linz, and Seymour Martin Lipset, 7 (Boulder, Colo: Lynne Rienner, 1989); Larry Diamond, ed., *The Democratic Revolution: Struggles for Freedom and Pluralism in the Developing World* (New York: Freedom House, 1992); and *Developing Democracy,* 219–21, 234–38.

15. Diamond and Linz, "Introduction," 1–58.

16. Renske Doorenspleet, *Democratic Transitions: Exploring the Structural Sources of the Fourth Wave* (Boulder, Colo: Lynne Rienner, 2005); Tatu Vanhanen, *Democratization: A Comparative Analysis of 170 Countries* (New York: Routledge, 2003).

17. Diamond, *Developing Democracy,* 65, 161.

18. Gabriel Almond and Sidney Verba, *The Civic Culture* (Newbury Park, Calif.: Sage Publications, 1989), 356; Sidney Verba, "Comparative Political Culture," in *Political Culture and Political Development,* ed. Lucien W. Pye and Sidney Verba, 513 (Princeton: Princeton University Press, 1965). See also Murray Edelman, *Constructing the Political Spectacle* (Chicago: University of Chicago Press, 1988).

19. Di Palma, esp. ch. 3.

20. Diamond, "Introduction," 21, and "Causes and Effects," 229–49, in *Political Culture and Democracy.*

21. Keith Michael Baker, ed., *The French Revolution and the Creation of Modern Political Culture,* Vol. 1: *The Political Culture of the Old Regime* (Oxford: Pergamon Press, 1987), xii. See also James Epstein, "Between Culture and Language," in *In Practice* (Stanford: Stanford University Press, 2003), 1–12, for an approach more rooted in British intellectual currents; and Ronald P. Formisano, "The Concept of Political Culture," *Journal of Interdisciplinary History* 31 (2001): 393–426, which argues for an approach closer to Antonio Gramsci's concept of hegemony.

22. Jürgen Habermas, *The Structural Transformation of the Public Sphere,* trans. Thomas Berger (Cambridge: MIT Press, 1989). Margaret Somers, "The Narrative Constitution of Identity: A Relational and Network Approach," *Theory and Society* 23 (1994), 605–49, attempts to combine social science and narrative approaches.

23. For critiques of Habermas, see especially Mary Ryan, "Gender and Public Access: Women's Politics in Nineteenth Century America," in *Habermas and the Public Sphere,* ed. Craig Calhoun, 259–88 (Cambridge: MIT Press, 1992); and Geoff Eley, "Nations, Publics, and Political Cultures: Placing Habermas in the Nineteenth Century," in Calhoun, 289–339; and Harold Mah, "Phantasies of the Public Sphere: Rethinking the Habermas of Historians," *Journal of Modern History* 72 (2000): 153–82.

24. Gary Thurston, *The Popular Theatre Movement in Russia, 1862–1919* (Evanston, Ill.: Northwestern University Press, 1998), 2, 16; Friedland, 167–227.

25. Frank R. Ankersmit, "Pygmalion: Rousseau and Diderot on the Theatre and on Representation," *Rethinking History* 7, no. 3 (2003): 315–39, esp. 332.

26. Calhoun, "Introduction," in *Habermas,* esp. 28.

27. Guy Debord, *La Société du Spectacle* (Paris: Gallimard, 1992), 16–19, 24.

28. Guy Debord, *Commentaires sur la société du spectacle* (Paris: Gallimard, 1992), 21–23.

29. Thomas Crow, *Painters and Public Life in Eighteenth-Century Paris* (New Haven: Yale University Press, 1985); Michael Fried, *Absorption and Theatricality: Image and Beholder in the Age of Diderot* (Berkeley and Los Angeles: University of California Press, 1980).

30. T. J. Clark, *The Painting of Modern Life: Paris in the Art of Manet and His Followers* (New York: Alfred A. Knopf, 1985), 15, 63. See also Theodore Reff, "Manet and the Paris of Haussmann and Baudelaire," in *Visions of the Modern City,* ed. William Sharpe and Leonard Wallock, 135–67 (Baltimore: Johns Hopkins University Press, 1987); and Michele Hannoosh, "Painters of Modern Life: Baudelaire and the Impressionists," in Sharpe and Wallock, 168–88.

31. Keith Tester, ed., *The Flâneur* (New York: Routledge, 1994); Rachel Bowlby, *Just Looking: Consumer Culture in Dreiser, Gissing and Zola* (New York: Methuen, 1985); Michael Miller, *The Bon Marché: Bourgeois Culture and the Department Store, 1869–1920* (Princeton: Princeton University Press, 1981); Rosalind Williams, *Dream Worlds: Mass Consumption in Late Nineteenth-Century France* (Berkeley and Los Angeles: University of California Press, 1982).

32. Ozouf; Avner Ben-Amos, *Funerals, Politics and Memory in Modern France 1789–1996* (New York: Oxford University Press, 2000); Matthew Truesdell, *Spectacular Politics: Louis-Napoleon Bonaparte and the Fête Imperiale* (New York: Oxford University Press, 1997); Olivier Ihl, *La Fête républicaine* (Paris: Gallimard, 1996).

33. Rosamonde Sanson, *Le 14ᵉ Juillet: fête et conscience nationale, 1789 1975* (Paris: Flammarion, 1976); Pascal Ory, *Une Nation pour mémoire, 1889, 1939, 1989: trois jubilés révolutionnaires* (Paris: Presses de la Fondation Nationale des Sciences Politiques, 1992); Steven Laurence Kaplan, *Farewell, Revolution: Disputed Legacies, France 1789/1989* (Ithaca: Cornell University Press, 1995); Alain Corbin, Noelle Gérôme, and Danielle Tartakowsky, eds., *Les Usages politiques des fêtes aux 19ᵉ–20ᵉ siècles* (Paris: Publications de la Sorbonne, 1994). For some methodological concerns, see Pascal Ory, "L'Histoire des politiques symboliques modernes: Un questionnement," *Revue d'histoire moderne et contemporaine* 47, no. 3 (2000): 525–36.

34. Maurice Agulhon, *Marianne au combat* (Paris: Flammarion, 1979); *Marianne au pouvoir* (Paris: Flammarion, 1989).

35. Eric Hobsbawm and Terence Ranger, eds., *The Invention of Tradition* (Cambridge: Cambridge University Press, 1983). See also Daniel O'Quinn, *Staging Governance: Theatrical Imperialism in London, 1770–1800* (Baltimore: Johns Hopkins University Press, 2005).

36. Simon Newman, *Parades and the Politics of the Street: Festive Culture in the Early American Republic* (Philadelphia: University of Pennsylvania Press, 1997), 120–30, 144; David Waldstreicher, *In the Midst of Perpetual Fetes: The Making of American Nationalism, 1776–1820* (Chapel Hill: University of North Carolina Press, 1997), 205.

37. Waldstreicher, 181, 201.

38. Mary Ryan, *Women in Public: Between Banners and Barricades, 1825–1880* (Baltimore: Johns Hopkins University Press, 1990); John Bodnar, *Remaking America: Public Memory, Commemoration, and Patriotism in the Twentieth Century* (Princeton: Princeton University Press, 1992).

39. Lynn Mally, *Revolutionary Acts: Amateur Theater and the Soviet State, 1917–1938* (Ithaca: Cornell University Press, 2000), 3–4, 35, 38; David Bradby and John McCormick, *People's Theatre* (London: Croom Helm, 1978), 45–59. On poster art, see Victoria Bonnell, *Iconography of Power: Soviet Political Posters under Lenin and Stalin* (Berkeley and Los Angeles: University of California Press, 1997); Denise J. Youngblood, *Movies for the Masses: Popular Cinema and Soviet Society in the 1920s* (Cambridge: Cambridge University Press, 1992), 2, 73, 83, 139–152.

40. James von Geldern, *Bolshevik Festivals, 1917–1920* (Berkeley and Los Angeles: University of California Press, 1993), 28.

41. Von Geldern, 42, 59, 66–71, 199–207.

42. Maurice Samuels, *The Spectacular Past: Popular History and the Novel in Nineteenth-Century France* (Ithaca: Cornell University Press, 2004), 12–15.

43. Vanessa Schwartz, *Spectacular Realities: Early Mass Culture in Fin-de-Siècle France* (Berkeley and Los Angeles: University of California Press, 1998), 3.

44. Schwartz, 4–10.

45. Victor Turner, "Introduction," in *From Ritual to Theatre* (New York: Performing Arts Journal Publications, 1982), 13.

46. Turner, "Acting in Everyday Life and Everyday Life in Acting," in *From Ritual to Theatre*, 104, 107–108.

47. Victor Turner, *Dramas, Fields, and Metaphors* (Ithaca: Cornell University Press, 1974), esp. 37–41, 99, 123; and *On the Edge of the Bush: Anthropology as Experience* (Tucson: University of Arizona Press, 1985), 300–301; Richard Schechner, *Performance Theory* (New York: Routledge, 1988).

48. Clifford Geertz, *Negara: The Theater State in Nineteenth-Century Bali* (Princeton: Princeton University Press, 1980), 13, 134–36.

49. Laurence Whitehead, *Democratization: Theory and Experience* (Oxford: Oxford University Press, 2002), 37–64, esp. 42–43. Both the metaphor and the theatrical aspects of democratization quickly disappear from Whitehead's book.

50. Victor Hugo, "Choses Vues: 15 Décembre 1840: Funérailles de l'Empereur. Notes Prises sur Place," in *Oeuvres Complètes: Histoire* (Paris: Robert Laffont, 1987), 805–22; Maurice Barrès, *Les Déracinés* (Paris: Félix Juven, n.d.), 442–51, 460–63.

51.   For accounts of the public roles of French intellectuals, see Sudhir Hazareesingh, *Political Traditions in Modern France* (Oxford: Oxford University Press, 1994), 33–64; Pascal Ory and Jean-François Sirinelli, *Les Intellectuels en France, de l'Affaire Dreyfus à nos jours* (Paris: Armand Colin, 1986); Jean-François Sirinelli, *Génération intellectuelle: khâgneux et normaliens dans l'entre-deux-guerres* (Paris: Fayard, 1992); and Jean-Pierre Rioux and Jean-François Sirinelli, eds., *La Guerre d'Algérie et les intellectuels français* (Paris: Editions Complexe, 1991). See also the special issue on "Interdisciplinary Perspectives on French History and Literature" of *French Historical Studies* 28, no. 3 (2005); Whitney Walton, *Eve's Proud Descendants: Four Women Writers and Republican Politics in Nineteenth-Century France* (Stanford: Stanford University Press, 2000); Jeffrey Ravel, *The Contested Parterre: Public Theater and French Political Culture, 1680–1791* (Ithaca: Cornell University Press, 1999); Sheryl Kroen, *Politics and Theater: The Crisis of Legitimacy in Restoration France, 1815–1830* (Berkeley and Los Angeles: University of California Press, 2000); Lenard Berlanstein, *Daughters of Eve: A Cultural History of French Theater Women from the Old Regime to the Fin-de-Siècle* (Cambridge: Harvard University Press, 2001); Jean Elisabeth Pedersen, *Legislating the French Family: Feminism, Theater, and Republican Politics, 1870–1920* (New Brunswick, N.J.: Rutgers University Press, 2003); Sally Debra Charnow, *Theatre, Politics, and Modernity in Fin-de-Siècle Paris* (New York: Palgrave Macmillan, 2005).

52.   Lynn Hunt, *The Family Romance of the French Revolution* (Berkeley and Los Angeles: University of California Press, 1992), xiii; Judith R. Walkowitz, *City of Dreadful Delight* (Chicago: University of Chicago Press, 1992), 83–90.

53.   M. H. Abrams, *A Glossary of Literary Terms,* 5th ed. (Chicago: Holt, Rinehart and Winston, 1988), 72–74; Alastair Fowler, *Kinds of Literature: An Introduction to the Theory of Genres and Modes* (Cambridge: Harvard University Press, 1982), 20–24.

54.   For brief introductions see John Carlos Rowe, "Structure," in *Critical Terms for Literary Study,* 2nd ed., ed. Frank Lentricchia and Thomas McLaughlin, 23–28 (Chicago: University of Chicago Press, 1995); and Paul A. Bové, "Discourse," in Lentricchia and McLaughlin, 50–65, esp. 58. See also Michel Foucault, "The Discourse on Language," in *The Archaeology of Knowledge,* trans. Rupert Swyer (New York: Pantheon, 1972). Richard Terdiman, *Discourse/Counter-Discourse: The Theory and Practice of Symbolic Resistance in Nineteenth-Century France* (Ithaca: Cornell University Press, 1985), is a particularly effective demonstration of the utility of discourse theory in understanding a wide range of cultural artifacts.

55.   Bové, 56.

56.   Charles Guilbert de Pixerécourt, *Coelina,* in *Théâtre choisi* (Geneva: Slatkine Reprints, 1971).

57.   Frank Rahill, *The World of Melodrama* (University Park: Pennsylvania State University Press, 1967), xiv; Jean-Marie Thomasseau, *Le Mélodrame* (Paris: Presses Universitaires de France, 1984); Maurice Descôtes, *Le Public du théâtre et son histoire* (Paris: Presses Universitaires de France, 1964), 220–43; Julia Przybos, *L'Entreprise mélodramatique* (Paris: Librairie José Corti, 1987); André Billaz, "Mélodrame et littérature: le cas de Pixerécourt," *Revue des sciences humaines* 41 (1976): 239–42; J. Paul Marcoux, *Guilbert de Pixerécourt: French Melodrama in*

the Early Nineteenth Century (New York: Peter Lang, 1992), 1–16. For American comparisons, see David Grimstead, *Melodrama Unveiled: American Theater and Culture 1800–1850* (Chicago: University of Chicago Press, 1968), and Michael R. Booth, *English Melodrama* (London: Herbert Jenkins, 1965).

58.   Peter Brooks, *The Melodramatic Imagination* (New Haven: Yale University Press, 1976), xi, 14–15, 203. Hunt emphasizes the family as the setting in which this moral action took place in the melodramas of the late 1790s. Hunt, 188.

59.   Brooks, 36, 199–201, 205. This is not the only way to read the revolutionary emphasis on virtue. Margaret Cohen argues that the leaders of the Revolution also elaborated a "sentimental" form of virtue, not "one term in a Manichean opposition but rather a response to the conflict between two equally valid imperatives, collective welfare and individual freedom." Margaret Cohen, *The Sentimental Education of the Novel* (Princeton: Princeton University Press, 1999), 74.

60.   Friedland, 296. The term "melodrama" has been adopted in film studies to describe Hollywood family melodramas of the 1950s and 1960s, but—while there is great debate as to the meaning of the term—it has tended to be used in ways different from those outlined by, for example, Peter Brooks. Nonetheless, we should note that in that usage, as well, the incompleteness of the plot resolution is significant. It is the impossibility of the characters living "happily ever after" that exposes the inability of melodrama to create a unified new world. In the words of film critic Geoffrey Nowell-Smith, this inability to "accommodate its problems either in a real present or an ideal future . . . lays them open in their contradictoriness." Melodrama, therefore, "opens a space which most Hollywood films have studiously closed off." Quoted by John Mercer and Martin Shingler, *Short Cuts* (London: Wallflower Press, 2004), 14. For the film studies debate, see Steve Neale, "'Melo Talk': On the Meaning and Use of the Term 'Melodrama' in the American Trade Press," *Velvet Light Trap* (Fall 1993): 66–89; and Rick Altman, "Reusable Packaging: Generic Products and the Recycling Process," in *Refiguring American Film Genres: History and Theory,* ed. Nick Browne (Berkeley and Los Angeles: University of California Press, 1998), 1–41.

61.   Brooks, 32.

62.   Marie-Pierre Le Hir, *Le Romantisme aux enchères: Ducange, Pixerécourt, Hugo* (Amsterdam: John Benjamins, 1992), 22, 36, 86–87, 111, 135–36; Brooks, 32, 89, 205; Jacky Bratton, Jim Cook, and Christine Gledhill, "Introduction," in *Melodrama: Stage, Picture, Screen* (London: British Film Institute, 1994), 3; Rahill, 297; Elaine Hadley, *Melodramatic Tactics: Theatricalized Dissent in the English Marketplace, 1800–1885* (Stanford: Stanford University Press, 1995).

63.   Bradby and McCormick, 16–17; Peter Brooks, "Melodrama, Body, Revolution," in Bratton, Cook, and Gledhill, esp. 19.

64.   Scott S. Bryson, *The Chastised Stage: Bourgeois Drama and the Exercise of Power* (Saratoga, Calif.: Anma Libri, 1991), 113–14.

65.   Christophe Campos, "Paris after the Revolution," *Theatre Quarterly* 1, no. 3 (1971): 63.

66. François Furet, "The French Revolution Is Over," in *Interpreting the French Revolution,* trans. Elborg Forster (Cambridge: Cambridge University Press, 1981), 1–79.

67. Furet, *Interpreting the French Revolution;* Keith Michael Baker, *Inventing the French Revolution* (Cambridge: Cambridge University Press, 1990); Colin Lucas, ed., *The French Revolution and the Creation of Modern Political Culture,* Vol. 2: *The Political Culture of the French Revolution* (New York: Pergamon Press, 1988). For some indications of concerns by French scholars about the utility of the kind of methods of cultural analysis used in this book, see Stéphane Van Damme, "Comprendre les *Cultural Studies," Revue d'histoire moderne et contemporaine* 51–54 bis (2004): 48–58.

68. François Furet, *La Révolution française* (Paris: Hachette, 1988), T. 1: 147, 153, 216, 252–54, 439–47; T. 2: 29, 67, 71–75; Maurice Agulhon, *La République* (Paris: Hachette, 1990), T. 1: 33–36, 77–78, 90–91, 139–40, 163–66, 353, 367; T. 2: 407–408, 422–24.

69. For similar examples see Robert Gildea, *The Past in French History* (New Haven: Yale University Press, 1994); Roger Price, *The French Second Empire* (Cambridge: Cambridge University Press, 2001); *People and Politics in France, 1848–1871* (Cambridge: Cambridge University Press, 2004); Jeremy Popkin, *A History of Modern France,* 3rd ed. (Saddle River, N.J.: Prentice-Hall, 2006).

2. Varieties of Performance in Nineteenth-Century Paris

1. Françoise Waquet, *Les Fêtes royales sous la Restauration ou l'Ancien Régime Retrouvé* (Geneva: Droz, 1981); Jo Burr Margadant, "Gender, Vice, and the Political Imaginary in Postrevolutionary France: Reinterpreting the Failure of the July Monarchy, 1830–1848," *American Historical Review* 104, no. 5 (December 1999): 1461–96.

2. Marvin Carlson, *The Theatre of the French Revolution* (Ithaca: Cornell University Press, 1966), 80; René Tarin, "Le Théâtre de la période révolutionnaire: un mal-aimé de la critique et de l'histoire littéraire," *Revue de la société d'histoire du théâtre* 48 (1996): 353–61; Emmet Kennedy, et al., *Theatre, Opera and Audiences in Revolutionary Paris: Analysis and Repertory* (Westport, Conn.: Greenwood Press, 1996); quote from Catherine Naugrette-Christophe, *Paris sous le Second Empire: Le Théâtre et la ville* (Paris: Librairie Théâtrale, 1998), 223.

3. John McCormick, *Popular Theatres of Nineteenth-Century France* (New York: Routledge, 1993), 148; Brooks, 89.

4. McCormick, 157–59.

5. Fabrice Labrousse, *La Bastille* (Paris: Chez Marchant, 1837).

6. Odile Krakovitch, "La Révolution à travers le théâtre de 1815 à 1870: à chaque génération sa peur," in *Le XIXᵉ Siècle et la Révolution française* (Paris: Editions Créaphis, 1992), 61.

7. Paul Gerbod, "La Scène parisienne et sa représentation de l'histoire nationale dans la première moitié du XIXᵉ siécle," *Revue historique* 266 (1981): 28.

8. Krakovitch, 65.

9. Dumanoir and Clairville, *Charlotte Corday* (Paris: Imprimerie Dondey-Dupré, 1847).

10. Naugrette-Christophe, 74–75, 112–13.

11. Ibid., 129–78, 211–13.

12. Victor Hallay-Dabot, *Histoire de la censure théâtrale en France* (Paris: E. Dentu, 1862), 329; François Ponsard, *Charlotte Corday,* in *Théâtre Complet de F. Ponsard* (Paris: Michel Lévy frères, 1851), 201–355.

13. Henri Bonnais, *Le 9 thermidor ou la mort de Robespierre: Drame historique, non représenté* (Paris: Moutardier, 1851), esp. i, 44–45, 87, 127.

14. On the political institutions of the Restoration, see Guillaume de Bertier de Sauvigny, *The Bourbon Restoration,* trans. Lynn M. Case (Philadelphia: University of Pennsylvania Press, 1966), 65–72.

15. On performative aspects of the revolutionary assemblies, as well as attempts to limit popular intervention in their deliberations, see Friedland, 267–94. See also the discussion of the impeachment trial of Warren Hastings in O'Quinn, 164–257.

16. *Archives Parlementaires,* Chambre des Députés, 26 janvier 1818 (Paris: Librairie Administratif de P. Dupont, 1862), 497–514, esp. 497.

17. Ibid., 508.

18. Ibid., 508–14; Charles Pouthas, *Guizot pendant la Restauration* (Paris: Plon-Nourrit et Cie, 1923), 185.

19. *Le Moniteur Universel* 29 (3 Vendémiaire An VI): 5, 22.

20. *Archives Parlementaires,* Chambre des Députés, 2 décembre 1819, 712–14; Ruth F. Necheles, *The Abbé Grégoire 1787–1831* (Westport, Conn.: Greenwood, 1971), 211–19.

21. *Archives Parlementaires,* Chambre des Députés, 2 décembre 1819, 712–14.

22. *Archives Parlementaires,* Chambre des Députés, 6 décembre 1819, 723–41.

23. Stanley Mellon, *The Political Uses of History* (Stanford: Stanford University Press, 1958), 36–43; *Archives Parlementaires,* Chambre des Députés, 6 décembre 1819, 729, 736.

24. On audience behavior in the theater, see F. W. J. Hemmings, *The Theatre Industry in Nineteenth-Century France* (Cambridge: Cambridge University Press, 1993), 82–83.

25. *Archives Parlementaires,* Chambre des Députés, 6 décembre 1819, 735, 736.

26. Alphonse Aulard, *L'éloquence parlementaire pendant la Révolution française* (Paris: Hachette, 1885–86); James R. Lehning, *To Be a Citizen: The Political Culture of the Early French Third Republic* (Ithaca: Cornell University Press, 2001), 14–34.

27. Joseph S. Meisel, *Public Speech and the Culture of Public Life in the Age of Gladstone* (New York: Columbia University Press, 2001), 51–106; Craig R. Smith, *Daniel Webster and the Oratory of Civil Religion* (Columbia: University of Missouri Press,

2005); Garry Wills, *Lincoln at Gettysburg: The Words That Remade America* (New York: Simon and Schuster, 1992).

28. *Archives Parlementaires,* Chambre des Députés, 26 janvier 1818, 499.

29. Rahill, 54–55.

30. Michael Marrinan, *Painting Politics for Louis Philippe: Art and Ideology in Orleanist France, 1830–1848* (New Haven: Yale University Press, 1988), 79–91.

31. Ibid., 103–105.

32. Ibid., 77–79.

33. Ibid., 79.

34. Hallay-Dabot, 291; Martin Meisel, *Realizations: Narrative, Pictorial, and Theatrical Arts in Nineteenth-Century England* (Princeton: Princeton University Press, 1983), 203.

35. Jean Tulard, "Le Retour des cendres," in *Les Lieux de mémoire: La Nation,* ed. Pierre Nora (Paris: Gallimard, 1986), 2:81–110.

36. Société des Amis de l'Egalité, *Celebration de l'anniversaire du 14 juillet* (Paris: Imprimerie de Demonville, s.d.), in *Révolutions du XIXe siècle,* 1er série (Paris: EDHIS, 1974), T. 1: 1–2.

37. *Doctrines Républicaines: Programmes de la Tribune* (31 janvier 1833) (Paris: Imprimerie de Auguste Mie, 1833), in *Révolutions du XIXe siècle,* 1er série, T. 11: 5–6, 11–14.

38. *Le Montagnard par le citoyen Rogeau* (Paris: Prevot, 1833), in *Révolutions du XIXe siècle,* 1er série, T. 1: 3, 5, 7.

39. *Le Moniteur* 115 (25 avril 1793): 213–14.

40. *Déclaration des Droits de l'Homme,* in *Révolutions du XIXe siècle,* 1er série, T. 1.

41. Paul Thureau-Dangin, *Histoire de la monarchie de Juillet* (Paris: Plon, 1888), T. 2: 214–15, 221, 246; Alain Faure, "Mouvements populaires et Mouvement Ouvrier à Paris (1830–1834)," *Le Mouvement Social* 88 (1974): 78–87; Robert J. Bezucha, *The Lyon Uprising of 1834* (Cambridge: Harvard University Press, 1974), 149–74.

42. *Petit Catéchisme Républicaine par un membre de la Société des Droits de l'Homme* (Paris: Chez Rouannet, 1832), 9, 12, in *Révolutions du XIXe siècle,* 1er série, T. 3.

43. J. J. Vignerte, *Au Rédacteur en chef du National, 4 août 1833* 2, in *Révolutions du XIXe siècle,* 1er série, T. 3.

44. *Société Marseillaise des Droits de l'Homme et du Citoyen* (Marseille: Mille et Serres, 1834), 4, 7, in *Révolutions du XIXe siècle,* 1er série, T. 3.

45. *Société des droits de l'Homme et du Citoyen, Comité Central de Grenoble* (Grenoble: Imprimerie de J.L. Barnel, s.d.), 2–3, in *Révolutions du XIXe siècle,* 1er série, T. 3.

46. Armand Carrel, "Rapport sur le manifeste de la Société des Droits de l'Homme, lu à la Société de défense commune de la liberté de la press, le 8 décembre 1833," in

Oeuvres politiques et littéraires d'Armand Carrel (Paris: Librairie de F. Chamerot, 1859), T. 5: 426–27, 430, 444.

47.   Thureau-Dangin, T. 2: 215; *Procès des citoyens Vignerte et Pagnerre, membres de la Société des Droits de l'homme, Cours d'Assises de Paris, 22 février 1834*, in *Révolutions du XIXᵉ siècle*, 1ᵉʳ série, T. 3: 4, 10, 12, 17, 20.

48.   *Procés des Vingt-Sept ou de la Société des droits de l'homme et des élèves de l'Ecole Polytéchnique* (Paris: Adolphe Riou, 1834), in *Révolutions du XIXᵉ siècle*, 1ᵉʳ série, 48.

49.   Thureau-Dangin, T. 3: 388–90.

50.   Louis Blanc, *Histoire de Dix Ans, 1830–1840* (Paris: Germer Baillière, n.d.), T. 5: 378.

51.   *Cours de Pairs. Affaire des 12 et 13 mai 1839. Rapport fait à la Cour les 11 et 12 juin 1839 par M. Merilhou* (Paris: Imprimerie Royale, 1839), in *Révolutions du XIXᵉ siècle*, 2ᵉᵐᵉ série (Paris: EDHIS, 1979), T. 9: 6, 7.

52.   *Banquets Démocratiques*. Extrait du *Journal du Peuple* du 5 juillet 1840, in *Révolutions du XIXᵉ siècle*, 2ᵉᵐᵉ série, T. 3: 3, 5, 8, 10.

53.   *Obsèques de Godefroy Cavaignac. Discours prononcés sur sa tombe* (Paris: Lange Levy et Cie, 1845), in *Révolutions du XIXᵉ siècle*, 2ᵉᵐᵉ série, T. 4: 10.

54.   Clark, esp. ch. 1.

55.   Naugrette-Christophe, 161–63.

56.   Truesdell, 59; *Oeuvre de Napoléon III* (Paris: Plon, 1869), T. 3: 357–60.

57.   Truesdell, 59–60.

58.   Ibid., 60–63.

59.   Quoted in ibid., 64.

60.   Ibid., 64–67. Albert Boime, *Thomas Couture and the Eclectic Vision* (New Haven: Yale University Press, 1980), 266–79. The painting was never finished.

61.   Emile Zola, *Son Excellence Eugène Rougon*, in *Les Rougon-Macquart* (Paris: Bibliothèque de la Pléiade, 1961), 2:85–86; *Le Figaro*, 19 juin 1856.

62.   Truesdell, 40, 75–78; Rosamonde Sanson, "Le 15 août: Fête nationale du Second Empire," in Corbin, Gérôme, and Tartakowsky, 119; Sudhir Hazareesingh, *The Saint-Napoleon: Celebrations of Sovereignty in Nineteenth-Century France* (Cambridge: Harvard University Press, 2004).

63.   Truesdell, 40–46.

64.   Vincent Robert, *Les chemins de la manifestation 1848–1914* (Lyon: Presses Universitaires de Lyon, 1996), 142.

65.   Truesdell, 77; Sanson, 123, 130, 131, 133, 134; Robert, 146.

66.   See for example Tocqueville's description of the invasion of the Assembly on May 15, 1848, and especially his characterization of Louis-August Blanqui in *The Recollections of Alexis de Tocqueville*, trans. by Alexander Teixera de Mattos (New York: Meridian Books, 1959), 125–40, esp. 130.

3. Boulevard Spectacles of the Third Republic

1.   See especially Schwartz.

2.   Pascal Ory, *1889: L'Expo Universelle* (Paris: Editions Complexe, 1989); Ben-Amos; Ihl; Lehning.

3.   Alfred Picard, *Exposition Universelle Internationale de 1889. Rapport General. T. I. Historiques des Expositions Universelles, Préliminaires de l'Exposition Universelle de 1889* (Paris: Imprimerie Nationale, 1891), 303.

4.   Ory, *Une Nation pour mémoire;* and "Le Centenaire de la Révolution Française," in *Les Lieux de mémoire: La République,* ed. Pierre Nora (Paris: Gallimard, 1984), 523–60.

5.   Ory, *Une Nation pour mémoire,* 59–60.

6.   Associations Générales des Etudiants de Paris, *Les fêtes de l'Université de Paris en 1889* (Paris: Georges Chamerot, 1890), 24, 26–28.

7.   Alice Gérard, *La Révolution française, mythes et interprétations 1789–1970* (Paris: Flammarion, 1970), 68–69; Eugène Melchior de Vogué, "A travers l'Exposition," *Revue des deux mondes* 94 (1 juillet 1889): 189.

8.   *Le Figaro,* 25 juin 1894.

9.   *Le Figaro,* 26 juin 1894.

10.   *Le Figaro,* 2 juillet 1894.

11.   Michel Winock, "Une Question de principe," in Pierre Birnbaum, *La France de l'Affaire Dreyfus* (Paris: Gallimard, 1994), 543–72, esp. 543.

12.   For what follows see *Le Figaro,* 12 février 1908. See also Henri Brisson, *Souvenirs: Affaire Dreyfus* (Paris: Cornély, 1908), esp. pp. 344–49, and Jean El Gammal, "Un Territoire de mots: rhétorique et politique," in Birnbaum, 309–36 and esp. 325–26.

13.   Brisson, 348–49.

14.   On *Uncle Tom's Cabin* see George M. Fredrickson, *The Black Image in the White Mind* (New York: Harper and Row, 1971), 97–129; and Sarah Meer, *Uncle Tom Mania: Slavery, Minstrelsy, and Transatlantic Culture in the 1850s* (Athens: University of Georgia Press, 2005), 103–30.

15.   Emile Zola, *Nos Auteurs dramatiques* (Paris: Bibliothèque Charpentier, 1909), 196.

16.   Victorien Sardou, *Monsieur Garat,* in *Théâtre complet* (Paris: Editions Albin Michel, 1955), T. 13: 351–473.

17.   Pim Den Boer, *History as a Profession: The Study of History in France, 1818–1914,* trans. Arnold J. Pomerans (Princeton: Princeton University Press, 1998); James Friguglietti, *Albert Mathiez: Historien Révolutionnaire (1874–1932)* (Paris: Société des Etudes Robespierristes, 1974); Albert Mathiez, "Taine historien," *Revue d'histoire moderne et contemporaine* 7 (1907): 257–84.

18.   Victorien Sardou, *Les Merveilleuses,* in *Théâtre complet,* T. 15: 561–742, esp. 613, 565, 566, 578–579, 585, 586–588, 589–592.

19. Ibid., 720.

20. Ibid., 735.

21. Victorien Sardou, *Paméla, marchande de frivolités* in *Théâtre Complet*, T. 7: 5–200.

22. Ibid., 26–27.

23. Ibid., 82–83.

24. Ibid., 94.

25. Ibid., 148.

26. Ibid., 149.

27. Ibid., 177.

28. Ibid., 199.

29. Sardou, *Les Merveilleuses*, 566; Sardou, *Paméla*, 42.

30. Jerome A. Hart, *Sardou and the Sardou Plays* (Philadelphia: J. B. Lippincott, 1913), 101–104.

31. Victorien Sardou and Emile Moreau, *Madame Sans-Gêne*, in Sardou, *Théâtre Complet*, T. IV: 24–25; Venita Datta, "'L'Appel au soldat': Visions of the Napoleonic Legend in Popular Culture of the Belle Epoque," *French Historical Studies* 28 (2005): 7–13.

32. Sardou and Moreau, *Madame Sans-Gêne*, 33–50.

33. Ibid., 54.

34. Ibid., 65.

35. Ibid., 87–99.

36. Ibid., 108–11.

37. Ibid., 129–33.

38. Ibid., 134–41.

39. Ibid., 186.

40. Ibid., 137, 88.

41. Ibid., 157.

42. Ibid., 185.

43. Ibid., 175.

44. Michelle Perrot, "The New Eve and the Old Adam: French Women's Condition at the Turn of the Century," in *Behind the Lines: Gender and the Two World Wars*, ed. Margaret R. Higonnet et al., 51–60 (New Haven: Yale University Press, 1987); Mary Louise Roberts, *Disruptive Acts: The New Woman in Fin-de-Siècle France* (Chicago: University of Chicago Press, 2002), 19–28.

45. Victorien Sardou, *Thermidor*, in *Théâtre Complet*, T. 6: 5–235.

46. Ibid., 151.

47. Ibid., 27, 28.

48. The debate is in *Journal Officiel de la République Française, Chambre de Députés* (hereafter *JOC*), 29 janvier 1891, 143–159. See also Eugen Weber, "About *Thermidor:* The Oblique Uses of Scandal," *French Historical Studies* 17 (1991): 330–42; Georges Mouly, *Les Papiers de Victorien Sardou* (Paris: Editions Albin Michel, 1934), 384–91; and Steven M. Beaudoin, "'Et les beaux rêves d'avenir?' Victorien Sardou and Fin-de-Siècle Attitudes on the French Revolution," M.A. thesis, University of Maine, 1990, esp. 39–48.

49. Gérard, 72; *JOC*, 29 janvier 1891, 144, 147.

50. *JOC*, 29 janvier 1891, 147.

51. Ibid., 151.

52. Ibid., 156.

53. Ibid., 148.

54. Ibid., 149–50.

55. Ibid., 154–55.

56. Ibid., 150–52.

57. Ibid., 153–54.

58. Ibid., 156.

59. Ibid., 156.

60. Ibid., 152.

61. Ibid., 157–58.

62. Ibid., 158.

63. Sardou, *Thermidor*, 211.

64. Ibid., 197, 235. See also Irena Filipowska, *Le Théâtre historique en France (1870–1914)* (Poznan: Uniwersytet Im. Adama Mickiewicza W Psnaniu, 1988), 185–89; Hemmings, 88.

65. Victorien Sardou, *Robespierre*, in *Théâtre Complet*, T. 6: 433–602.

66. Ibid., 597–600.

67. Ibid., 603.

68. Hart, 112–14. Sardou condemned the violence of the Paris Commune of 1871, but was a Dreyfusard. Georges Mouly, *Vie Prodigieuse de Victorien Sardou* (Paris: Albin Michel, 1931), 274, 182–85, 195, 296–300.

69. Antoine de Baecque, *Glory and Terror: Seven Deaths under the French Revolution*, trans. Charlotte Mandell (New York: Routledge, 2001), 157–60.

70. Sardou, *Robespierre*, 461–62.

71. Zola, *Nos Auteurs dramatiques,* 203.

72. Victorien Sardou, *Les Femmes fortes,* in *Théâtre complet,* T. XIV: 221–363, esp. 282, 289, 296.

73. Ibid., 296.

74. Ibid., 341–61.

75. See Cohen, 47–48; and Pedersen.

76. Carol Blum, *Rousseau and the Republic of Virtue: The Language of Politics in the French Revolution* (Ithaca: Cornell University Press, 1986), 153–68, discusses the connection between virtue and the policies of the First Republic; for concerns about public virtue in the Third Republic see Lehning, esp. 76–77, and Edward Berenson, *The Trial of Madame Caillaux* (Berkeley and Los Angeles: University of California Press, 1992), 89–132.

77. See Joan Wallach Scott, *Only Paradoxes to Offer: French Feminists and the Rights of Man* (Cambridge: Harvard University Press, 1996).

78. Loren Kruger, *The National Stage: Theatre and Cultural Legitimation in England, France, and America* (Chicago: University of Chicago Press, 1992), 42–44; David James Fisher, "The Origins of the French Popular Theatre," *Journal of Contemporary History* 12 (1977): 465–66; Charnow.

79. Romain Rolland, *The People's Theatre,* trans. Barrett H. Clark (New York: Henry Holt and Company, 1918), 47, 65.

80. Ibid., 76–78, 97; see also R. Dadoun, *La Dramaturgie de R. Rolland, Histoire littéraire de la France* (Paris: Editions sociales, 1978).

81. David James Fisher, "Romain Rolland and the Ideology and Aesthetics of French People's Theatre," *Theatre Quarterly* 9, no. 33 (1979): 86; Venita Datta, "Romain Rolland and the Théâtre de la Révolution: A Historical Perspective," *CLIO* 20, no. 3 (1991): 213–23.

82. Gérard, 76; David James Fisher, *Romain Rolland and the Politics of Intellectual Engagement* (Berkeley and Los Angeles: University of California Press, 1988), 20–22.

83. Romain Rolland, *Le 14 Juillet,* in *Théâtre de la Révolution* 1 (Paris: Editions Albin Michel, 1972), 102.

84. Ibid., 118–19.

85. Ibid., 123, 127, 140–41.

86. Ibid., 143.

87. Ibid., 156–57.

88. Ibid., 198–203.

89. Fisher, *Romain Rolland,* 23–24.

90. Rolland, *Le 14 Juillet,* 203, 211–14.

91. Valérie Battaglia, "Romain Rolland et le *Théâtre de la Révolution*," *Revue d'histoire du théâtre* 41 (1989): 184.

92. Rolland, *Le 14 Juillet*, 220–26.

93. Fisher, "French Popular Theatre," 471–73.

94. They proved more useful during labor demonstrations: at a textile strike in the Nord in 1900, for example, his play *Danton* was performed as a part of a demonstration that also featured a speech by the socialist leader Jean Jaurès. Productions of his plays became rare, and more frequently they were read. The director Firmin Gémier staged *Le Jeu de l'amour et de la mort* in 1928 at the Odéon as a part of a long series of plays chronicling the history of France. By the mid-1930s, with increased labor agitation and the rise of the Popular Front, they drew more attention. Performances sometimes seemed to re-create revolutionary festivals. In 1936 a performance of *Le 14 Juillet* marked the formation of the Popular Front government, and *Danton* was a part of the *fête nationale* that summer. *Le Jeu de l'amour et de la mort* was performed at the Comédie-Française as a part of the Sesquicentennial Celebration of the Revolution in 1939. In 1945 Rolland's *Danton* was used to celebrate the liberation of the city of Paris from German occupation. *Les Loups* was revived by the Théâtre de la Région Parisienne in 1966. Dorothy Knowles, *French Drama of the Inter-War Years, 1918–1939* (London: George G. Harrap, 1967), 292–93, 308–309.

95. Rolland, *People's Theater*, 103–106, 114–15; Fisher, "Ideology and Aesthetics of French Popular Theatre," 97–98.

96. Shanny Peer, *France on Display: Peasants, Provincials and Folklore in the 1937 Paris World's Fair* (Albany: State University of New York Press, 1998); Peter Jelavich, *Munich and Theatrical Modernism: Politics, Playwriting, and Performance, 1890–1914* (Cambridge: Harvard University Press, 1985), 217; Karen Petrone, *Life Has Become More Joyous, Comrades: Celebrations in the Time of Stalin* (Bloomington: Indiana University Press, 2000).

4. Spectacles of Light and Darkness between the World Wars

1. For the most important general arguments, see Paul Fussell, *The Great War and Modern Memory* (Oxford: Oxford University Press, 1975), 35; Modris Eksteins, *Rites of Spring: The Great War and the Birth of the Modern Age* (Boston: Houghton Mifflin, 1989), 128, 328; Jay M. Winter, *Sites of Memory, Sites of Mourning: The Great War and European Cultural History* (Cambridge: Cambridge University Press, 1995), 2; and Samuel Hynes, *A War Imagined: The First World War and English Culture* (New York: Atheneum, 1990), esp. xiii, 236–37, 421. On Great Britain, see Adrian Gregory, *The Silence of Memory: Armistice Day 1919–1946* (Oxford: Berg, 1994); Alex King, *Memorials of the Great War in Britain: The Symbolism and Politics of Remembrance* (Oxford: Berg, 1998); Philip Longworth, *The Unending Vigil: A History of the Commonwealth War Graves Commission 1917–1984* (London: Secker and Warburg, 1985); Geoffrey Moorhouse, *Hell's Foundations: A Social History of the Town of Bury in the Aftermath of the Gallipoli Campaign* (New York: Henry Holt, 1992); David W. Lloyd, *Battlefield Tourism: Pilgrimage and the Commemoration of the Great War in*

Britain, Australia and Canada, 1919–1939 (New York: Berg, 1998). On Germany, see George L. Mosse, *Fallen Soldiers: Reshaping the Memory of the World Wars* (New York: Oxford University Press, 1990); and Robert Weldon Whalen, *Bitter Wounds: German Victims of the Great War, 1914–1939* (Ithaca: Cornell University Press, 1984).

2.　Danielle Tartakowsky, *Les Manifestations de rue en France, 1918–1968* (Paris: Publications de la Sorbonne, 1997), 68, 54. See also Sanson; Miguel Rodriquez, *Le 1ᵉʳ Mai* (Paris: Gallimard, 1990); Antoine Prost, *Les Anciens combattants et la société française, 1914–1939* (Paris: Presses de la fondation nationale des sciences politiques, 1977).

3.　Daniel J. Sherman, *The Construction of Memory in Interwar France* (Chicago: University of Chicago Press, 1999).

4.　Prost, I:70–71; *Le Figaro,* 14 juillet 1919.

5.　*Le Figaro,* 15 juillet 1919.

6.　*Le Figaro,* 12 novembre 1920.

7.　Annette Becker, *War and Faith: The Religious Imagination in France, 1914–1930* (New York: Berg, 1998), 124, 170–76.

8.　Ibid., 160.

9.　See Schwartz; Meisel, 436; A. Nicholas Vardac, *Stage to Screen: Theatrical Method from Garrick to Griffith* (Cambridge: Harvard University Press, 1949).

10.　Richard Abel, *The Ciné Goes to Town: French Cinema 1896–1914* (Berkeley and Los Angeles: University of California Press, 1994), 9–58; Susan Hayward, *French National Cinema* (London: Routledge, 1993), 68–71; Rémi Fournier Lanzoni, *French Cinema from Its Beginnings to the Present* (New York: Continuum, 2002), 23–52; McCormick, 51.

11.　Abel, *Ciné Goes to Town,* 91, 94, 96.

12.　Ibid., 267–69, 274–76, 302–303.

13.　Richard Abel, *French Cinema: The First Wave, 1915–1929* (Princeton: Princeton University Press, 1984), 14.

14.　Hayward, 88; Abel, *French Cinema,* 70–71.

15.　For a survey of Gance's career, see Steven Philip Kramer and James Michael Welsh, *Abel Gance* (Boston: Twayne, 1978).

16.　Norman King, *Abel Gance: A Politics of Spectacle* (London: BFI Publishing, 1984), 3–4.

17.　Obituary by Jean-Luc Douin in *Télérama,* 18 November 1981, quoted in King, 1. For the history of the film, see Kevin Brownlow, *Napoleon: Abel Gance's Classic Film* (New York: Alfred A. Knopf, 1983). Brownlow was responsible for reconstructing, over several decades, the film. Abel, *French Cinema,* 428–45, provides a more aesthetic and technical analysis of the film.

18.　King, 168, 149, notes that the sound version of 1935 "could have been dedicated to Pétain" given its appeal for a strong authority and loyal, devoted subjects. He also notes that the tendency of the Brownlow and the Coppola versions to cut out peripheral material and focus on Napoleon himself also tends to "focus attention very much more on Bonaparte as authoritarian leader."

19. Brownlow, 110.

20. The shooting script is quoted at length in King, 101–105. While some parts of the scene appear to have been filmed, only fragments remain in the reconstructed version of the film.

21. Robert Lang, "The Birth of a Nation: History, Ideology, Narrative Form," in *The Birth of A Nation: D. W. Griffith, Director,* ed. Robert Lang (New Brunswick, N.J.: Rutgers University Press, 1994), 3–24.

22. Samuels.

23. Debord, *La Société du Spectacle.*

24. Alan Williams, *Republic of Images: A History of French Filmmaking* (Cambridge: Harvard University Press, 1992), 166–68; Lanzoni, 75–100; Jonathan Buchsbaum, *Cinéma Engagé: Film in the Popular Front* (Urbana: University of Illinois Press, 1988), 90–93.

25. Hayward, 139; Buchsbaum, 250, 263, 268. A scene involving a lengthy conversation between Robespierre and Brissot, which Renoir thought was the principal scene in the film, was in the original script but was cut.

26. Jackson, 142.

27. Williams, 232; Roy Armes, *French Cinema* (New York: Oxford University Press, 1985), 106.

28. Martin O'Shaughnessy, "Nation, History and Gender in the Films of Jean Renoir," in *France in Focus: Film and National Identity,* ed. Elizabeth Ezra and Sue Harris (New York: Berg, 2000), 127–41, esp. 129, 132–34.

29. Tartakowsky, 386, 64, 301.

30. Maurice Agulhon, *Les Métamorphoses de Marianne* (Paris: Flammarion, 2001), 86.

31. Serge Berstein, "L'Affrontement simulé des années 1930," *Vingtième Siècle* 5 (1985): 51; Herman Lebovics, *True France: The Wars over Cultural Identity, 1900–1945* (Ithaca: Cornell University Press, 1992).

32. Danielle Tartakowsky, "Stratégies de la Rue, 1934–1936," *Le Mouvement Social* 135 (1986): 31–63.

33. *Le Figaro,* 14 juillet 1935; *Le Figaro,* 15 juillet 1935.

34. Tartakowsky, *Les Manifestations en rue,* 340, 344, 345; Julian Jackson, *The Popular Front in France: Defending Democracy, 1934–38* (Cambridge: Cambridge University Press, 1988), 115, 7.

35. *Le Figaro,* 15 juillet 1935.

36. *Le Figaro,* 13 juillet 1936.

37. *Le Figaro,* 15 juillet 1936.

38. Jackson, 115, 284; *Le Figaro,* 15 juillet 1936; Tartakowsky, *Les Manifestations de rue,* 401, 413.

39. Annie Kriegel, *The French Communists: Profile of a People,* trans. by Elaine P. Halperin (Chicago: University of Chicago Press, 1972), 114; Berstein, 50.

40. Jackson, 120.

41. Jean-Pierre Azéma, "Anticommunismes et anticommunistes," in *Le Parti communiste français des années sombres, 1938–1941,* ed. Jean-Pierre Azéma, Antoine Prost, and Jean-Pierre Rioux (Paris: Editions du Seuil, 1986), 32.

42. Jackson, 136.

43. Ory, *Une Nation pour mémoire,* 41–43; Tartakowsky, *Les Manifestations de rue,* 434; Pascal Ory, *Les Expositions Universelles de Paris* (Paris: Editions Ramsay, 1982); Pierre Caron, "Le Cent-Cinquantenaire de la Révolution française," *Annales historiques de la Révolution française* 18 (1946): 98–101. Caron was the director of the Archives Nationales de France at the time, and served as vice president of the committee named to implement plans for the state celebration.

44. *Le Populaire,* 2 février 1939; Caron, 104n6.

45. Jacques Duclos, *Mémoires 1935–1939: Aux jours ensoleillés du Front Populaire* (Paris: Fayard, 1969), 365–66.

46. *Le Populaire,* 6 mai 1939.

47. Edouard Herriot, *Lyon n'est plus* (Paris: Hachette, 1937–40); Ory, *Une Nation pour mémoire,* 170.

48. *Le Populaire,* 6 mai 1939.

49. *Le Figaro,* 5, 6 mai 1939.

50. *Le Populaire,* 24 juin 1939. This is the entire story, buried on p. 2. See also *Le Figaro,* 24 juin 1939.

51. See Roger Martelli, "Héritiers de la Révolution française," in Azéma, Prost, and Rioux, 198–200.

52. Duclos, 389.

53. Pascal Ory, *Une Nation pour mémoire,* 131–32, 190.

54. *Le Figaro,* 15 juillet 1939.

55. Berstein, 40–53; Jackson, 287.

56. Daniel Cordier, *Jean Moulin: L'Inconnu du Panthéon* (Paris: J. C. Lattès, 1993), III:247; Pierre Laborie, *Résistants Vichyssois et autres* (Paris: Editions du C.N.R.S., 1980), 238, 297; Julian Jackson, *France: The Dark Years, 1940–1944* (Oxford: Oxford University Press, 2001), 486.

57. Agulhon, *Les Métamorphoses de Marianne,* 111.

58. Henri Frenay, *The Night Will End,* trans. Dan Hofstadter (New York: McGraw-Hill, 1976), 165.

59. Gérard, 91; Georges Lefebvre, "Documents," *Annales historiques de la révolution française* 198 (1969): 570–82.

60. Frenay, 185; Charles Rickard, *La Savoie dans la Résistance* (Rennes: Editions Ouest-France, 1993), 52–53.

61. Rickard, 320. See also Pascal Ory, *Les Collaborateurs 1940–1945* (Paris: Editions du Seuil, 1976).

5. Commercial Spectacles in Postwar Paris

1. Bernard Zimmer, "Charlotte Corday," in *Theatre II* (Paris: La Table Ronde, 1968), 151.

2. For a survey of the canonical figures in French theater, see Georges Versini, *Le Théâtre français depuis 1900* (Paris: Presses Universitaires de France, 1970).

3. See David Bradby, *Modern French Drama 1940–1990* (Cambridge: Cambridge University Press, 1991), esp. 87–165.

4. Ibid., 94–98; Anne Dhoquois, "La réception théâtrale de Bertolt Brecht en France (1945–1963)," *Revue de la société d'histoire du théâtre* 47 (1995): 39–52.

5. Bradby, 142–43.

6. Thérèse Marachy, "*Pauvre Bitos* d'Anouilh: l'éclatement théâtral d'un mythe," *Revue d'histoire du théâtre* 41 (1989): 196–201; Joseph Epoka Mwantuali, "Anouilh et l'humanité: *Pauvre Bitos* ou le miroir des siècles," *Revue d'histoire du théâtre* 49 (1997): 55–68; Bradby, 98–100.

7. Jean Anouilh, *Pauvre Bitos ou le dîner aux têtes,* in *Pièces Grinçantes* (Paris: La Table Ronde, 1973).

8. Knowles, 177.

9. Anouilh, 416.

10. Campos, "Paris after the Revolution," 63–71.

11. Christophe Campos, "Experiments for the People of Paris," *Theatre Quarterly* 2, no. 8 (1972): 61–62.

12. Catherine Mounier, "Deux créations collectives du Théâtre du Soleil: *1793, L'Age d'Or,*" in *Les Voies de la création théâtrale 5,* ed. Denis Bablet and Jean Jacquot, 125–26 (Paris: Editions du CNRS, 1977).

13. Mounier, 126; Adrian Kiernander, *Ariane Mnouchkine and the Théâtre du Soleil* (New York: Cambridge University Press, 1993), 45–64.

14. Emile Copfermann, "Entretiens avec Ariane Mnouchkine," in *Différent: Le Théâtre du Soleil* (supplément à *Travail Théâtrale,* fevrier 1976), 7.

15. Robert Abirached, "Au théâtre: 1789 et la perfection du bonheur," *Nouvelle Revue Française* 219 (Mars 1971): 111.

16. Campos, "Experiments for the People of Paris," 59.

17. André Alba, Jules Isaac, and Charles H. Pouthas, *L'Epoque révolutionnaire 1789–1851: Classe de première* (Paris: Hachette, 1950), 54, 74–76, 83–84, 86. See also Jean-Marie Baldner et al., "A l'école primaire," in *Manuels Scolaires et Révolution Française,* ed. Jean-Yves Mollier, 80–96 (Paris: Editions Messidor, 1990); and Eric Mesnard et al., "Dans le secondaire," in Mollier, 99–104.

18. Alba, Isaac, and Pouthas, 101, 123–138.

19. Ibid., 157, 185.

20. Emile Copfermann, "Où est la différence? Première entretien avec les membres de la troupe," in *Différent,* 17; Françoise Kourilsky, "De '1789' à '1793': Entretien avec Ariane Mnouchkine," in *Différent,* 17; David Williams, ed., *Collaborative Theatre: The Théâtre du Soleil Sourcebook* (London: Routledge, 1999), 41; "Document: 1793 à la Cartoucherie: La Cité Révolutionnaire est de ce monde," *Les lettres françaises* (14 mai 1972): 16.

21. Bradby, 195–200; for a description of the production from the perspective of the audience, see Victoria Nes Kirby, " *1789* at the Cartoucherie," in David Williams, *Collaborative Theatre,* 3–15.

22. Sophie Lemasson and Jean-Claude Penchenat, *1789* (Paris: Stock, 1971), 11, 12.

23. Ibid., 16.

24. Ibid., 46.

25. Ibid., 47–48.

26. Ibid., 53.

27. Ibid., 55.

28. Ibid., 67, 68.

29. Ibid., 70.

30. Ibid., 74.

31. Mounier, 126; Bradby, 195.

32. "Document," 16.

33. Renée Saurel, "Le Pain noir de l'égalité: *1793,*" *Les Temps Modernes* 312–13 (Juillet-Août 1972): 319, 321.

34. Gilbert Chateau, " *1793* et le théâtre politique," *La Nouvelle Revue Française* 236 (1972): 109.

35. Théâtre du Soleil, *1793: la cité révolutionnaire est de ce monde* (Paris: Stock, 1973), 7.

36. *1793,* 13.

37. Ibid., 95.

38. Ibid., 25–31.

39. Ibid., 42–46.

40. Ibid., 51, 75, 116.

41. Ibid., 120–30.

42. Jean Decock, " *1793:* Le Cité Révolutionnaire est de ce monde," *French Review* 47, no. 1 (October 1973): 240–41.

43. *1793,* 38.

44. Ibid., 105.

45. Chateau, 109.

46. Jean Ristat, "Le Théâtre de la différence," *Les Lettres Françaises* (14 juin 1972): 17.

47. For a summary of the events in Paris, see Kaplan, 302–307. See also Patrick Garcia, *Le Bicentenaire de la Révolution française* (Paris: CNRS Editions, 2000).

48. Jean-Noel Jeanneny, *Le Bicentenaire de la Révolution Française: Rapport du Président de la Mission du Bicentenaire de la République sur les activités de cet organisme et les dimensions de la célébration. 5 mars 1990* (Paris: La Documentation Française, 1990), 90–91.

49. Garcia, 54.

50. Kaplan, 307.

51. Ibid., 307–13.

52. Ibid., 314.

53. See ibid., 338–42; and Ben-Amos, 372–74, for descriptions of the pantheonization.

54. Kaplan, 342.

55. Ibid., 342.

56. *Le Figaro,* 11 décembre 1989.

57. "L'Eglise, la Révolution et les Droits de l'Homme: Cardinal Jean-Marie Lustiger, entretien avec François Furet," in *1789: La Commémoration* (Paris: Gallimard, 1999), 137, 138–39, 167.

58. "L'Eglise, la Révolution et les Droits de l'Homme," 139, 172. Lustiger notes the ceremony on December 11 and the negotiations leading up to it in a note appended to the interview in 1998.

59. Annie Kriegel, "Un Hommage Critiquable," *Le Figaro* (12 décembre 1989): 2; on the Affaire, see Miriam Feldblum, *Reconstructing Citizenship: The Politics of Nationality Reform and Immigration in Contemporary France* (Albany: State University of New York Press, 1999), 129–45.

60. Michel Riquet, S.J., "Un Hommage merité," *Le Figaro* (12 décembre 1989): 2.

61. Jeanneny, 125.

62. Ibid., 211–13; *L'Officiel des Spectacles* 2218 (28 juin—4 juillet 1989): 67; *L'Officiel des Spectacles* 2219 (5 juillet—11 juillet 1989): 7, 11, 13, 80.

63. See David Williams, "Introduction," and the essays on *L'Indiade* in *Collaborative Theatre*, ed. David Williams, xii–xiii, 131–178; on *Sihanouk* and *L'Indiade*, see Kiernander, 28–44 and 123–134.

64. Bradby, 267.

6. Conclusion

1. Richard Rose, William Mishler, and Christian Haerpfer, *Democracy and Its Alternatives: Understanding Post-Communist Societies* (Baltimore: Johns Hopkins University Press, 1998), 51.

2. Stanley Hoffman, *In Search of France* (New York: Harper and Row, 1965); Hazareesingh, *Political Traditions in Modern France;* Alexis de Tocqueville, *Democracy in America,* trans. George Lawrence (New York: Knopf, 1994), 513–24; Duncan MacRae, *Parliament, Parties and Society in France 1946–1958* (New York: Saint Martin's Press, 1967), 28–32.

3. Habermas; Calhoun.

4. Ravel; Crow.

5. David A. Bell, *The Cult of the Nation in France: Inventing Nationalism 1680–1800* (Cambridge: Harvard University Press, 2001), 91. For English comparisons, see Jeremy Osborn, "India and the East India Company in the Public Sphere of Eighteenth-Century Britain," in *The Worlds of the East India Company,* ed. H. V. Bowen, Margarette Lincoln, and Nigel Rigby, 201–22 (Woodbridge: Boydell Press, 2002); H. J. Barker, *Newspapers, Politics and Public Opinion in Late Eighteenth-Century England* (Oxford: Clarendon Press, 1998).

6. Keith Michael Baker, "Enlightenment and the Institution of Society: Notes for a Conceptual History," in *Civil Society: History and Possibilities,* ed. Sudipta Kaviraj and Sunil Khilnani, 84–104 (Cambridge: Cambridge University Press, 2001); Lucas.

7. James Livesey, *Making Democracy in the French Revolution* (Cambridge: Harvard University Press, 2001).

8. Raymond Huard, "Political Association in Nineteenth-Century France: Legislation and Practice," in *Civil Society Before Democracy: Lessons from Nineteenth-Century Europe,* ed. Nancy Bermeo and Philip Nord, 135–53 (New York: Rowman and Littlefield, 2000); Peter H. Amann, *Revolution and Mass Democracy: The Paris Club Movement in 1848* (Princeton: Princeton University Press, 1975); Carol E. Harrison, *The Bourgeois Citizen in Nineteenth-Century France: Gender, Sociability, and the Uses of Emulation* (Oxford: Oxford University Press, 1999); Berlanstein, 154; Philip Nord, *The Republican Moment* (Cambridge: Harvard University Press, 1995).

9. Hazareesingh, *From Subject to Citizen: The Second Empire and the Emergence of Modern French Democracy* (Princeton: Princeton University Press, 1998); and *Intellectual Founders of the Republic: Five Studies in Nineteeth-Century French Republican Political Thought* (Oxford: Oxford University Press, 2001), 203;

Stéphane Gerson, *The Pride of Place: Local Memories and Political Culture in Nineteenth-Century France* (Ithaca: Cornell University Press, 2003).

10. Tartakowsky, 804.

11. Larry Diamond, "Introduction: Political Culture and Democracy," in *Political Culture and Democracy,* 5.

12. Diamond, *Developing Democracy,* 162; "Introduction: In Search of Consolidation," in *Consolidating the Third Wave Democracies,* ed. Larry Diamond et al., xix (Baltimore: Johns Hopkins Univsity Press, 1997).

13. Robert Putnam, *Making Democracy Work: Civic Traditions in Modern Italy* (Princeton: Princeton University Press, 1993), 111; "Bowling Alone," *Journal of Democracy* 6 (1995): 65–78.

14. Ronald Inglehart, "Culture and Democracy," in *Culture Matters,* ed. Lawrence E. Harrison and Samuel P. Huntington, 80–97 (New York: Basic Books, 2000).

15. Putnam, *Making Democracy Work,* 87, 99–104.

16. Diamond, *Developing Democracy,* 225–28, 242.

17. For fuller discussions of different versions of social capital, see Pierre Bourdieu, "The Forms of Capital," in *Handbook of Theory and Research for the Sociology of Education,* ed. John Richardson, 241–58 (New York: Greenwood Press, 1986); James S. Coleman, "Social Capital in the Creation of Human Capital," *American Journal of Sociology* (supplement) 94 (1988): S95–S120; Bob Edwards, Michael W. Foley, and Mario Diani, "Social Capital Reconsidered," in *Beyond Tocqueville: Civil Society and the Social Capital Debate in Comparative Perspective,* ed. Bob Edwards and Michael W. Foley, 266–80 (Hanover, N.H.: University Press of New England, 2001). For a critique of the concept, see Michael W. Foley and Bob Edwards, "Is It Time to Disinvest in Social Capital?" *Journal of Public Policy* 19 (1999): 141–73.

18. Muthiah Alagappa, "Civil Society and Political Change: An Analytical Framework" and "Introduction," in *Civil Society and Political Change in Asia,* ed. Muthiah Alagappa, 40–43, 10–11 (Stanford: Stanford University Press, 2004); Philip Nord, "Introduction," in Bermeo and Nord, xxxi.

19. Richard L. Wood, "Political Culture Reconsidered: Insights on Social Capital from an Ethnography of Faith-based Community Organizing," in Edwards and Foley, 260, 263. See also David Laitin, *Hegemony and Culture: Politics and Religious Change among the Yoruba* (Chicago: University of Chicago Press, 1986), 1–20.

20. This is similar to the recommendation by Ronald Formisano that American political historians adopt a conceptualization of political culture that is closer to Antonio Gramsci's concept of hegemony. See Formisano, 393–426.

21. Gary Wilder, "Practicing Citizenship in Imperial Paris," in *Civil Society and the Political Imagination in Africa: Critical Perspectives,* ed. John L. Comaroff and Jean Comaroff (Chicago: University of Chicago Press, 1999), 50; Claude Nicolet, *L'Idée républicaine en France* (Paris: Gallimard, 1982), 331.

22. Diamond, *Developing Democracy,* 19, 64–116.

Selected Bibliography

Abel, Richard. *The Ciné Goes to Town: French Cinema 1896–1914.* Berkeley: University of California Press, 1994.

———. *French Cinema: The First Wave, 1915–1929.* Princeton: Princeton University Press, 1984.

Abirached, Robert. "Au théâtre: 1789 et la perfection du bonheur." *Nouvelle Revue Française* 219 (mars 1971): 109–11.

Abrams, M. H. *A Glossary of Literary Terms,* 5th ed. Chicago: Holt, Rinehart and Winston, 1988.

Agulhon, Maurice. *La République.* Paris: Hachette, 1990.

———. *Les Métamorphoses de Marianne.* Paris: Flammarion, 2001.

———. *Marianne au combat.* Paris: Flammarion, 1979.

———. *Marianne au pouvoir.* Paris: Flammarion, 1989.

Alagappa, Muthiah, ed. *Civil Society and Political Change in Asia.* Stanford: Stanford University Press, 2004.

Alba, André, Jules Isaac, and Charles H. Pouthas. *L'Epoque révolutionnaire 1789–1851: Classe de première.* Paris: Hachette, 1950.

Almond, Gabriel, and Sidney Verba. *The Civic Culture.* Newbury Park, Calif.: Sage Publications, 1989.

Altman, Rick. "Reusable Packaging: Generic Products and the Recycling Process." In *Refiguring American Film Genres: History and Theory,* ed. Nick Browne, 1–41. Berkeley: University of California Press, 1998.

Amann, Peter H. *Revolution and Mass Democracy: The Paris Club Movement in 1848.* Princeton: Princeton University Press, 1975.

Anderson, Lisa, ed. *Transitions to Democracy.* New York: Columbia University Press, 1999.

Ankersmit, Frank R. "Pygmalion: Rousseau and Diderot on the Theatre and on Representation." *Rethinking History* 7, no. 3 (2003): 315–39.

Anouilh, Jean. *Pièces Grinçantes.* Paris: La Table Ronde, 1973.

Archives Parlementaires. Chambre des Députés, 26 janvier 1818. Paris: Librairie Administratif de P. Dupont, 1862.

Armes, Roy. *French Cinema.* New York: Oxford University Press, 1985.

Associations Générales des Etudiants de Paris. *Les fêtes de l'Université de Paris en 1889.* Paris: Georges Chamerot, 1890.

Aulard, Alphonse. *Le Culte de la raison et le culte de l'Etre Suprême.* Paris: F. Alcan, 1892.

———. *L'éloquence parlementaire pendant la Révolution française.* Paris: Hachette, 1885–86.

Azéma, Jean-Pierre, Antoine Prost, and Jean-Pierre Rioux, eds. *Le Parti communiste français des années sombres, 1938–1941.* Paris: Editions du Seuil, 1986.

Bablet, Denis, and Jean Jacquot. *Les Voies de la création théâtrale 5.* Paris: Editions du CNRS, 1977.

Baecque, Antoine de. *Glory and Terror: Seven Deaths under the French Revolution.* Trans. Charlotte Mandell. New York: Routledge, 2001.

Baker, Keith Michael, "Enlightenment and the Institution of Society: Notes for a Conceptual History." In *Civil Society: History and Possibilities,* ed. Sudipta Kaviraj and Sunil Khilnani, 84–104. Cambridge: Cambridge University Press, 2001.

———, ed. *The French Revolution and the Creation of Modern Political Culture.* Vol. 1: *The Political Culture of the Old Regime.* Oxford: Pergamon Press, 1987.

———. *Inventing the French Revolution.* Cambridge: Cambridge University Press, 1990.

Baldner, Jean-Marie, et al. "A l'école primaire." In *Manuels Scolaires et Révolution Française,* ed. Jean-Yves Mollier, 80–96. Paris: Editions Messidor, 1990.

Barker, H. J. *Newspapers, Politics and Public Opinion in Late Eighteenth-Century England.* Oxford: Clarendon Press, 1998.

Barrès, Maurice. *Les Déracinés.* Paris: Félix Juven, n.d.

Battaglia, Valérie. "Romain Rolland et le *Théâtre de la Révolution.*" *Revue d'histoire du théâtre* 41 (1989): 178–95.

Beaudoin, Steven M. "'Et les beaux rêves d'avenir?' Victorien Sardou and Fin-de-Siècle Attitudes on the French Revolution." M.A. thesis, University of Maine, 1990.

Becker, Annette. *War and Faith: The Religious Imagination in France, 1914–1930.* New York: Berg, 1998.

Bell, David A. *The Cult of the Nation in France: Inventing Nationalism 1680–1800.* Cambridge: Harvard University Press, 2001.

Ben-Amos, Avner. *Funerals, Politics and Memory in Modern France 1789–1996.* New York: Oxford University Press, 2000.

Berenson, Edward. *The Trial of Madame Caillaux.* Berkeley and Los Angeles: University of California Press, 1992.

Berlanstein, Lenard. *Daughters of Eve: A Cultural History of French Theater Women from the Old Regime to the Fin-de-Siècle.* Cambridge: Harvard University Press, 2001.

Bermeo, Nancy, and Philip Nord, eds. *Civil Society before Democracy: Lessons from Nineteenth-Century Europe.* New York: Rowman and Littlefield, 2000.

Berstein, Serge. "L'Affrontement simulé des années 1930." *Vingtième Siècle* 5 (1985): 39–53.

Bertier de Sauvigny, Guillaume de. *The Bourbon Restoration.* Trans. Lynn M. Case. Philadelphia: University of Pennsylvania Press, 1966.

Bezucha, Robert J. *The Lyon Uprising of 1834.* Cambridge: Harvard University Press, 1974.

Billaz, André. "Mélodrame et littérature: le cas de Pixerécourt." *Revue des sciences humaines* 41 (1976): 239–42.

Birnbaum, Pierre, ed. *La France de l'Affaire Dreyfus.* Paris: Gallimard, 1994.

Blanc, Louis. *Histoire de Dix Ans, 1830–1840.* Paris: Germer Baillière, n.d.

Blum, Carol. *Rousseau and the Republic of Virtue: The Language of Politics in the French Revolution.* Ithaca: Cornell University Press, 1986.

Bodnar, John. *Remaking America: Public Memory, Commemoration, and Patriotism in the Twentieth Century.* Princeton: Princeton University Press, 1992.

Boime, Albert. *Thomas Couture and the Eclectic Vision.* New Haven: Yale University Press, 1980.

Bonnais, Henri. *Le 9 thermidor ou la mort de Robespierre: Drame historique, non représenté.* Paris: Moutardier, 1851.

Bonnell, Victoria. *Iconography of Power: Soviet Political Posters under Lenin and Stalin.* Berkeley and Los Angeles: University of California Press, 1997.

Booth, Michael R. *English Melodrama.* London: Herbert Jenkins, 1965.

Bourdieu, Pierre. "The Forms of Capital" In *Handbook of Theory and Research for the Sociology of Education,* ed. John Richardson, 241–58. New York: Greenwood Press, 1986.

Bové, Paul A. "Discourse." In *Critical Terms for Literary Study,* 2nd ed., ed. Frank Lentricchia and Thomas McLaughlin, 50–65. Chicago: University of Chicago Press, 1995.

Bowlby, Rachel. *Just Looking: Consumer Culture in Dreiser, Gissing and Zola.* New York: Methuen, 1985.

Bradby, David. *Modern French Drama 1940–1990.* Cambridge: Cambridge University Press, 1991.

Bradby, David, and John McCormick. *People's Theatre.* London: Croom Helm, 1978.

Bratton, Jacky, Jim Cook, and Christine Gledhill, eds. *Melodrama: Stage, Picture, Screen.* London: British Film Institute, 1994.

Brisson, Henri. *Souvenirs: Affaire Dreyfus.* Paris: Cornély, 1908.

Brooks, Peter. "Melodrama, Body, Revolution." In *Melodrama: Stage, Picture, Screen,* ed. Jacky Bratton, Jim Cook, and Christine Gledhill. London: British Film Institute, 1994.

———. *The Melodramatic Imagination.* New Haven: Yale University Press, 1976.

Browne, Nick, ed. *Refiguring American Film Genres: History and Theory.* Berkeley and Los Angeles: University of California Press, 1998.

Brownlow, Kevin. *Napoleon: Abel Gance's Classic Film.* New York: Alfred A. Knopf, 1983.

Bryson, Scott S. *The Chastised Stage: Bourgeois Drama and the Exercise of Power.* Saratoga, Calif.: Anma Libri, 1991.

Buchsbaum, Jonathan. *Cinéma Engagé: Film in the Popular Front.* Urbana: University of Illinois Press, 1988.

Calhoun, Craig, ed. *Habermas and the Public Sphere.* Cambridge: MIT Press, 1992.

Campos, Christophe. "Experiments for the People of Paris." *Theatre Quarterly* 2, no. 8 (1972): 57–67.

———. "Paris after the Revolution." *Theatre Quarterly* 1, no. 3 (1971): 63–71.

Carlson, Marvin. *The Theatre of the French Revolution.* Ithaca: Cornell University Press, 1966.

Caron, Pierre. "Le Cent-Cinquantenaire de la Révolution française." *Annales historiques de la Révolution française* 18 (1946): 98–101.

Carrel, Armand. *Oeuvres politiques et littéraires d'Armand Carrel.* Paris: Librairie de F. Chamerot, 1859.

Charnow, Sally Debra. *Theatre, Politics, and Modernity in Fin-de-Siècle Paris.* New York: Palgrave Macmillan, 2005.

Chateau, Gilbert. "1793 et le théâtre politique." *La Nouvelle Revue Française* 236 (1972): 109.

Clark, T. J. *The Painting of Modern Life: Paris in the Art of Manet and His Followers.* New York: Alfred A. Knopf, 1985.

Cohen, Margaret. *The Sentimental Education of the Novel.* Princeton: Princeton University Press, 1999.

Coleman, James S. "Social Capital in the Creation of Human Capital." *American Journal of Sociology* (supplement) 94 (1988): S95–S120.

Copfermann, Emile. "Entretiens avec Ariane Mnouchkine." In *Différent: Le Théâtre du Soleil,* supplément à *Travail Théâtrale,* fevrier 1976.

———. "Où est la différence? Première entretien avec les membres de la troupe." In *Différent: Le Théâtre du Soleil,* supplément à *Travail Théâtrale,* fevrier 1976.

Corbin, Alain, Noelle Gérôme, and Danielle Tartakowsky, eds. *Les Usages politiques des fêtes aux 19e–20e siècles.* Paris: Publications de la Sorbonne, 1994.

Cordier, Daniel. *Jean Moulin: L'Inconnu du Panthéon.* Paris: J. C. Lattès, 1993.

Crow, Thomas. *Painters and Public Life in Eighteenth-Century Paris.* New Haven: Yale University Press, 1985.

Dadoun, R. *La Dramaturgie de R. Rolland, Histoire littéraire de la France.* Paris: Editions sociales, 1978.

Dahl, Robert. *Polyarchy: Participation and Opposition.* New Haven: Yale University Press, 1971.

Datta, Venita. "'L'Appel au soldat': Visions of the Napoleonic Legend in Popular Culture of the Belle Epoque." *French Historical Studies* 28 (2005): 7–13.

———. "Romain Rolland and the Théâtre de la Révolution: A Historical Perspective," *CLIO* 20, no. 3 (1991): 213–23.

Debord, Guy. *Commentaires sur la société du spectacle*. Paris: Gallimard, 1992.

———. *La Société du Spectacle*. Paris: Gallimard, 1992.

Decock, Jean. "1793: Le Cité Révolutionnaire est de ce monde." *French Review* 47, no. 1 (October 1973): 240–41.

Den Boer, Pim. *History as a Profession: The Study of History in France, 1818–1914*. Trans. Arnold J. Pomerans. Princeton: Princeton University Press, 1998.

Descôtes, Maurice. *Le Public du théâtre et son histoire*. Paris: Presses Universitaires de France, 1964.

Dhoquois, Anne. "La réception théâtrale de Bertolt Brecht en France (1945–1963)." *Revue de la société d'histoire du théâtre* 47 (1995): 39–52.

Di Palma, Giuseppe. *To Craft Democracies: An Essay on Democratic Transitions*. Berkeley and Los Angeles: University of California Press, 1990.

Diamond, Larry, ed. *The Democratic Revolution: Struggles for Freedom and Pluralism in the Developing World*. New York: Freedom House, 1992.

———. *Developing Democracy: Toward Consolidation*. Baltimore: Johns Hopkins University Press, 1999.

———, ed. *Political Culture and Democracy in Developing Countries*. Boulder, Colo.: Lynne Rienner, 1994.

Diamond, Larry, Juan J. Linz, and Seymour Martin Lipset, eds. *Democracy in Developing Countries*. Vol. 4: *Latin America*. Boulder, Colo.: Lynne Rienner, 1989.

Diamond, Larry, et al., eds. *Consolidating the Third Wave Democracies*. Baltimore: Johns Hopkins University Press, 1997.

Différent: Le Théâtre du Soleil. Supplément à *Travail Théâtrale* (février 1976).

"Document: *1793* à la Cartoucherie: La Cité Révolutionnaire est de ce monde" *Les lettres françaises* (17 mai 1972): 16.

Doorenspleet, Renske. *Democratic Transitions: Exploring the Structural Sources of the Fourth Wave*. Boulder, Colo.: Lynne Rienner, 2005.

Duclos, Jacques. *Mémoires 1935–1939: Aux jours ensoleillés du Front Populaire*. Paris: Fayard, 1969.

Dumanoir and Clairville. *Charlotte Corday*. Paris: Imprimerie Dondey-Dupré, 1847.

Edelman, Murray. *Constructing the Political Spectacle*. Chicago: University of Chicago Press, 1988.

Edwards, Bob, Michael W. Foley, and Mario Diani, eds. *Beyond Tocqueville: Civil Society and the Social Capital Debate in Comparative Perspective*. Hanover: University Press of New England, 2001.

Eksteins, Modris. *Rites of Spring: The Great War and the Birth of the Modern Age*. Boston: Houghton Mifflin, 1989.

El Gammal, Jean. "Un Territoire de mots: rhétorique et politique." In *La France de l'Affaire Dreyfus*, ed. Pierre Birnbaum, 309–36. Paris: Gallimard, 1994.

Eley, Geoff. "Nations, Publics, and Political Cultures: Placing Habermas in the Nineteenth Century." In *Habermas and the Public Sphere*, ed. Craig Calhoun, 289–339. Cambridge: MIT Press, 1992.

Epstein, James. *In Practice*. Stanford: Stanford University Press, 2003.

Faure, Alain. "Mouvements populaires et Mouvement Ouvrier à Paris (1830–1834)." *Le Mouvement Social* 88 (1974): 51–92.

Feldblum, Miriam. *Reconstructing Citizenship: The Politics of Nationality Reform and Immigration in Contemporary France*. Albany: State University of New York Press, 1999.

Filipowska, Irena. *Le Théâtre historique en France (1870–1914)*. Poznan: Uniwersytet Im. Adama Mickiewicza W Psnaniu, 1988.

Fisher, David James. "The Origins of the French Popular Theatre." *Journal of Contemporary History* 12 (1977): 461–97.

———. "Romain Rolland and the Ideology and Aesthetics of French People's Theatre." *Theatre Quarterly* 9, no. 33 (1979): 83–103.

———. *Romain Rolland and the Politics of Intellectual Engagement*. Berkeley and Los Angeles: University of California Press, 1988.

Foley, Michael W., and Bob Edwards. "Is It Time to Disinvest in Social Capital?" *Journal of Public Policy* 19 (1999): 141–73.

Formisano, Ronald P. "The Concept of Political Culture." *Journal of Interdisciplinary History* 31 (2001): 393–426.

Foucault, Michel. "The Discourse on Language." In *The Archaeology of Knowledge*, trans. Rupert Swyer. New York: Pantheon, 1972.

Fowler, Alastair. *Kinds of Literature: An Introduction to the Theory of Genres and Modes*. Cambridge: Harvard University Press, 1982.

Fredrickson, George M. *The Black Image in the White Mind*. New York: Harper and Row, 1971.

Frenay, Henri. *The Night Will End*. Trans. Dan Hofstadter. New York: McGraw-Hill, 1976.

Fried, Michael. *Absorption and Theatricality: Image and Beholder in the Age of Diderot*. Berkeley and Los Angeles: University of California Press, 1980.

Friedland, Paul. *Political Actors: Representative Bodies and Theatricality in the Age of the French Revolution*. Ithaca: Cornell University Press, 2002.

Friguglietti, James. *Albert Mathiez: Historien Révolutionnaire (1874–1932)*. Paris: Société des Etudes Robespierristes, 1974.

Furet, François, *Interpreting the French Revolution*. Trans. Elborg Forster. Cambridge: Cambridge University Press, 1981.

————. *La Révolution française.* Paris: Hachette, 1988.

Fussell, Paul. *The Great War and Modern Memory.* Oxford: Oxford University Press, 1975.

Garcia, Patrick. *Le Bicentenaire de la Révolution française.* Paris: CNRS Editions, 2000.

Geertz, Clifford. *Negara: The Theater State in Nineteenth-Century Bali.* Princeton: Princeton University Press, 1980.

Gérard, Alice. *La Révolution française, mythes et interprétations 1789–1970.* Paris: Flammarion, 1970.

Gerbod, Paul. "La Scène parisienne et sa représentation de l'histoire nationale dans la première moitié du XIXᵉ siécle." *Revue historique* 266 (1981): 1–30.

Gerson, Stéphane. *The Pride of Place: Local Memories and Political Culture in Nineteenth-Century France.* Ithaca: Cornell University Press, 2003.

Gildea, Robert. *The Past in French History.* New Haven: Yale University Press, 1994.

Gregory, Adrian. *The Silence of Memory: Armistice Day 1919–1946.* Oxford: Berg, 1994.

Grimstead, David. *Melodrama Unveiled: American Theater and Culture 1800–1850.* Chicago: University of Chicago Press, 1968.

Habermas, Jürgen. *The Structural Transformation of the Public Sphere.* Trans. Thomas Berger. Cambridge: MIT Press, 1989.

Hadley, Elaine. *Melodramatic Tactics: Theatricalized Dissent in the English Marketplace, 1800–1885.* Stanford: Stanford University Press, 1995.

Hallay-Dabot, Victor. *Histoire de la censure théâtrale en France.* Paris: E. Dentu, 1862.

Hannoosh, Michele. "Painters of Modern Life: Baudelaire and the Impressionists." In *Visions of the Modern City,* ed. William Sharpe and Leonard Wallock, 168–88. Baltimore: Johns Hopkins University Press, 1987.

Harrison, Carol E. *The Bourgeois Citizen in Nineteenth-Century France: Gender, Sociability, and the Uses of Emulation.* Oxford: Oxford University Press, 1999.

Hart, Jerome A. *Sardou and the Sardou Plays.* Philadelphia: J. B. Lippincott, 1913.

Hayward, Susan. *French National Cinema.* London: Routledge, 1993.

Hazareesingh, Sudhir. *From Subject to Citizen: The Second Empire and the Emergence of Modern French Democracy.* Princeton: Princeton University Press, 1998.

————. *Intellectual Founders of the Republic: Five Studies in Nineteenth-Century French Republican Political Thought.* Oxford: Oxford University Press, 2001.

————. *Political Traditions in Modern France.* Oxford: Oxford University Press, 1994.

————. *The Saint-Napoleon: Celebrations of Sovereignty in Nineteenth-Century France.* Cambridge: Harvard University Press, 2004.

Hemmings, F. W. J. *The Theatre Industry in Nineteenth-Century France.* Cambridge: Cambridge University Press, 1993.

Herriot, Edouard. *Lyon n'est plus.* Paris: Hachette, 1937–40.

Hobsbawm, Eric, and Terence Ranger, eds. *The Invention of Tradition.* Cambridge: Cambridge University Press, 1983.

Hoffman, Stanley. *In Search of France.* New York: Harper and Row, 1965.

Huard, Raymond. "Political Association in Nineteenth-Century France: Legislation and Practice." In *Civil Society Before Democracy: Lessons from Nineteenth-Century Europe,* ed. Nancy Bermeo and Philip Nord, 135–53. New York: Rowman and Littlefield, 2000.

Hugo, Victor. "Choses Vues: 15 Décembre 1840: Funérailles de l'Empereur. Notes Prises sur Place." In *Oeuvres Complètes: Histoire,* 805–22. Paris: Robert Laffont, 1987.

Hunt, Lynn. *The Family Romance of the French Revolution.* Berkeley and Los Angeles: University of California Press, 1992.

Huntington, Samuel P. *The Third Wave: Democratization in the Late Twentieth Century.* Norman: University of Oklahoma Press, 1991.

Hynes, Samuel. *A War Imagined: The First World War and English Culture.* New York: Atheneum, 1990.

Ihl, Olivier. *La Fête républicaine.* Paris: Gallimard, 1996.

Inglehart, Ronald. "Culture and Democracy." In *Culture Matters,* ed. Lawrence E. Harrison and Samuel P. Huntington, 80–97. New York: Basic Books, 2000.

"Interdisciplinary Perspectives on French History and Literature." Special issue, *French Historical Studies* 28, no. 3 (2005).

Jackson, Julian. *France: The Dark Years, 1940–1944.* Oxford: Oxford University Press, 2001.

———. *The Popular Front in France: Defending Democracy, 1934–38.* Cambridge: Cambridge University Press, 1988.

Jeanneny, Jean-Noel. *Le Bicentenaire de la Révolution Française: Rapport du Président de la Mission du Bicentenaire de la République sur les activités de cet organisme et les dimensions de la célébration. 5 mars 1990.* Paris: La Documentation Française, 1990.

Jelavich, Peter. *Munich and Theatrical Modernism: Politics, Playwriting, and Performance, 1890–1914.* Cambridge: Harvard University Press, 1985.

Kaplan, Steven Laurence. *Farewell, Revolution: Disputed Legacies, France 1789/1989.* Ithaca: Cornell University Press, 1995.

Kaviraj, Sudipta, and Sunil Khilnani, eds. *Civil Society: History and Possibilities.* Cambridge: Cambridge University Press, 2001.

Kennedy, Emmet, et al. *Theatre, Opera and Audiences in Revolutionary Paris: Analysis and Repertory.* Westport, Conn.: Greenwood Press, 1996.

Kiernander, Adrian. *Ariane Mnouchkine and the Théâtre du Soleil.* New York: Cambridge University Press, 1993.

King, Alex. *Memorials of the Great War in Britain: The Symbolism and Politics of Remembrance.* Oxford: Berg, 1998.

King, Norman. *Abel Gance: A Politics of Spectacle.* London: BFI Publishing, 1984.

Kirby, Victoria Nes. "*1789* at the Cartoucherie." In *Collaborative Theatre: The Théâtre du Soleil Sourcebook,* ed. David Williams. London: Routledge, 1999.

Knowles, Dorothy. *French Drama of the Inter-War Years, 1918–1939.* London: George G. Harrap, 1967.

Kourilsky, Françoise. "De '1789' à '1793': Entretien avec Ariane Mnouchkine." In *Différent: Le Théâtre du Soleil,* supplément à *Travail Théâtrale,* fevrier 1976.

Krakovitch, Odile. "La Révolution à travers le théâtre de 1815 à 1870: à chaque génération sa peur. " In *Le XIXe Siècle et la Révolution française,* 57–74. Paris: Editions Créaphis, 1992.

Kramer, Steven Philip, and James Michael Welsh. *Abel Gance.* Boston: Twayne, 1978.

Kriegel, Annie. *The French Communists: Profile of a People.* Trans. Elaine P. Halperin. Chicago: University of Chicago Press, 1972.

———. "Un Hommage Critiquable." *Le Figaro* (12 décembre 1989): 2.

Kroen, Sheryl. *Politics and Theater: The Crisis of Legitimacy in Restoration France, 1815–1830.* Berkeley: University of California Press, 2000.

Kruger, Loren. *The National Stage: Theatre and Cultural Legitimation in England, France, and America.* Chicago: University of Chicago Press, 1992.

Laborie, Pierre. *Résistants Vichyssois et autres.* Paris: Editions du C.N.R.S., 1980.

Labrousse, Fabrice. *La Bastille.* Paris: Chez Marchant, 1837.

Laitin, David. *Hegemony and Culture: Politics and Religious Change among the Yoruba.* Chicago: University of Chicago Press, 1986.

Lang, Robert, ed. *The Birth of A Nation: D. W. Griffith, Director.* New Brunswick, N.J.: Rutgers University Press, 1994.

Lanzoni, Rémi Fournier. *French Cinema from Its Beginnings to the Present.* New York: Continuum, 2002.

LaPlace, Roselyne, ed. *Monvel: Théâtre, discours politiques et réflexions diverses.* Paris: Honoré Champion, 2001.

Le Hir, Marie-Pierre. *Le Romantisme aux enchères: Ducange, Pixerécourt, Hugo.* Amsterdam: John Benjamins, 1992.

Lebovics, Herman. *True France: The Wars over Cultural Identity, 1900–1945.* Ithaca: Cornell University Press, 1992.

Lefebvre, Georges. "Documents." *Annales historiques de la révolution française* 198 (1969): 570–82.

Lehning, James R. *To Be a Citizen: The Political Culture of the Early French Third Republic.* Ithaca: Cornell University Press, 2001.

Lemasson, Sophie, and Jean-Claude Penchenat. *1789*. Paris: Stock, 1971.

Lentricchia, Frank, and Thomas McLaughlin, eds. *Critical Terms for Literary Study*, 2nd ed. Chicago: University of Chicago Press, 1995.

Linz, Juan J. *The Breakdown of Democratic Regimes*. Baltimore: Johns Hopkins University Press, 1978.

Livesey, James. *Making Democracy in the French Revolution*. Cambridge: Harvard University Press, 2001.

Lloyd, David W. *Battlefield Tourism: Pilgrimage and the Commemoration of the Great War in Britain, Australia and Canada, 1919–1939*. New York: Berg, 1998.

Longworth, Philip. *The Unending Vigil: A History of the Commonwealth War Graves Commission 1917–1984*. London: Secker and Warburg, 1985.

Lucas, Colin, ed. *The French Revolution and the Creation of Modern Political Culture*. Vol. 2: *The Political Culture of the French Revolution*. New York: Pergamon Press, 1988.

MacRae, Duncan. *Parliament, Parties and Society in France 1946–1958*. New York: Saint Martin's Press, 1967.

Mah, Harold. "Phantasies of the Public Sphere: Rethinking the Habermas of Historians." *Journal of Modern History* 72 (2000): 153–82.

Mally, Lynn. *Revolutionary Acts: Amateur Theater and the Soviet State, 1917–1938*. Ithaca: Cornell University Press, 2000.

Marachy, Thérèse. "*Pauvre Bitos* d'Anouilh: l'éclatement théâtral d'un mythe." *Revue d'histoire du théâtre* 41 (1989): 196–201.

Marcoux, J. Paul. *Guilbert de Pixérécourt: French Melodrama in the Early Nineteenth Century*. New York: Peter Lang, 1992.

Margadant, Jo Burr. "Gender, Vice, and the Political Imaginary in Postrevolutionary France: Reinterpreting the Failure of the July Monarchy, 1830–1848." *American Historical Review* 104, no. 5 (December 1999): 1461–96.

Marrinan, Michael. *Painting Politics for Louis Philippe: Art and Ideology in Orleanist France, 1830–1848*. New Haven: Yale University Press, 1988.

Martelli, Roger. "Héritiers de la Révolution française." In *Le Parti communiste français des années sombres, 1938–1941*, ed. Jean-Pierre Azéma, Antoine Prost, and Jean-Pierre Rioux, 198–200. Paris: Editions du Seuil, 1986.

Maslan, Susan. *Revolutionary Acts: Theater, Democracy, and the French Revolution*. Baltimore: Johns Hopkins University Press, 2005.

Mathiez, Albert. "Taine historien." *Revue d'histoire moderne et contemporaine* 7 (1907): 257–84.

McCormick, John. *Popular Theatres of Nineteenth-Century France*. New York: Routledge, 1993.

Meer, Sarah. *Uncle Tom Mania: Slavery, Minstrelsy, and Transatlantic Culture in the 1850s*. Athens: University of Georgia Press, 2005.

Meisel, Joseph S. *Public Speech and the Culture of Public Life in the Age of Gladstone.* New York: Columbia University Press, 2001.

Meisel, Martin. *Realizations: Narrative, Pictorial, and Theatrical Arts in Nineteenth-Century England.* Princeton: Princeton University Press, 1983.

Melchior de Vogué, Eugène. "A travers l'Exposition." *Revue des deux mondes* 94 (1 juillet 1889): 183–90.

Mellon, Stanley. *The Political Uses of History.* Stanford: Stanford University Press, 1958.

Mercer, John, and Martin Shingler. *Short Cuts.* London: Wallflower Press, 2004.

Mesnard, Eric, et al. "Dans le secondaire." In *Manuels Scolaires et Révolution Française,* ed. Jean-Yves Mollier, 99–104. Paris: Editions Messidor, 1990

1789: La Commémoration. Paris: Gallimard, 1999.

Miller, Michael. *The Bon Marché: Bourgeois Culture and the Department Store, 1869–1920.* Princeton: Princeton University Press, 1981.

Moland, Louis, ed. *Théâtre de la Révolution.* Paris: Garnier Frères, 1877.

Mollier, Jean-Yves, ed. *Manuels Scolaires et Révolution Française.* Paris: Editions Messidor, 1990.

Moorhouse, Geoffrey. *Hell's Foundations: A Social History of the Town of Bury in the Aftermath of the Gallipoli Campaign.* New York: Henry Holt, 1992.

Mosse, George L. *Fallen Soldiers: Reshaping the Memory of the World Wars.* New York: Oxford University Press, 1990.

Mouly, Georges. *Les Papiers de Victorien Sardou.* Paris: Editions Albin Michel, 1934.

———. *Vie Prodigieuse de Vistorien Sardou.* Paris: Albin Michel, 1931.

Mounier, Catherine. "Deux créations collectives du Théâtre du Soleil: *1793, L'Age d'Or.*" In *Les Voies de la création théâtrale 5,* ed. Denis Bablet and Jean Jacquot, 125–26. Paris: Editions du CNRS, 1977.

Mwantuali, Joseph Epoka. "Anouilh et l'humanité: *Pauvre Bitos* ou le miroir des siècles." *Revue d'histoire du théâtre* 49 (1997): 55–68.

Naugrette-Christophe, Catherine. *Paris sous le Second Empire: Le Théâtre et la ville.* Paris: Librairie Théâtrale, 1998.

Neale, Steve. "'Melo Talk': On the Meaning and Use of the Term 'Melodrama' in the American Trade Press." *Velvet Light Trap* (Fall 1993): 66–89.

Necheles, Ruth F. *The Abbé Grégoire 1787–1831.* Westport, Conn.: Greenwood, 1971.

Newman, Simon. *Parades and the Politics of the Street: Festive Culture in the Early American Republic.* Philadelphia: University of Pennsylvania Press, 1997.

Nicolet, Claude. *L'Idée républicaine en France.* Paris: Gallimard, 1982.

Nord, Philip. *The Republican Moment.* Cambridge: Harvard University Press, 1995.

Oeuvre de Napoléon III. Paris: Plon, 1869.

O'Quinn, Daniel. *Staging Governance: Theatrical Imperialism in London, 1770–1800*. Baltimore: Johns Hopkins University Press, 2005.

Ory, Pascal. *Les Collaborateurs 1940–1945*. Paris: Editions du Seuil, 1976.

———. *Les Expositions Universelles de Paris*. Paris: Editions Ramsay, 1982.

———. "L'Histoire des politiques symboliques modernes: Un questionnement." *Revue d'histoire moderne et contemporaine* 47, no. 3 (2000): 525–36.

———. *1889: L'Expo Universelle*. Paris: Editions Complexe, 1989.

———. *Une Nation pour mémoire, 1889, 1939, 1989: trois jubilés révolutionnaires*. Paris: Presses de la Fondation Nationale des Sciences Politiques, 1992.

Ory, Pascal, and Jean-François Sirinelli. "Le Centenaire de la Révolution Française." In *Les Lieux de mémoire: La République*, ed. Pierre Nora, 523–560. Paris: Gallimard, 1984.

———. *Les Intellectuels en France, de l'Affaire Dreyfus à nos jours*. Paris: Armand Colin, 1986.

Osborn, Jeremy. "India and the East India Company in the Public Sphere of Eighteenth-Century Britain." In *The Worlds of the East India Company*, ed. H. V. Bowen, Margarette Lincoln, and Nigel Rigby, 201–22. Woodbridge: Boydell Press, 2002.

O'Shaughnessy, Martin. "Nation, History and Gender in the Films of Jean Renoir." In *France in Focus: Film and National Identity*, ed. Elizabeth Ezra and Sue Harris, 127–41. New York: Berg, 2000.

Ozouf, Mona. *Festivals and the French Revolution*. Trans. Alan Sheridan. Cambridge, Mass.: Harvard University Press, 1988.

Pedersen, Jean Elisabeth. *Legislating the French Family: Feminism, Theater, and Republican Politics, 1870–1920*. New Brunswick, N.J.: Rutgers University Press, 2003.

Peer, Shanny. *France on Display: Peasants, Provincials and Folklore in the 1937 Paris World's Fair*. Albany: State University of New York Press, 1998.

Perrot, Michelle. "The New Eve and the Old Adam: French Women's Condition at the Turn of the Century." In *Behind the Lines: Gender and the Two World Wars*, ed. Margaret R. Higonnet et al., 51–60. New Haven: Yale University Press, 1987.

Petrone, Karen. *Life Has Become More Joyous, Comrades: Celebrations in the Time of Stalin*. Bloomington: Indiana University Press, 2000.

Picard, Alfred. *Exposition Universelle Internationale de 1889. Rapport General. T. I. Historiques des Expositions Universelles, Préliminaires de l'Exposition Universelle de 1889*. Paris: Imprimerie Nationale, 1891.

Pixerécourt, Charles Guilbert de. *Théâtre choisi*. Geneva: Slatkine Reprints, 1971.

Ponsard, François. *Théâtre Complet de F. Ponsard*. Paris: Michel Lévy frères, 1851.

Popkin, Jeremy. *A History of Modern France*, 3rd ed. Saddle River, N.J.: Prentice-Hall, 2006.

Pouthas, Charles. *Guizot pendant la Restauration*. Paris: Plon-Nourrit et Cie, 1923.

Price, Roger. *The French Second Empire.* Cambridge: Cambridge University Press, 2001.

———. *People and Politics in France, 1848–1871.* Cambridge: Cambridge University Press, 2004.

Prost, Antoine. *Les Anciens combattants et la société française, 1914–1939.* Paris: Presses de la fondation nationale des sciences politiques, 1977.

Przybos, Julia. *L'Entreprise mélodramatique.* Paris: Librairie José Corti, 1987.

Putnam, Robert. "Bowling Alone." *Journal of Democracy* 6 (1995): 65–78.

———. *Making Democracy Work: Civic Traditions in Modern Italy.* Princeton: Princeton University Press, 1993.

Pye, Lucien W., and Sidney Verba, eds. *Political Culture and Political Development.* Princeton: Princeton University Press, 1965.

Rahill, Frank. *The World of Melodrama.* University Park: Pennsylvania State University Press, 1967.

Ravel, Jeffrey. *The Contested Parterre: Public Theater and French Political Culture, 1680–1791.* Ithaca: Cornell University Press, 1999.

Reff, Theodore. "Manet and the Paris of Haussmann and Baudelaire." In *Visions of the Modern City,* ed. William Sharpe and Leonard Wallock, 135–67. Baltimore: Johns Hopkins University Press, 1987.

Révolutions du XIXe siècle. Paris: EDHIS, 1974, 1979.

Rickard, Charles. *La Savoie dans la Résistance.* Rennes: Editions Ouest-France, 1993.

Rioux, Jean-Pierre, and Jean-François Sirinelli, eds. *La Guerre d'Algérie et les intellectuels français.* Paris: Editions Complexe, 1991.

Riquet, Michel, S.J. "Un Hommage merité." *Le Figaro* (12 décembre 1989): 2.

Ristat, Jean. "Le Théâtre de la difference." *Les Lettres Françaises* (14 juin 1972): 17.

Robert, Vincent. *Les chemins de la manifestation 1848–1914.* Lyon: Presses Universitaires de Lyon, 1996.

Roberts, Mary Louise. *Disruptive Acts: The New Woman in Fin-de-Siècle France.* Chicago: University of Chicago Press, 2002.

Rodriquez, Miguel. *Le 1er Mai.* Paris: Gallimard, 1990.

Rolland, Romain. *The People's Theatre.* Trans. Barrett H. Clark. New York: Henry Holt, 1918.

———. *Théâtre de la Révolution* 1. Paris: Editions Albin Michel, 1972.

Root-Bernstein, Michèle. *Boulevard Theater and Revolution in Eighteenth-Century Paris.* Ann Arbor, Mich.: UMI Research Press, 1984.

Rose, Richard, William Mishler, and Christian Haerpfer. *Democracy and Its Alternatives: Understanding Post-Communist Societies.* Baltimore: Johns Hopkins University Press, 1998.

Rowe, John Carlos. "Structure." In *Critical Terms for Literary Study,* 2nd ed., ed. Frank Lentricchia and Thomas McLaughlin, 23–28. Chicago: University of Chicago Press, 1995.

Rustow, Dankwart A. "Transitions to Democracy: Towards a Dynamic Model." *Comparative Politics* 2 (1970): 337–63.

Ryan, Mary. "Gender and Public Access: Women's Politics in Nineteenth Century America." In *Habermas and the Public Sphere,* ed. Craig Calhoun, 259–88. Cambridge: MIT Press, 1992.

———. *Women in Public: Between Banners and Barricades, 1825–1880.* Baltimore: Johns Hopkins University Press, 1990.

Samuels, Maurice. *The Spectacular Past: Popular History and the Novel in Nineteenth-Century France.* Ithaca: Cornell University Press, 2004.

Sanson, Rosamonde. *Le 14ᵉ Juillet: fête et conscience nationale, 1789–1975.* Paris: Flammarion, 1976.

———. "Le 15 août: Fête nationale du Second Empire." In *Les Usages politiques des fêtes aux 19ᵉ–20ᵉ siècles,* ed. Alain Corbin, Noelle Gérôme, and Danielle Tartakowsky, 119. Paris: Publications de la Sorbonne, 1994.

Sardou, Victorien. *Théâtre complet.* Paris: Editions Albin Michel, 1955.

Saurel, Renée. "Le Pain noir de l'égalité: *1793.*" *Les Temps Modernes* 312–13 (Juillet–Août 1972): 319–22.

Schechner, Richard. *Performance Theory.* New York: Routledge, 1988.

Schwartz, Vanessa. *Spectacular Realities: Early Mass Culture in Fin-de-Siècle France.* Berkeley and Los Angeles: University of California Press, 1998.

Scott, Joan Wallach. *Only Paradoxes to Offer: French Feminists and the Rights of Man.* Cambridge, Mass.: Harvard University Press, 1996.

Sharpe, William, and Leonard Wallock, eds. *Visions of the Modern City.* Baltimore: Johns Hopkins University Press, 1987.

Sherman, Daniel J. *The Construction of Memory in Interwar France.* Chicago: University of Chicago Press, 1999.

Sirinelli, Jean-François. *Génération intellectuelle: khâgneux et normaliens dans l'entre-deux-guerres.* Paris: Fayard, 1992.

Smith, Craig R. *Daniel Webster and the Oratory of Civil Religion.* Columbia: University of Missouri Press, 2005.

Tarin, René. "Le Théâtre de la période révolutionnaire: un mal-aimé de la critique et de l'histoire littéraire." *Revue de la société d'histoire du théâtre* 48 (1996): 353–61.

Tartakowsky, Danielle. *Les Manifestations de rue en France 1918–1968.* Paris: Publications de la Sorbonne, 1997.

———. "Stratégies de la Rue, 1934–1936." *Le Mouvement Social* 135 (1986): 31–63.

Terdiman, Richard. *Discourse/Counter-Discourse: The Theory and Practice of Symbolic Resistance in Nineteenth-Century France.* Ithaca: Cornell University Press, 1985.

Tester, Keith, ed. *The Flâneur.* New York: Routledge, 1994.

Théâtre du Soleil. *1793: la cité révolutionnaire est de ce monde.* Paris: Stock, 1973.

Thomasseau, Jean-Marie. *Le Mélodrame.* Paris: Presses Universitaires de France, 1984.

Thureau-Dangin, Paul. *Histoire de la monarchie de Juillet.* Paris: Plon, 1888.

Thurston, Gary. *The Popular Theatre Movement in Russia, 1862–1919.* Evanston, Ill.: Northwestern University Press, 1998.

Tocqueville, Alexis de. *Democracy in America.* Trans. George Lawrence. New York: Knopf, 1994.

———. *The Recollections of Alexis de Tocqueville.* Trans. Alexander Teixera de Mattos. New York: Meridian Books, 1959.

Truesdell, Matthew. *Spectacular Politics: Louis-Napoleon Bonaparte and the Fête Imperiale.* New York: Oxford University Press, 1997.

Tulard, Jean. "Le Retour des cendres." In *Les Lieux de mémoire: La Nation,* ed. Pierre Nora, 81–110. Paris: Gallimard, 1986

Turner, Victor. *Dramas, Fields, and Metaphors.* Ithaca: Cornell University Press, 1974.

———. *From Ritual to Theatre.* New York: Performing Arts Journal Publications, 1982.

———. *On the Edge of the Bush: Anthropology as Experience.* Tucson: University of Arizona Press, 1985.

Van Damme, Stéphane. "Comprendre les *Cultural Studies.*" *Revue d'histoire moderne et contemporaine* 51, 4 bis (2004): 48–58.

Vanhanen, Tatu. *Democratization: A Comparative Analysis of 170 Countries.* New York: Routledge, 2003.

Vardac, A. Nicholas. *Stage to Screen: Theatrical Method from Garrick to Griffith.* Cambridge, Mass.: Harvard University Press, 1949.

Versini, Georges. *Le Théâtre français depuis 1900.* Paris: Presses Universitaires de France, 1970.

von Geldern, James. *Bolshevik Festivals, 1917–1920.* Berkeley and Los Angeles: University of California Press, 1993.

Vovelle, Michel. *The Revolution against the Church: From Reason to the Supreme Being.* Trans. Alan José. Columbus: Ohio State University Press, 1991.

Waldstreicher, David. *In the Midst of Perpetual Fetes: The Making of American Nationalism, 1776–1820.* Chapel Hill: University of North Carolina Press, 1997.

Walkowitz, Judith R. *City of Dreadful Delight.* Chicago: University of Chicago Press, 1992.

Walton, Whitney. *Eve's Proud Descendants: Four Women Writers and Republican Politics in Nineteenth-Century France.* Stanford: Stanford University Press, 2000.

Waquet, Françoise. *Les Fêtes royales sous la Restauration ou l'Ancien Régime Retrouvé.* Geneva: Droz, 1981.

Weber, Eugen. "About *Thermidor:* The Oblique Uses of Scandal." *French Historical Studies* 17 (1991): 330–42.

Whalen, Robert Weldon. *Bitter Wounds: German Victims of the Great War, 1914–1939.* Ithaca: Cornell University Press, 1984.

Whitehead, Laurence. *Democratization: Theory and Experience.* Oxford: Oxford University Press, 2002.

Wilder, Gary. "Practicing Citizenship in Imperial Paris." In *Civil Society and the Political Imagination in Africa: Critical Perspectives,* ed. John L. Comaroff and Jean Comaroff, 44–71. Chicago: University of Chicago Press, 1999.

Williams, Alan. *Republic of Images: A History of French Filmmaking.* Cambridge, Mass.: Harvard University Press, 1992.

Williams, David, ed. *Collaborative Theatre: The Théâtre du Soleil Sourcebook.* London: Routledge, 1999.

Williams, Rosalind. *Dream Worlds: Mass Consumption in Late Nineteenth-Century France.* Berkeley and Los Angeles: University of California Press, 1982.

Wills, Garry. *Lincoln at Gettysburg: The Words That Remade America.* New York: Simon and Schuster, 1992.

Winock, Michel. "Une Question de principe." In *La France de l'Affaire Dreyfus,* ed. Pierre Birnbaum, 543–72. Paris: Gallimard, 1994.

Winter, Jay M. *Sites of Memory, Sites of Mourning: The Great War and European Cultural History.* Cambridge: Cambridge University Press, 1995.

Wood, Richard L. "Political Culture Reconsidered: Insights on Social Capital from an Ethnography of Faith-based Community Organizing." In *Beyond Tocqueville: Civil Society and the Social Capital Debate in Comparative Perspective,* ed. Bob Edwards, Michael W. Foley, and Mario Diani, 254–265. Hanover: University Press of New England, 2001.

Youngblood, Denise J. *Movies for the Masses: Popular Cinema and Soviet Society in the 1920s.* Cambridge: Cambridge University Press, 1992.

Zimmer, Bernard. *Theatre II.* Paris: La Table Ronde, 1968.

Zola, Emile. *Nos Auteurs dramatiques.* Paris: Bibliothèque Charpentier, 1909.

———. *Son Excellence Eugène Rougon.* In *Les Rougon-Macquart.* Paris: Bibliothèque de la Pléiade, 1961.

Index

Ponsard, François, 23, 61
Le Populaire, 96
Popular Front, 18, 84–85, 90, 92–93
Pouthas, Charles, 105
Public Sphere, 5–6

Quartorze Juillet, 17, 32, 76–77, 91–92, 94, 119–120
Le 14 Juillet, 66, 70, 73, 108
Quatre-vingt-treize, 70

Racine, Jean, 20
Raspail, François-Vincent, 36
Rebérioux, Madeleine, 106
Reinach, Joseph, 60–63
Réjane, Gabrielle, 52
Renoir, Jean, 84–90, 98, 101
Resistance, 98–99, 102–103
Restoration, 24–25
La Révolution française, 22
Revue de la Révolution Française, 48
Rewbell, Jean-François, 53
Reynaud, Paul, 16, 96
Riquet, Michel, 119
Ristat, Jean, 113
Robespierre, Maximilien, 1–3, 13, 17, 19, 22–24, 32–38, 43, 52, 61–62, 65–66, 71, 74, 82, 85, 88, 93, 97, 100, 102, 106, 110, 123, 132–133
Robespierre, 65, 120
Rocque, Colonel François de la, 92
Roland, Mme Manon, 65
Rolland, Romain, 66, 69–71, 73–74, 89, 107–108, 120, 127
La Roue, 80
Rouget de L'Isle, Claude Joseph, 93
Rousseau, Jean-Jacques, 6, 8, 10
Roux, Jacques, 111
Rue de Grenelle, 23
The Rules of the Game, 85

Le Sacre de Napoléon, 80
Saint Denis, 102
Saint-Just, Louis Antoine de, 13, 24, 32, 36, 82
Saint-Napoleon, 41–42
Sakharov, Andrey, 117
Samuels, Maurice, 9, 14

Sardou, Victorien, 18, 52, 54, 58–59, 61–62, 64–67, 69, 73–75, 89, 101
Sartre, Jean-Paul, 101
Sartrouville, 102
Scheurer-Kestner, Auguste, 49, 50
Schwartz, Vanessa, 9, 14, 40, 45, 51
Second Empire, 20, 39, 41, 129
Second Republic, 129
Shakespeare, William, 101
Sieyès, Abbé Emmanuel Joseph, 115
Simon, Jules, 48
Soboul, Albert, 106
Société de Défense Commune de la Liberté de la Presse, 35
Société des Amis de l'Egalité, 32
Société des Amis du Peuple, 36
Société des Droits de l'Homme, 34–36
Société des Familles, 37
Société des Montagnards, 33
Société des Saisons, 37
Solidarité Française, 91
Sorbonne, 47–48
Spectacle, 6–9, 15, 17–18, 114, 116, 120–121, 126–128, 133
Stowe, Harriet Beecher, 51

Taine, Hippolyte, 52
Tallien, J-L, 24, 65
Tambours du Bronx, 116
Tartakowsky, Danielle, 76
Tchador, Affaire du, 119
Telluride Film Festival, 81
Terror, 22, 35, 44, 128
Théâtre de l'Ambigu-Comique, 12
Théâtre de l'Odéon, 20–23
Théâtre de l'Opéra-Comique, 23
Théâtre de la Porte-Saint-Antoine, 22
Théâtre de la Porte-Saint-Martin, 64
Théâtre de la Rénaissance-Gémier, 73
Théâtre des Pays du Nord, 119
Théâtre du people, 69
Théâtre du Soleil, 18, 101, 104–114, 120, 125
Théâtre-Français, 20–23
Théâtre-Italien, 23
Théâtre National Populaire, 101–102
Théâtre Populaire de Lorraine, 102
Théâtre Romain Rolland, 120
Thermidor, 59

James R. Lehning is Professor of History at the University of Utah and author of *To Be a Citizen: The Political Culture of the Early French Third Republic* and *Peasant and French: Cultural Contact in Rural France during the Nineteenth Century.*

Printed and bound by CPI Group (UK) Ltd, Croydon, CR0 4YY

13/04/2025

14656546-0003